MULTICULTURAL POLICIES AND MODES OF CITIZENSHIP IN EUROPEAN CITIES

In memory of Hans Mahnig (1966-2001)

DAMES

Dansk Center for Migration
og Etniske Studier

EUROPEAN RESEARCH CENTRE
ON MIGRATION & ETHNIC RELATIONS

Multicultural Policies and Modes of Citizenship in European Cities

Edited by
ALISDAIR ROGERS
University of Oxford

JEAN TILLIE
University of Amsterdam

Ashgate

Aldershot • Burlington USA • Singapore • Sydney

Published by
Ashgate Publishing Limited
Gower House
Croft Road
Aldershot
Hants GU11 3HR
England

Ashgate Publishing Company
131 Main Street
Burlington, VT 05401-5600 USA

Ashgate website: http://www.ashgate.com

British Library Cataloguing in Publication Data
Multicultural policies and modes of citizenship in European
    cities. - (Research in migration and ethnic relations
    series)
    1. Multiculturalism - Europe 2. Minorities - Legal status,
    laws, etc. - Europe 3. Immigrants - Legal status, laws, etc.
    - Europe 4. Immigrants - Cultural assimilation - Europe
    5. Citizenship - Europe 6. Urban policy - Europe
    I. Rogers, Alisdair II. Tillie, Jean
    323.1'4

Library of Congress Control Number: 2001089060

ISBN 0 7546 1555 3

Printed in Great Britain by
Antony Rowe Ltd, Chippenham, Wiltshire

Contents

List of Contributors

Michael Alexander is a PhD candidate at the Amsterdam Study Centre for the Metropolitan Environment, University of Amsterdam, the Netherlands.

Nadia Auriat is a sociologist working at the UNESCO MOST Programme, Paris, France.

John Crowley is a research fellow at the Centre d'Etudes et de Recherches Internationales, Fondation Nationale des Sciences Politiques, Paris, France.

Romain Garbaye is affiliated to Worcester College, Oxford University, United Kingdom.

Dirk Jacobs has a degree in sociology and is a PhD in social sciences. He is currently a research associate at the Institute of Political Sociology and Methodology, Catholic University of Brussels, Belgium.

Riva Kastoryano is CNRS research fellow at the Centre d'Etudes et de Recherches Internationales, Fondation Nationale des Sciences Politiques, Paris, France.

Karen Kraal is an anthropologist and research assistant at the Institute for Migration and Ethnic Studies, University of Amsterdam, the Netherlands.

Hans Mahnig worked as a political scientist at the Swiss Forum for Migration Studies in Neuchâtel, Switzerland.

M. Margarida Marques is a professor in the Department of Sociology and researcher in SociNova, Faculty of Social and Human Sciences, Lisbon New University, Portugal.

Damian Moore is doctor in political science at the Université de Droit, d'Economie et des Sciences d'Aix-Marseille, Institut d'Etudes Politiques d'Aix-en-Provence, France.

Ricard Morén-Alegret is a social scientist and works at the Departament de Geografia, Universitat Autònoma de Barcelona and the Centre for Research in Ethnic Relations, University of Warwick, United Kingdom.

Marina Petronoti is a social anthropologist and researcher at the National Centre for Social Research, Athens, Greece.

Lubomira Rochet is an economist, University of Paris-Evry, France.

Alisdair Rogers is a college lecturer at Keble College and the School of Geography and the Environment, University of Oxford, United Kingdom.

Rui Santos is a professor in the Department of Sociology and researcher in SociNova, Faculty of Social and Human Sciences, Lisbon New University, Portugal.

Jean Tillie is senior researcher and programme leader at the Institute for Migration and Ethnic Studies, University of Amsterdam, the Netherlands. While working on this book he was fellow-in-residence at the Netherlands Institute for the Advanced Study in the Humanities and Social Sciences (NIAS), Wassenaar, the Netherlands.

Steven Vertovec is director of the ESRC Transnational Communities Programme at the Institute of Social and Cultural Anthropology, University of Oxford, United Kingdom.

Andreas Wimmer is professor and director of the Department for Political and Cultural Change of the Centre of Development Studies, University of Bonn, Germany.

Preface

NADIA AURIAT AND LUBOMIRA ROCHET

Globalisation is without doubt a dominant feature of the past decades. One of the most salient phenomena characterising our contemporary world, which results from this process, is the tremendous increase in international population movements. These massive population flows have been facilitated by a series of factors, such as the development of communication, transport, technologies and global networks which have significantly contributed to the increased immigration of refugee workers and their families to developed countries – particularly to Western European countries.

At least two models of migration can be accounted for. First, there is the migration of highly skilled individuals, due to the rise of multinational companies. Second, there is the migration of low skilled workers from poor underdeveloped countries to richer countries, which is one of the major features of globalisation. Until about 1974, the arrival of unskilled workers was welcomed and even stimulated by governments of receiving countries, as they represented a cheap workforce. This began to change when Europe underwent a considerable economic recession in the 1970s, but even during that period unsolicited immigration continued. It is this category in particular that is perceived as a threat to national cohesion in the eyes of receiving societies. The phenomenon engendered growing international recognition that the traditional models for coping with previous waves of integration, namely the assimilation and the integration models, were no longer appropriate for addressing the changing patterns of inter-ethnic relations. This concern is particularly challenging in the case of 'new countries of immigration' such as Greece, which had traditionally been an emigration country.

This issue is closely relevant to the emergence of cities as arenas of accelerated social transformations. Cities have always been confronted with ethnic diversity, but today they have become the visible and tangible face of globalisation, concentrating within their periphery some of the best, as well as the worst, features of our time. Since the newcomers tend to settle in large urban areas, these become *loci* of human diversity, where people from different socio-economic and ethnic backgrounds attempt to build a shared future. This visionary and utopian dimension of the city has always

ix

existed. Let us recall here that the word 'citizenship' derives from 'city', and implicitly conveys the notion of community. Today's cities are faced with huge responsibilities as they enter into the twenty-first century.

From a philosophical point of view, cities must place the citizen at the centre of public policy and reinvent the concept of the city to meet the challenges engendered by globalisation and increased diversity. Creating the city of the democratic age requires first and foremost achieving the full participation of all citizens in the public debate and promoting integration through social well-targeted policies.

Furthermore, large cities are under strain to weave together the various communities into a reasonably cohesive whole, accommodating the new diversity since nation states have lost their prominence and efficiency in managing ethnic diversity. The perception that a process of economic and cultural internationalisation is undermining the autonomy and policy-making capacity of the state is widely shared nowadays. As a result of these tendencies, nation states are confronted with claims to decentralise policies to lower levels. This is particularly true with regard to immigration policies and the management of ethnic diversity. Even if migration and admission policies are mainly national and continue to be set up at national or even regional levels, local authorities are actually in charge of the day-to-day management of diversity: the concrete consequences of migration movements are dealt with at municipal levels, where the immigrants live.

Major steps must be taken since the situation of immigrants and ethnic minorities are all too often characterised by marginalisation and exclusion. Often they are formally excluded from the political decision-making system, but they are also the subject of numerous other modes of exclusion. In the socio-economic domain, these include restricted access to the labour market, or denial or differential provision of social welfare resources. In the cultural and religious domain, immigrants and ethnic minorities have limited possibilities for satisfying their ethnic, cultural and religious needs and recognition of such identities are often problematic. This condition is particularly challenging since the international community has pledged itself to enhancing and operationalising rights for indigenous people and people belonging to ethnic minorities. In 1948, for the first time, the Universal Declaration of Human Rights provided for the respect of cultural rights in article 22 which states that everyone is entitled to realisation of the cultural rights indispensable for dignity and the free development of personality. Furthermore, the 1992 Declaration on the Rights of Persons belonging to National or Ethnic, Religious and Linguistic Minorities extended these rights to persons belonging to minorities to effectively participate in cultural, religious, social, economic and public life as well as in the decision-making process concerning the minority to which they belong.

The case studies presented here all concentrate on the two fundamental notions of citizenship and participation. In the research project underpinning this volume, Multicultural Policies and Modes of Citizenship in European Cities (MPMC), researchers from a range of social science disciplines conducted comparative analyses within various cities selected for the size and prominence of immigrant and ethnic minority groups. As detailed in the Introduction to this volume, the researchers worked with policy-makers and members of local organisations. Their aim was

> to assess the development and interplay of both "bottom-up" (community-led) initiatives and "top-down" (municipality-created) policies aimed at improving the integration of immigrant and ethnic minorities in public decision-making processes (p. 8).

The project focused particularly on what are termed 'channels of activation and mobilisation' in European cities, that is,

> organisations, actions or institutions through which immigrant and ethnic minority communities are supposed to make their interests and concerns known to municipal decision-makers and other significant actors in the various societal domains (p. 8).

As we can learn from these case studies, the relationship between citizenship and participation is not a simple and univocal one. Participation in policy-making by immigrant and ethnic minority groups is significantly hindered by the fact that many do not possess the status of legal citizenship. However, even in those states where some form of citizenship applies, other social and political factors prevent their full public participation. The editors explain in their Introduction that this lack of participation and/or acceptance in all social domains prevents the full development of citizenship by immigrants and ethnic minorities. As they state:

> If citizenship is considered as being full participation in the public domain and the exclusion from citizenship is seen as the exclusion from participation, the concept of citizenship is not only relevant in the political-juridical sphere, but also in the social-economic and social-cultural sphere' (p. 6).

In all three societal domains the concept of citizenship raises the issue of 'integration through participation'. Therefore, ensuring full citizenship and active participation in the public decision-making process requires integrating these notions within the broader framework of Human Rights.

Beyond these formal rules and regulations, one of the outstanding interests of this book is to give an in-depth and well-documented view of the practice of citizenship and participation. It is through the detailed study of the interactions between the local authorities and the immigrant associations and ethnic networks that we can learn the processes adopted by cities to deal with diversity. This accounts for the methodological standpoint adopted in the implementation of the project. All the authors looked at citizenship and participation from two different perspectives.

The first is the 'top-down' approach. Here the institutional framework of the society of settlement is taken as a starting point and the question is raised regarding the extent to which it is already open to participation by immigrants and ethnic minorities, or will be opened and activated over the course of time. In this approach the concepts of inclusion/exclusion and 'opportunity structure' are key concepts concerning the first part of that question. As regards the second part, i.e. measures to stimulate participation, activation seems to be the appropriate concept (as distinct from bottom-up mobilisation).

The second perspective is the 'bottom-up' approach. Here the central focus is on the initiatives taken by immigrants, ethnic minorities and their organisations to stand up for their political, social and cultural interests irrespective of institutional structures, either alone or in conjunction with other actors. The basic concept here is mobilisation. The analytical distinction between top-down and bottom-up, and activation and mobilisation makes it possible to systematically study the interaction between the two processes.

This provides fruitful insight because it clearly designates immigrants and ethnic minorities as actors, who profit by the institutional organisation of the hosting society and mobilise alternative and informal mechanisms and strategies to influence political decisions. One of the most fascinating aspects of these case studies is the precision applied to the description of the immigrants' strategies for gaining legitimacy in public and political spheres, mainly through the establishment of ethnic associations or informal networks.

The scope, openness, expertise and rigour of the works collected here under the auspices of the UNESCO MOST Programme (Management Of Social Transformations) makes this volume relevant to both the academic and policy-making communities. The methodological requirements were carefully followed resulting in a common groundwork for extensive comparability.

All these issues are of particular concern to UNESCO insofar as it embodies the ideal of reconciling respect for diversity with concerns for societal cohesion and the promotion of universally shared values and norms. While UNESCO's Constitution stresses the 'fruitful diversity of cultures' its highest principle is 'the intellectual and moral solidarity of mankind'. It is therefore quite natural that this project has found its place in the framework of the UNESCO MOST Programme.

The specific theme of 'cities as arenas of accelerated social transformations' is a core subject in the programme. The choice of such a theme demonstrates MOST's interest in understanding how social transformations affect the city of today and tomorrow. Furthermore, the study of multiculturalism is one of the three issues defined for the programme and the MPMC project is at the *nexus* of these two problematics.

The mission of UNESCO's Social and Human Sciences Sector is to contribute to generating and transferring social science knowledge to policy-makers and civil society. For this purpose, the MOST Programme was created in 1994 with the goals of improving understanding by generating policy-relevant knowledge on three major issues of our time: managing multi-ethnicity and multiculturalism, city governance, and coping with the impact of globalisation; and improving the communication between researchers and decision-makers.

Understanding social processes that take place in urban centres is a prerequisite for guiding and changing urban development policies. This approach is of relevance to decision-makers and stakeholders in the relationships between the state and civil society. It involves the implementation of both 'bottom-up' and 'top-down' strategies to favour active participation of all those concerned in open negotiations, transparent decision-making mechanisms, and the formulation of urban-management policies.

In these fields the MPMC project has marked considerable advances and has vastly contributed to a better understanding of immigration and urban-related issues. The project is also a model for comparative interdisciplinary research – not always an easy task. We are grateful to all those who have devoted their time and expertise to making this project a success.

We are very pleased to present this volume as a result of an UNESCO sponsored research project.

Acknowledgements

This book is the result of a joint effort of researchers in the 'Multicultural Policies and Modes of Citizenship in European Cities' (MPMC) project. This project is financed by the UNESCO MOST Programme (Management Of Social Transformations). We want to thank UNESCO for this support and for making this volume possible.

Furthermore we want to thank Rinus Penninx (director of the Institute for Migration and Ethnic Studies at the University of Amsterdam), Steven Vertovec (director of the ESRC Transnational Communities Programme (ESRC), Institute of Social and Cultural Anthropology, University of Oxford) and Marco Martiniello (Centre d'Etudes de l'Etnicité et des Migrations, Liege) for the necessary space and time needed to work on this volume. We also want to thank Karen Kraal for keeping the whole thing together and last, but not least, we want to thank Heleen Ronden at the Institute for Migration and Ethnic Studies for the layout of the manuscript.

1 Introduction: Multicultural Policies and Modes of Citizenship in European Cities

ALISDAIR ROGERS, JEAN TILLIE AND STEVEN VERTOVEC

Introduction

Now in their second and third generations, people whose origins lie in post-war immigration have become essentially permanent residents throughout Europe. Estimates of the number of non-EU nationals resident in EU countries range between 15 and 17.5 million, or over 4 per cent of the EU population. The 'foreign' population therefore outnumbers ten of the fifteen EU members, without including a similar number of second- and third-generation migrant-origin individuals. Furthermore, there is every indication that the absolute and relative significance of this population will increase. In the early 1990s there were over a million immigrants a year into the EU, double the numbers of the 1980s. The flow declined in the second half of the decade. Nonetheless, in 1996, immigrants accounted for three-quarters of the population growth of the EU, whose countries generally possess low birth rates. By some estimates the EU will need to admit 50 to 70 million newcomers by 2050 to counteract the declining and ageing population.[1] In November 2000 the EU Commission formally recognised this situation and began a debate on a common European immigration and integration policy. This 'foreign-origin' population has legitimate needs, demands, rights and duties with respect to the (national and local) 'host societies'. These needs are legitimate because they have contributed much through their labour, taxes, commercial services, participation in schools and neighbourhoods, and by enriching urban cultural landscapes. However, in every country of Europe immigrants and ethnic minorities have suffered disproportionately from a variety of forms of exclusion. As a result, they often endure among the worst social-economic circumstances of all of Europe's inhabitants.

Numerous policies, resources and recommendations have arisen at all levels of governance in all of the EU member states that address these

1

conditions. Municipal authorities are included in this process. Yet all too often immigrant and ethnic minority groups have had little say in the public decisions that affect them. Therefore, such decisions, and their consequent policies and resources often do not meet the needs of, or are not sufficiently engaged with or made use of by, immigrant and ethnic minority groups. This is a major obstacle to the successful economic incorporation of millions of Europeans.

Citizenship

The relative lack of immigrant and ethnic minority participation in policy-making is significantly conditioned by the fact that many do not have the legal status of citizenship. However, even in those states where some form of citizenship is available, other social and political factors prevent their full public participation. The political marginalisation or exclusion of socially and economic contributing residents challenges basic liberal democratic values, core institutional procedures, and even fundamental questions of morality. Together with the political concerns which have been directly voiced by immigrant and ethnic minority groups themselves (characterised by ever more effective forms of organisation), this state of affairs has recently stimulated much rethinking with regard to the concept of social citizenship in its broadest sense and the idea of a civil society.

Our task in this project is not to rehearse the burgeoning debate on citizenship, which has been the focus of several recent volumes (see for example Aleinikoff and Klusmeyer, 2000: Bauböck, 1994; Favell, 1998; Jopke, 1999; Kymlicka and Norman, 2000). It is increasingly difficult to pin down a clear definition. From a focus on the relationship between individuals, states and rights, it has broadened to include more sociological questions such as the access to resources, inequality, membership in a political community and identity. From its origins in political philosophy and political science, the debate has expanded into sociology, anthropology, urban studies, international relations and transnational studies. Under the influence of new social movements, citizenship has been extended from formal matters of belonging to some nation-state to more substantive ones of civil, political, social, economic and cultural rights and obligations.

As a result, citizenship theory has exposed the limitations of classical analyses such as T.H. Marshall's (1992) distinction between legal, political and social forms of citizenship. Among the new questions being advanced are whether there are rights in other spheres, such as economic rights in the workplace, cultural rights of recognition or even animal rights and to what degree should rights be matched by responsibilities and obligations? Should passive protections flowing from the state be accompanied by active engagement, making participation itself the purpose of citizenship? Are rights cumulative, evolutionary and progressive, or are there reversals and unevenness? Some, such as Soysal (1994), have argued that a post-national citizenship based on the universal discourse of human rights has displaced older national forms and provided European migrants and foreigners with almost all the social and economic rights open to full citizens. Other commentators, for example Stasiulis (1997), detect a widespread retreat from inclusive forms of citizenship towards more hierarchical situations. Finally, there are a series of questions arising from the fact that Marshall presupposed a culturally homogeneous society. This debate pits communitarians and nationalists on the one hand against certain liberals, postmodernists and theorists of identity politics on the other. Do the benefits of citizenship only flow from prior and committed membership of a political community, for example through naturalisation? Or, as Bauböck (1992) has argued, are they universal and egalitarian and so precede membership? Can liberal states allow group rights for national minorities or further, should they extend differentiated rights and special representation to oppressed groups (Young, 1990)? Aside from who has it and how, how has citizenship itself been socially constructed through gender, class, race and sexual differences?

It is no coincidence that theories of citizenship have appeared so frequently in discussions of European politics and identity. The legal status of citizenship, or nationality, is not universally available to migrants or, in some cases, to their children. Countries differ substantially in both their rules of naturalisation and their ideologies of nationhood, as the chapters in this volume show. Many countries are favourably inclined to dual citizenship but some, notoriously Germany, are not or have not been. Ireland, the Netherlands, Sweden, Denmark and Norway grant local voting rights to non-citizens, as do some local states within Germany and Switzerland.

Although non-citizens often enjoy many of the social and economic rights of citizens, these are mainly the property of guest workers long resident in Europe. Since the 1980s however, there has been a drastic increase in the number of marginalised migrants, seasonal and contract workers, street hawkers, women forced into the sex industry, female domestic workers, refugees, illegal immigrants and, at the other end of the spectrum, transient professionals and their families. There is evidence of this new migrant population in our case studies of Athens and Oeiras, Lisbon for example. In many cases, their lack of citizenship is functional in their exploitation. But in others it does not prevent them from accessing some of the services and benefits of the cities in which they reside. Moreover, even if residence were to become more widely accepted as the basis for formal citizenship, many marginal and transnational migrants are not, and may not intend being, permanently resident in any one country. An increasing number lead transnational lives.

Cities and Citizenship

> Cities are challenging, diverging from, and even replacing nations as the important space of citizenship – as the lived space not only of its uncertainties but also of its emergent forms (Holston and Appadurai, 1995, p. 189).

The significance of an urban focus on 'foreign-origin' communities, multiculturalism and citizenship can be gauged from the fact that even in the one country most renown for making citizenship inaccessible, Germany, the rate of naturalisation by the Berlin government easily outstripped the rest of the country. It would not be too inaccurate to claim that Western Europe has 'monocultural' nations but multicultural cities (Rogers, 2000).

As elsewhere in the world, migrants and their descendants in Europe are overwhelmingly concentrated in cities. Furthermore, they are overrepresented in large metropolitan areas and national capitals. For example, 55 per cent of Portugal's foreigners are in Lisbon and over 40 per cent of the Netherlands' minorities are found in the four largest urban centres. As a result, a number of European cities contain foreign-origin (defined in different ways in different cities) communities of between a tenth and a third of their total inhabitants. These include increasingly cosmopolitan centres such as Brussels, Copenhagen, Amsterdam, and London, where both EU and non-EU nationals are found. They also include former industrial and port cities such as Rotterdam, Frankfurt, Antwerp, Marseille and Birmingham. In general, Southern European cities – including Barcelona and Athens – have immigrant communities of around five per cent of local population.

John Crowley, in his concluding essay, examines the case for a 'local' citizenship. There are at least five main reasons why there might be a theoretical connection between cities and citizenship (Rogers, 2000; see also Holston, 1999). To begin with, revival of philosophical interest in citizenship often returns to its antecedents in Athens, Rome, the medieval borough and the many local sites of citizenship swept away by the emergence of the nation-state. Within some quarters there seems to be a nostalgia for the pre-modern European independent city-state and the leagues of mercantile cities. Secondly, it is often argued that the rescaling of politics, particularly in Europe, means that the nation-state can no longer exhaust the possibilities of citizenship or meet its challenges. Into this democratic gap enters the city, mediating local and global processes and networking with other cities. Thirdly, in so far as current debates on citizenship raise questions about the relationship between membership in some form of community and the formal aspects of citizenship, cities are the sites of the most profound questions of belonging and identity. The assumption of shared community and culture as the basis for citizenship becomes most problematic in the city. Metropolitan areas are where the contradictions between universal and differentiated conceptions of citizenship become most evident.

Cities are also the most productive sites of alternative citizenship or challenges from below, for example the Franco-Maghrebian struggle for citizenship in the French *banlieues*. But at the same time, cities can also be the site of exclusionary discourses of citizenship, as found among the neo-Nazi campaigns for 'foreigner-free' zones in former eastern Germany which began in the 1990s.

Fifthly, there are significant local variations in both the forms of citizenship and its substance. Whether or not there are such local differences and whether they are meaningful is a matter of empirical study. For example, in a comparison of Moroccan political mobilisation in Lille and Utrecht, Bousetta (1997) discovered the anticipated contrast between non-ethnic and ethnic based collective politics, but concluded that neither strategy was more successful than the other was.

If there are theoretical grounds for associating cities and citizenship, then what is most obviously missing is systematic and comparative empirical inquiry across national contexts. This is the prime aim of the MPMC project, which focuses on channels of mobilisation as a way of investigating citizenship and participation.

Modes of Citizenship and 'Channels of Mobilisation'

Beyond the political sphere and the issues of representative liberal democracy, there are numerous other modes of exclusion affecting immigrants and ethnic minorities. These include restricted access to the labour market (including public sector employment); limited opportunities for self-employment and small business formation; denial or differential provision of social welfare resources (including programmes for financial assistance, training, health, housing, insurance, and old age pensions); and limited possibilities to openly express cultural identity.

Not participating in these various societal domains prevents the full development of social citizenship by immigrants and ethnic minorities. This means that the concept of citizenship can be successfully deployed to *analyse* the position of immigrants and ethnic minorities in a broad range of societal domains. If citizenship is considered as being full participation in the public domain and the exclusion from citizenship is seen as the exclusion from participation, the concept of citizenship is not only relevant in the political-juridical sphere, but also in the social-economic and social-cultural sphere. That is, in all three societal domains the citizenship concept raises the issue of integration through participation.

With respect to participation (and thus integration) in the *social-cultural* domain the key questions might include: what (if any) conditions are created for immigrants and ethnic minorities to express their own religious identity; what initiatives are taken by the ethnic communities themselves to express this identity? In the *social-economic* sphere the issue concerns questions of equal participation, for example, restricted access to the labour market or limited possibilities for self-employment. In the *political-juridical* domain the concept of citizenship relates to issues of political participation, the fight against racism and discrimination, but also the juridical position of immigrants as members of the national community.

For each domain *channels of mobilisation* can be identified. Through these channels immigrants can be mobilised in order to participate in the public domain, and so mitigate forms of social, economic and political exclusion.

In the social-cultural sphere one can think of, for example, religious or cultural organisations of immigrants; participation in primary or secondary school activities; participation in various educational programmes (including education in their own language) or the development of specific policies directed towards the expression of identity. In the social-economic domain channels of mobilisation may be immigrant-owned small businesses, economic self-organisations and trade unions. Concerning the political-juridical domain, one can think of immigrants and ethnic minorities participating in existing political parties; the establishment of 'immigrant parties' or action groups and the so-called consultative bodies. That is, throughout Europe

– especially at the level of cities – a range of parallel institutions and policies have been created by way of the common objective of liaisons with immigrants and ethnic minorities. According to Anderson (1990) these include consultative bodies such as:

- contact and co-ordination groups (created for the inclusion of all majority and minority groups with a broad remit to improve relations);
- working and co-ordination groups (comprised mainly of government departments dealing with immigrants and ethnic minorities, with very few actual members of the latter groups; for the purpose of sharing information and co-ordinating programmes and activities);
- parliaments or forums of migrant workers or ethnic minorities (made up of representatives of immigrant/ethnic minority groups only, in order to articulate their interests and press for the implementation of policies);
- advisory councils (perhaps the most common type of institution, including representatives of both immigrant/ethnic minority groups and members of government, with broad scope for sharing information, expressing concerns, distributing resources, and lobbying for interests);
- committees on migrant or ethnic minority affairs (established by government, with variable makeup but sometimes with decision-making powers).

However, such participatory institutions and policies have been established or have developed very differently in terms of structure, intent, and relation to regional and national policy; their degrees and evidence of success and failure have differed considerably as well. These variations are not simply cross-national. There are significant differences among, and therefore lessons to be learned from, European cities.

The MPMC Research Project

The research project Multicultural Policies and Modes of Citizenship in European Cities (MPMC) has been organised under the auspices of UNESCO's Management of Social Transformation (MOST) Programme as one project in the theme of Multicultural and Multi-ethnic Societies.[2] Social scientists from a variety of disciplines have undertaken research and comparative analyses within selected urban contexts characterised by a substantial presence and activity of immigrant and ethnic minority groups.

Working with policy-makers and members of local organisations, their task was to assess the development and interplay of both 'bottom-up' (community-led) initiatives and 'top-down' (municipality-created) policies aimed at improving the integration of immigrant and ethnic minorities in public decision-making processes. Of central concern to the project is what we have termed above *channels of mobilisation*. These are organisations, actions or institutions through which immigrant and ethnic minority communities are supposed to make their interests and concerns known to municipal decision-makers and other significant actors in the various societal domains.

A rigorous comparison and evaluation of structures, processes, strategies and activities in both 'top-down' and 'bottom-up' levels surrounding channels of mobilisation in European cities has two aims relevant to current political and policy-related debates. The first involves the advancement of social scientific theories and typologies concerning social integration, most particularly through extending the concept of social citizenship. The second concerns proposals – assessed together with community groups and policy-makers – for a set of 'best practices' and policy recommendations involving the integration of social-culturally, social-economically and politically excluded groups into the sphere of urban governance.

In each city, the research team was charged with providing answers to the following questions:

- How do immigrant and ethnic minority groups gain access, or have been confronted with obstacles, to relevant channels of mobilisation within the social-cultural, the social-economic and political-juridical domains?
- What are the social-cultural, social-economic, and political-juridical conditions affecting immigrant and ethnic minority groups, including their own patterns and processes of mobilisation and expression of interests?
- How do immigrant and ethnic minority groups gain access, or have been confronted with obstacles, to decision-making processes?
- How do local authority frameworks for immigrants and ethnic minorities (for example consultative bodies, forums, and ombudsmen) and municipal policies (including regulations, institutions, and structures) develop in terms of structure, intent and relation to regional and national policies?

The Project Cities

The cities identified for research under the MPMC project come from right across West Europe. They vary in at least two dimensions. Some are found in countries with a relatively long history of overseas immigration and settlement, by European standards at least. They include Birmingham (United Kingdom), Amsterdam (the Netherlands), Brussels (Belgium) and Zurich (Switzerland). Other cities have no more than one generation of experience with immigration, such as Athens and Lisbon. There is already traffic in policy and research between northern and southern countries and city governments. The cases presented here contribute research essential to this policy exchange.

Secondly, the cities are located in countries with notably different concepts, practices and laws of citizenship in all its forms. Do such differences reach down to the municipal level as well? Are there significant urban modes of citizenship within these national-level regimes? And, above all, do such top-down differences explain variations in mobilisation and participation among the cities described? A substantial body of research comparing and contrasting national citizenship exists, but there are fewer examples of inquiry at lower levels.

Several of the cities featured here have undergone significant changes at the level of governance – Amsterdam, Birmingham and Brussels to name but three. To what extent do these changes impact upon immigrant and minority ethnic communities? Were such communities actively involved in the reorganisation of governance? And are there trends among European cities, towards both participation and multiculturalism on the one hand, or neo-liberalism and social exclusion on the other?

This Volume

In this volume the above-mentioned 'channels of mobilisation' are an important topic of inquiry. For Amsterdam, Athens, Barcelona, Birmingham, Brussels, Marseille, Oeiras (Lisbon), Paris, Tel Aviv and Zurich, multicultural policies are analysed and examples of immigrant mobilisation are studied. In addition, the historical cycles of migration and the actual composition of the immigrant population are reported for each city. Further, specific immigrant communities are studied in depth (that is, the importance of this community in the city, their organisations; their links to other (local) societal actors, their formal and informal links to the municipality, the most important community issues etc.).

A close study of the way multicultural policies are developed and the way immigrant communities mobilise in these cities, shows that in each city policies and mobilisation can be classified in terms of the answers to the following questions:

Political rights
- Are local voting rights granted to ethnic minorities in so far as they are non-citizens?

Immigrant communities
- Do immigrant/ethnic organisations exist and, if yes, what are their main goals and activities?
- Are there specific political issues on which immigrant/ethnic communities are mobilised (such as (re)housing or education)?
- Are there coalitions between immigrant communities and other societal actors, such as, trade unions, churches, political parties, anti-racist organisations or other NGOs?
- Can one speak of transnational communities in the specific city?

Local policies
- Can the policies which are developed, be characterised as *group specific*, i.e. directed specifically towards ethnic minorities, for example, supporting ethnic association activities) or *general (issue-based)*, i.e. directed to people in need irrespective of their ethnic background? For example, is some kind of consultative structure between the city and the immigrant population established (see also Anderson's typology of consultative bodies mentioned above)?
- Are there any differences between the official policies developed, for instance at national level, and *de facto* policies as practised at the local level?
- What is the relation between local levels of government and other levels, such as the state or EU?

In her chapter on *Amsterdam* Karen Kraal summarises city politics in terms of a move from group-specific to problem-oriented, or general, policies. In the 1980s the focus was on ethnic and cultural differences and the maintaining of their cultural identity. Now a so-called diversity policy is developed which no longer focuses on groups but on problems. The central aim of the diversity policy is participation of all individuals in society and politics. By contrast, as Marina Petronoti shows, in *Athens* there are no regulations whatsoever (at least until 1998). Such policies as are developed can be labelled 'ad-hoc measures'. The number of ethnic associations is increasing. However, they lack basic political resources and are highly dependent on churches, ant-racist organisations and other NGOs. Ricard Morén-Alegret demonstrates that in *Barcelona* predominantly general policies are developed with respect to ethnic minorities. Immigrants have no voting rights (except those from EU countries). As far as ethnic organisations are concerned there is a development from protest organisations to service organisations.

Romain Garbaye states in his *Birmingham* chapter that the role of the national and local Labour Party was (and is) important. As in Amsterdam, in Birmingham there is a pragmatic development towards general policies. A high level of community organisation does exist. Special attention is paid to the Standing Consultative Forum (SCF), a tentative association of ethnic groups to the City Council's policies, consisting of nine umbrella groups. In *Brussels*, 'a hybrid region in a multination state' as Dirk Jacobs puts it, the power struggle between the two national communities (the Flemish and the Francophone) both enables and frustrates political incorporation of ethnic minorities. The Flemish mainly adhere to group-specific policies, while the Francophones are more influenced by the individual republican model of France. Jacobs argues that this Flemish-Francophone struggle strongly inhibits formal enfranchisement of foreign residents.

In *Marseille* foreigners have no local voting rights (except EU residents). In the tradition of the French republican model, general policies with respect to social, educational and housing needs are developed and implemented. However, as Damian Moore argues in his chapter on the 'city of migrations', at the beginning of the 1980s, when local authorities launched urban regeneration policies in the northern areas of Marseille, a group of 'mediators' emerged between the North African minority and public institutions. These mediators gradually pushed the local authorities into creating formal and informal political and institutional opportunity structures for the North African minority and for other ethnic minorities in Marseille.

In their chapter on *Oeiras (Lisbon)* Margarida Marques and Rui Santos explicitly discuss the relation between the local governmental level and higher levels of government (national and EU level). For example, re-housing issues are local issues that affect immigrants, their legal status however is a national issue. At the national Portuguese level there is the High Commissioner for Immigration and Ethnic Minorities (HCIEM). The appointed HCIEM created a national Consultative Council to advise him.

This proved to be a major mobilisation event for national and local immigrants' associations. Furthermore, there is the EU URBAN Programme that has a strong local policy influence.

The *Paris* chapter, written by Riva Kastoryano and John Crowley, focuses on four contiguous *communes* in the north-western part of the near suburban area: Saint-Denis, Saint-Ouen, Épinay-sur-Seine and Clichy, of which the first two are profiled in more detail. Two developments, a law of 1982 which fundamentally reshaped local government, replacing the hierarchical relationship between the *préfet* and the local authorities by partnership and, in the same period, the removal of restrictions on the creation of voluntary organisations by foreign residents, transformed the local opportunity structure for migrant activity. Kastoryano and Crowley argue, however, that the 'local' still occupies an ambiguous position within the French model of nationhood.

Although *Tel Aviv* is not in Europe, Michael Alexander argues that it can be compared to European cities with regard to the interaction between cities and migrants. Alexander notes that Israeli national policy has created a paradoxical situation where undocumented migrants are mobilising more openly than 'legal' labour migrants. Tel Aviv still does not know how to deal with the overseas migrants who have replaced Palestinian workers, however the city's relatively benign attitude, such as the opening of a municipal aid centre serving migrants regardless of their legal status, contrasts with the national policy.

Hans Mahnig and Andreas Wimmer point to the 'contradictions of inclusion' in a direct democracy. In their chapter on *Zurich* they conclude that the town's political opportunity structure did not have a positive impact on the inclusion of migrants. The writers argue that the failure of attempts for more inclusive policies can first and foremost be explained by the opposition of important parts of the population who can express their hostility towards migrants through the instruments of direct democracy.

The book concludes with an after word by John Crowley. Crowley re-addresses the issue of 'local citizenship'. Is it possible to develop a concept of 'local citizenship' that is coherent, usable and useful? He is sceptical. Reviewing the cases presented in this book, he states that empirical evidence that local politics might constitute a local political field is so far woefully lacking. The exchanges among the empirical chapters and between them and this concluding reflection on the concept of citizenship provide rich material for discussion.

Notes

1 See the report of the Population Division of the Department of Economic and Social Affairs, United Nations, 'Replacement Migration: Is it a Solution to Declining and Ageing Populations?', March 2000.
2 Full details of the UNESCO Management of Social Transformation Programme can be found at http://www.unesco.org/most.

References

Aleinikoff, T.A. and Klusmeyer, D. (eds) (2000), *From Migrants to Citizens: Membership in a Changing World*, Carnegie Endowment for International Peace, Washington, DC.

Anderson, U. (1990), 'Consultative Institutions for Migrant Workers', in Z. Layton-Henry (ed.), *Political Rights of Migrant Workers in Western Europe*, Sage, London, pp. 113-26.

Bauböck, R. (1992), *Immigration and the Boundaries of Citizenship*, Monographs in Ethnic Relations no. 4, Centre for Research in Ethnic Relations, University of Warwick, Coventry.

Bauböck, R. (ed.) (1994), *From Aliens to Citizens: Redefining the Status of Immigrants in Europe*, Avebury, Aldershot.

Bousetta, H. (1997), 'Citizenship and Political Participation in France and the Netherlands: Reflections on Two Local Cases', *New Community* vol. 23, pp. 215-31.

Favell, A. (1998), *Philosophies of Integration: Immigration and the Idea of Citizenship*, Oxford University Press, Oxford.

Holston, J. (ed.) (1999), *Cities and Citizenship*, Duke University Press, Durham, NC.

Holston, J. and Appadurai, A. (1996), 'Cities and citizenship', *Public Culture* vol. 8, pp. 187-204.

Jopke, C. (1999), *Immigration and the Nation-State*, Oxford University Press, Oxford.

Kymlicka, W. and Norman, W. (eds) (2000), *Citizenship in Diverse Societies*, Oxford University Press, Oxford.

Marshall, T.H. (1992) [1950], 'Citizenship and Social Class', in T.H. Marshall and T. Bottomore, *Citizenship and Social Class*, part I, Pluto Press, London, pp. 3-51.

Rogers, A. (2000), 'Citizenship, Multiculturalism and the European City', in G. Bridge and S. Watson (eds), *A Companion to the City*, Blackwell, Oxford, pp 282-91.

Soysal, Y.N. (1994), *Limits of Citizenship: Migrants and Postnational Membership in Europe*, University of Chicago Press, Chicago.

Stasiulis, D.K. (1997), 'International Migration, Rights, and the Decline of "Actually Existing Liberal democracy"', *New Community* vol. 23, pp. 197-214.

Young, I.M. (1990), *Justice and the Politics of Difference*, Princeton University Press, Princeton.

2 Amsterdam: From Group-Specific to Problem-Oriented Policy

KAREN KRAAL

Introduction

For centuries Amsterdam has been a destination for immigrants, first Europe and then from across the world. In this chapter various aspects of migration to and migrants in Amsterdam will be described and placed in line based on diverse researches. In the first part the focus is on the history of migration, the composition of the current immigrant minority population and the social-economic position. In the second part the political opportunity structure of the city is presented. Special attention is given to the change of a group specific to a problem-oriented policy aimed at combating disadvantages of all inhabitants of the city. In 1999 the city decided that they had not succeeded to combat the disadvantaged position of migrants and that a new policy was needed. A new draft memorandum was therefore published. The two memorandums on which current policy is based are each discussed in a different paragraph. In the third part of this chapter we analyse how immigrants do politically participate and mobilise themselves in the described opportunity structure. We look at local elections (last held in 1998), the organisations founded by immigrants and we present a case study of various selected Turkish organisations in Amsterdam. In the fourth and last section the interaction between activation policies of authorities and mobilisation of ethnic minorities as well as district variations will be discussed. Two case studies are the core of this section, one conducted by Alink and Berger (1999) on the city districts Bos en Lommer and Zeeburg and one conducted by Van Heelsum and Penninx (1999) in the city district Oost. The differences between ethnic specific policies and more general policies shall be attended in this section.

Amsterdam: City of Migrants

The first great migration to Amsterdam took place in the late sixteenth century when more than 100,000 South Netherlanders fled from Spain's imperial forces, fearing prosecution for their Protestant belief's. They were mainly highly specialised craftsmen and workers and were welcomed with open arms. Between 1531-1606 Amsterdam's population grew from 30,000 to 60,000 partly as a result. A second immigration wave took place at the end of the seventeenth century, when Louis XIV ended the protection of the Protestant Huguenots who then fled to Amsterdam. Here they were permitted to settle and in a short period the city received 12,000 new inhabitants. From the seventeenth till the late nineteenth century, thousands of German men came for seasonal work. A lot of them settled and started their own businesses like bakeries and butcher's shops. At the end of the nineteenth century many German Catholic textile-entrepreneurs settled in Amsterdam.

There were also refugees and immigrants from further afield. For example, Jews from Portugal (at the beginning of the seventeenth century, who fled for persecution by Philip II) and Middle and Eastern Europe (in the eighteenth century especially, who fled for the pogroms in Poland and Russia) found refuge and the opportunity to exercise their rituals and beliefs.

More recent cycles of migration for the city correspond closely to cycles of migration for the country. Since 1945 the Netherlands has received several more inflows from abroad, similar to other North-western European countries. These include former colonists and settlers, colonised 'minorities', guest workers and, more recently, refugees and labour migrants. Amsterdam is one of the main Dutch cities to which immigrants go.[1]

These cycles of migrations are influenced by economic developments similar to developments in other European countries. By the mid-1950s, the economy had begun to grow and this process led to a labour shortage in certain sectors, such as mining and industry. A system of 'temporary guest workers' was devised to fill these vacancies. Initially Italian workers were recruited on a small scale. Then workers from Spain, Portugal, Turkey, Greece, Morocco, Yugoslavia and Tunisia followed. The number of 'guest workers' increased even more through spontaneous immigration from these countries, to 74,000 by 1967.

After 1973 the economy stagnated and labour recruitment stopped. Immigration from recruitment countries however (especially from Turkey and Morocco), continued, through family reunification, and more recently, marriage migration. Recruited workers as well as those immigrating through family reunification were predominantly unskilled and semi-skilled people from rural areas in sending countries (Penninx et al., 1994).

Following family reunification, the residence of migrant workers began to take on a permanent character. This was stimulated by both poor labour market conditions in source countries (Turkey, Morocco etc.) and by official Dutch policy (Penninx, 1979, pp. 104-7). The labour market position of immigrant workers in the Netherlands deteriorated in the second half of the 1970s and in the 1980s and unemployment increased (Kloosterman, 1994).

Another immigration wave took place before the independence of the former Dutch colony of Surinam (1974-1975) followed by a second peak after the decolonisation (1979-1980). This migration was not triggered by labour market considerations. Before Surinam's independence, the Surinamese were Dutch citizens and free to settle in the Netherlands. After the independence of Surinam in November 1975, Surinamese had in principle become aliens and thus subject to restrictive admission policies. The Netherlands remained a destination of sizeable migration movements of all ages and educational backgrounds (Van Amersfoort and Cortie, 1996).

The immigration of another important group, the Antilleans, is largely determined by shifts in the economic circumstances in the country of origin. The Netherlands Antilles forms part of the Kingdom of the Netherlands and there are no bars to their migration. Since the 1990s this immigration has returned to low levels (Lucassen and Penninx, 1997).

Between 1960 and 1995 the immigrant population grew from 117,000 to 757,000, excluding naturalisation (Heijs, 1995, pp. 206-11; Penninx et al., 1994, p. 17; Tesser et al, 1996, pp. 20-23).[2]

Composition of the Immigrant Minority Population

In the period 1968-1981 the immigrant population in Amsterdam more than doubled. Between 1981 and 1992 the share of non-native residents increased annually by approximately 1 per cent, although after 1992 this increase has levelled off. In 1999 316,875 allochtonous people lived in Amsterdam. This is 42 per cent of the total population of Amsterdam and 12 per cent of all immigrants in the Netherlands (CBS, 1999).[3] Of all inhabitants of the city 35.8 per cent belong to an ethnic group.[4] The most important groups are Turks, Moroccans, Surinamese and Antilleans.

Table 2.1 shows the numbers for ethnic groups in Amsterdam in 1982-1996, and in 2000. In contrast to the native population the ethnic minority population in Amsterdam is growing due to a higher birth rate and continuing immigration.[5]

Table 2.1   **Population of Amsterdam, according to ethnic groups[a], January 1st 1989-1996; January 1st 2000**

	1989	*1990*	*1992[a]*	*1994*	*1996*	*2000*
Surinamese	52,757	54,839	62,045	67,900	69,600	71,760 (9.8%)
Antilleans	8,473	9,063	10,684	10,600	10,500	11,623 (1.6%)
Turks	21,028	22,405	28,664	30,900	31,000	33,623 (4.6%)
Moroccans[b]	32,274	33,701	41,623	46,100	48,000	55,043 (7.5%)
South Europeans[c]	11,210	11,278	14,489	16,100	16,300	17,066 (2.3%)
NIC[d]	16,248	15,763	50,151	57,000	59,700	72,066 (9.0%)
IC[e]	23,479	23,707	70,132	71,100	69,500	69,651 (9.5%)
Dutch	529,521	524,465	435,705	424,600	413,600	400,027 (54.7%)
Total	694,990	695,221	713,493	724,200	718,100	731,289 (100.0%)

[a] The broad definition is used from 1992 till 1999: those who are born in the country of origin mentioned, plus those who have at least one parent who is born there
[b] Between 1989 and 1992, including Tunisians and Algerians
[c] Italians, Portuguese, Spaniards and (former) Yugoslavians
[d] Non-industrialised countries
[e] Industrialised countries

Source: BSM-GA, 1996; O+S, 2000.

The distribution of the ethnic groups across the city's 13 districts is rather spatially uneven. There are some districts in which the percentage of minorities is lowest (between 12.4 per cent and 18 per cent): Buitenveldert, Watergraafsmeer, Zuid, Binnenstad and Rivierenbuurt; and other districts in which the concentration of minorities is highest (between 50 per cent and 57.2 per cent): Zuidoost, Zeeburg and Bos en Lommer. This uneven distribution is partly attributed to the settlement procedure of immigrants. In the 1960s and 1970s, middle and high income native-Dutch moved to surrounding towns where large owner-occupied properties were available. They left their small (two or three bedroom flats) and cheap houses behind. These cheap houses which belong mainly to the social housing stock, offered suitable accommodations for immigrants. After a short time, however, these houses could no longer satisfy the requirements of large immigrant families. After family reunification in the second half of the 1970s and in the 1980s immigrants had to seek larger houses (3 or 4 bedrooms) in suburbs, as Bos en Lommer, Geuzenveld/Slotermeer, Osdorp and Zeeburg. The prices of these houses were moderate, just payable for large immigrant families. Recent research by the Amsterdam Statistic and Research Bureau, O+S (Van Vlijmen, 1996), shows that Moroccan and Turkish households often live in tight houses with an average rent of 570 Guilders (259 Euro).

Despite the uneven distribution of minorities over the various districts Amsterdam has a moderate level of segregation compared to cities such as Brussels, Dusseldorf, Frankfurt, London, Paris, Stockholm and Toronto (Ostendorf, 1996). This is partly because the Municipality has an important role in the construction and management of housing. Moreover, the Dutch government supports the purchasing power of low-income households by rent subsidies. Twenty per cent of the total households in Amsterdam receive rent subsidy. The percentage is about 33 per cent among Surinamese, Antillean and Moroccan households but a relative small number of Turkish households and households from non-industrialised countries have applied for this subsidy.

Social-economic Position

Most of the ethnic minorities from Mediterranean countries such as Italy, Spain, Portugal, Turkey and Morocco, were recruited in the 1960s and in the beginning of the 1970s for unskilled/low-paid jobs in the traditional industry. Unemployment began to rise at a great pace just after the first oil crisis of 1973 and the collapse of traditional sectors. In the period of 1970-1983, industrial production decreased by an average of 1 per cent annually but remained stabile between 1983-1995. At the same time, the productivity of labour (in terms of hourly production) rose sharply as a result of technical and organisational innovations. The direct consequence of these two developments in the Amsterdam-area was the decrease of number of jobs in industry from 148,000 in 1970 to 89,000 in 1995. By contrast jobs in the service sector, especially in commercial services, increased sharply. While the structure of employment changed in favour of relative high-educated workers, the education level of ethnic minorities has remained below average and they have become increasingly unemployed (Klooster-man, 1994).[6]

Not all ethnic minority groups have the same unfavourable labour market position. Surinamese and Antillean people are less frequently unemployed than Turks and Moroccans. Moreover, the distribution of employed Surinamese and Antilleans over different sectors shows more similarities to that of Dutch people.

Ethnic minorities have started their own small firms in reaction to their declining opportunities in the regular labour market, in sectors where the production is labour-intensive, profit margins are low and little start-up capital is required. Sectors like the clothing industry, retail trade and catering industry. The number of firms owned by ethnic minorities increased strongly in the last two decades. But not all minority groups are equally successful in establishing their own enterprises. Turks and Italians are more frequently entrepreneurs than Surinamese, Moroccans and (other) South Europeans. The degree of entrepreneurship is also high among some other small minority groups, i.e. Chinese, Egyptians, Pakistanis and Indians (Choenni, 1997).

Political Structures[7]

The reunification of immigrant families and the deterioration of the labour market position of immigrant workers encouraged the government to adjust its policy relating to immigrants. The assumption of temporary presence was replaced by the expectation of permanent presence. Some political rights like passive and active voting rights for local elections and an active labour market policy directed to (unemployed) immigrants followed. In the 1980s the policy aimed at minorities was based on the idea that minorities should integrate while also maintaining their cultural identity. Target groups were seen as disadvantaged in some way and ethnically and culturally different. The policies were aimed at reducing disadvantages especially in the domain of labour, education and housing. During the 1990s the accent moved from 'minority policy' towards 'integration policy'. Newcomers should not run the risk to fall into a disadvantaged state and be 'absorbed' in society. The current policy towards ethnic minorities is called 'diversity policy' and goes away from group-specific policy. The policy is still in development and is based on two memorandums.

The Memorandum of 1989

In 1989 the City of Amsterdam published the memorandum *Municipal Minorities Policy* (*'Raamnota Gemeentelijk Minderhedenbeleid'*). In this memorandum the City Administration concluded that 'after a decade of efforts of government and of private initiatives the position of ethnic minority groups seems not to be improved' and 'the effects of the minorities policy, which took form from the beginning of the seventies, (…) appear not to be encouraging'. Apparently changes were needed to make the city's minorities' policy more successful. According to the memorandum of 1989 the minorities policy would have two main objectives:

- Abolishing the disadvantaged position of immigrants by increasing the accessibility of scarce goods and services (in fields like labour, education, housing, health and welfare) and by stimulating a proportional use of these goods.
- Tackling the neglect of immigrants by combating discrimination and racism. The foundation of this objective was put down in the 1985 note *Anti-racism policy*. The basic principles of this policy are: a) the equality of all individuals in Amsterdam and b) a better functioning of agencies and institutions by applying the instrument of positive (or affirmative) action.

The memorandum mentions four different opportunities for migrant communities to influence policy:

- Participation in neighbourhood-oriented projects. According to the City Council, inhabitants of migrant origin are not enough involved in the development of public space and facilities. This situation must be improved by neighbourhood projects.

- Participation by immigrant support organisations. These organisations are a structural and (by policy recognised as) official form of participation to support and promote the interests of migrants and their organisations. At the moment there are three support organisations: the ACB (the Amsterdam Centre of Migrants), Forsa Amsterdam (support organisation for Antilleans and Arubans in Amsterdam) and SSA (support organisation for Surinamese Dutch). FSM (Federation Support Organisations Minorities Policy in the Region of Amsterdam) is the umbrella body for the three organisations (see also Figure 2.1).
- Advisory councils. Advisory councils are the most important forms of structural participation. The councils give advice (both solicited and unsolicited) directly to the Mayor, Aldermen and the City Council on the Amsterdam policy in general, but also on matters concerning migrants especially.[8] The Mayor, Aldermen and the City Council are compelled to react within a certain period. There is structural consultation between the city government and the advisory councils. There are five advisory councils: one for Turks (TDM), one for Moroccans (SRM), one for Surinamese, Antillian, Moluccan and Ghanese people (SAAMGha), one for refugees, Chinese and Pakistanis (VluChiPa) and one for South Europeans (ZEG). The members of the councils are chosen by the boards of the affiliated migrant organisations. The councils have their own secretary and budget that they receive from the municipality.
- Migrant organisations. According to the memorandum, migrant organisations play a keyrole concerning the position of migrants in society. They can connect to groups that are difficult for local government to reach, in case of governmental projects and initiatives on policies. In the opinion of the Administration organisations have to be more involved in the implementation of policy, especially in the fields of education and labour. The participation of migrant organisations is still too much focused on the preparation and evaluation phases of the policy process. To promote more active involvement, migrant organisations, welfare organisations and institutions have to co-operate more. Any costs arising from this co-operation will be subsidised by the city. In principle, all migrant organisations are eligible for subsidies. The most important criterion of eligibility is the accessibility of facilities. However, nationalist organisations that emphasise and promote their own national identity and are intolerant of out-group influences are excluded from the subsidy-policy.

Figure 2.1   **Structure of policy participation of immigrants in Amsterdam**

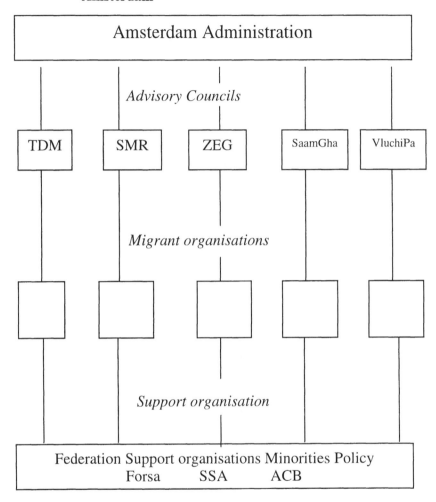

The Draft-memorandum of 1999

The above described policy has not abolished the disadvantaged position of immigrants and has not tackled the neglect of immigrants. Therefore the need was felt for a new strategy. In 1999 the city published the draft-memorandum *The Force of a Diverse City* (*'De Kracht van een Diverse Stad'*) which sets out the plans and targets of the Administration concerning 'diversity policy'. This draft-memorandum shows that the Administration considers the 1989 minorities policy as out-dated. On the one hand, the

Administration judged that minorities policy has worked well to make the problems of 'minority' groups (not only ethnic minorities, but also women, the disabled, and gays and lesbians) visible and to put them on the political agenda. On the other hand, a negative effect of minorities policy has been the stigmatisation of individual members of minority groups and the neglect of a diversity of individuals varying from 'problematical cases' – school drop outs, unemployed etc. – who need a maximum of governmental support to be able to participate in society to those who can find their way in society on their own. Combating disadvantage in fields such as education, labour, housing, use of public services has led for the Administration to focus on *problems* and not *a priori* on *target-groups* anymore. However, within this general approach, specific policies are possible, where necessary. The Administration cherishes diversity within its municipal borders and considers it as an enrichment of society.

The central aim of the diversity policy will be that all inhabitants of Amsterdam feel at home in their city and that everyone has the opportunity to contribute to this ideal situation. The Administration wants a city where:

- everyone has equal opportunities (in fields such as education, labour, housing and care);
- everyone has respect for the other and exclusion is actively combated;
- everyone can participate and make decisions together.

The Administration is planning to accomplish this by the following policy objectives:

- a better tuning of policy to the diverse composition of the population (especially in the fields of Labour, Housing and Liveability, Care, Sports and Recreation, Art and Culture, Education – also for the of aged – and youth policy);
- making the composition of the civil service and the organisational culture of municipal services and companies representative for the diversity of the population;
- stimulating the participation of all the inhabitants and actively combating negative formation, prejudice and exclusion;
- initiating a broad coalition in society that aims for a positive use of Amsterdam's diversity.

In the 1999 draft-memorandum eleven concrete measures are mentioned to improve the participation of all citizens in three fields: political participation; participation in advisory councils and other municipal councils; and participation in decision making processes.

The attention and the efforts of the Administration will be more focused on individual immigrants and less on migrant organisations. The Advisory Council of Minorities Policy will retain its important position in the policy process as a partner of the Administration, but only as long as other general advisory structures are not diverse enough in ethnic composition.

The draft-memorandum contains plans for the future. It still only exists on paper and it is unclear how it will develop. At the moment the formal structure for the participation of migrants in policy is as depicted in Figure 2.1.

Participation and Mobilisation

Participation in Local Elections

Following Denmark, Sweden and Ireland, the Dutch government awarded voting rights to non-Dutch people for District Council elections in 1980 and for City Council elections in 1985. These people must have a residence permit and have lived (continuously) in the Netherlands for at least five years in order to qualify. Non-Dutch people can, in principle, be elected as Aldermen. The position of Mayor is reserved for people with Dutch nationality. Non-Dutch people do not have voting rights for elections for Provincial States and Parliament (Heijs, 1995).

Since ethnic minorities achieved the right to vote for local elections, four local elections took place: in 1986, 1990, 1994 and 1998. During these elections researches were conducted on the turn out and voting behaviour of minority voters (all having Dutch nationality or not) in different cities, including in Amsterdam (Pennings, 1987; Tillie, 1994, 2000).

We may, on basis of these four elections, conclude that the turnout differs by elections, ethnic group and municipality/district, and that the turnout of minority voters is, in general, lower than native voters. The overall turnout of Turkish voters is the highest, followed by Moroccans, Surinamese and Antilleans. In 1994 the turnout rates of Turkish voters in some cities is even higher than native voters.

The turnout of minority groups in 1998 in Amsterdam amounted to 39 per cent for Turks, 23 per cent for Moroccans and 21 per cent for Surinamese/Antillean, a total turnout of 25 per cent (Tillie, 2000). The turnout of all inhabitants was 47 per cent.

The voting behaviour of the various ethnic groups in 1998 is presented in Table 2.2. The PvdA (Labour Party) clearly received most of the minority votes, followed by Groen Links (Green Left) and the CDA (Christian-democrats). The voting behaviour of minorities in general is explained primarily by ideological differences. An additional determinant is the participation of candidates from the own ethnic group which is most important for Turks, than Surinamese and Moroccan, but it plays no role for Antilleans (Tillie, 2000).

Table 2.2   Voting behaviour in Amsterdam (1998)

	Turks	*Moroccans*	*Surinam./ Antilleans*	*Total*
PvdA (Labour Party)	47	57	56	53
D66 (Prog. Liberal)	7	3	3	4
Groen Links (Green Left)	18	33	20	23
VVD (Liberal)	1	1	4	2
CDA (Christ. Democrats)	18	2	3	8
SGP/GPV/RPF (Christ. Conservative)	0	1	0	0
SP (Socialist Party)	1	0	3	2
Others	9	3	11	8
Total	100	100	100	100
N	336	247	379	962

Source: Tillie, 2000.

Despite having voting rights, ethnic minorities are not sufficiently represented in political institutions and social organisations in relation to the size of their populations. Although on the national level the largest political parties have at least one parliament member from the minority population, since the elections of 1994 there is no member of non-Dutch origin among members of the Provincial Executive, the Upper Chamber, Council of State and Mayors (Rath and Tillie, 1998).

Migrant Organisations

Ethnic minorities are active in various areas of the social and political life of Amsterdam through their own organisations. In the 1960s ethnic groups organised themselves to create their own space in a new culture. Since the 1990s, they have concentrated more on fulfilling their needs, improving their societal position and influencing the surrounding society. National origin, ethnic identity and political or religious affiliation are the main grounds on which organisations are based. Some provide religious services while others aim to promote political participation or influence public decision making processes.

The historical development of so-called self-organisations differs for each group. Among the determinants of these patterns are length of residence, ethnic-cultural background, the specific problems of the different groups and governmental policy towards them. In recent years the growth of organisations has stabilised, but new organisations are still being established which deal with subjects such as education or elderly people. On the national level initiatives are bundled in national (and multinational) umbrella organisations.

Many organisations are subsidised by the city, the city district(s) or other government levels. At the top level are the immigrant support organisations financed by the municipality of Amsterdam and the province (see Figure 2.1). Relevant minority organisations that are known to the city are registered in the so-called *Social Map of Multicultural Amsterdam*. Recent research by Tillie and Fennema (1997) on Turkish organisations indicated that 106 active organisations of/for the Turkish community in Amsterdam were registered (see also to Alink et al, 1998, for Moroccan organisations). This implies that there exist many more migrant organisations than the number of organisations which are reported in the *Social Map*. Table 2.3 shows the number of organisations per ethnic group.

Table 2.3   Number of self-organisations per ethnic group

Ethnic group	Number of persons (1)	Number of self-organisations (2)	(1):(2)
Antilleans	10,619	43	247
Turks	30,852	106	291
Moroccans	49,000	106	462
Surinamese	70,093	91	770

Source: Fennema and Tillie, 1999.

The Turkish Community

Here we will describe in more depth the mobilisation of one ethnic group, namely the Turks, by focusing on their organisations. As was shown in above paragraphs Turks vote more than other ethnic groups and have raised (equal to Moroccans) more organisations than the Surinamese and Antilleans. This observation inspired Tillie and Fennema (1997 to start their research on the mobilisation of ethnic groups in the Turkish community (see also Fennema and Tillie, 1999; Fennema et al. 2000). In this section I shall present part of this research, namely the material referring to the kind of organisations that were raised, the way members of these organisations worked with each other and the reasons for such co-operation.[9]

The nature of migration and the varying origins of the migrant workers within Turkey itself, both geographically and ethnically, have far-reaching consequences for the internal organisation of the community both in Amsterdam and in the Netherlands. Their aspirations upon arrival were to earn as much money as possible in the shortest time and go back. In addition, they were individually recruited or came to the Netherlands on their own initiative and did not form a group before arrival (Penninx, 1979, pp. 112-15).

Turkish workers established their first organisations in Amsterdam in the 1970s. This often took place with the support of local government that hoped that organisations would form a link between the Turkish community and Dutch society. Most organisations did not satisfy this expectation however. Instead they provided an opportunity for Turkish people to shelter in a 'recreated' Turkish social sphere and did not serve to protect their collective interests or their social position in Dutch society. This may be related to a couple of factors on the side of Turkish migrants: the lack of a tradition of protection of collective interests, their initial orientation towards return to Turkey and mutual differences of opinion within the community. The Dutch state allowed and indeed stimulated the emergence of migrant organisations, which were expected to participate in decision making processes on behalf of their own communities. Yet in the eyes of officials, 'grass-roots' organisations, comparable to the immigrant organisations in the USA at the beginning of the twentieth century, would be less needed (Böcker, 1994).

In Amsterdam, the first well-known organisation was the Turkish Cultural Centre (TKC) which provided a meeting place. After a couple of years, divisions related to regional origin, ethnic groups religious differences, political preferences began to emerge, parallel with the polarisation process in the country of origin. This led to the establishment of new organisations, mainly differentiated along political and religious lines. In the second half of 1970s, the left-wing Dutch-Turkish Workers Association (HTIB) was established on a national level as a counterpart of the TKC, which meanwhile organised right wing oriented Turks.

In the course of time, further polarisation took place within left-wing and right-wing organisations and the number of Turkish organisations increased largely. Local Turkish organisations started to form federations on the national level in three main streams: left wing, religious and nationalistic. In each major stream, there are many organisations, whose activities cover different areas, from sports to religion.

Fennema and Tillie (1997) have made an inventory of all official registrated Turkish organisations in Amsterdam. Further they gathered information on the members of the boards and tried to find out if boards did overlap. Resulting from the latter several networks were constructed. In these networks a line between two organisations is the result from one person seating in boards of both organisations. Figure 2.2 depicts such a network upon which further research was based.[10]

For a precise description of the organisations in the network I refer to Fennema et al. (2000). Here I only indicate that organisations grouped around Hilal (left side of the figure) can be called right/extreme right, organisations grouped around the TDM (right side of the figure) can be called left or religious and the isolated three organisations (figure below) can be called cultural. The network figure thus shows us that right-wing organisa-tions have many mutual links caused by the overlapping of boards as have left-wing organisations, religious organisations and cultural organisations.

Figure 2.2   Two components of the network of Turkish organisations in Amsterdam

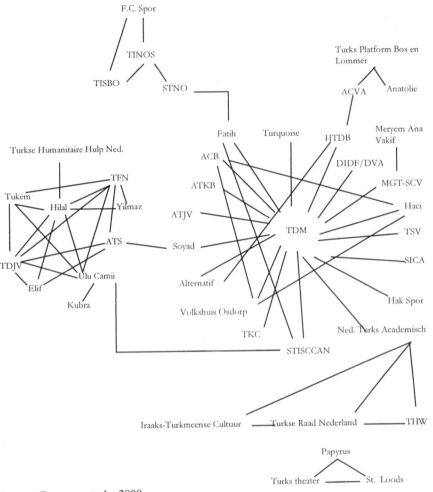

Source: Fennema et al., 2000.

In 1999 and 2000 several chairmen of a selected amount of organisations of Figure 2.2 were approached for an interview in which they were asked with whom they worked together and why. The results correspond with the figure made in 1997 and can be summarised as follows:

- religious organisations co-operate mainly with other religious organisations;
- left-wing organisations predominantly co-operate with other left-wing organisations and with cultural organisations; most of them co-operate with the TDM; left-wing organisations are also the only ones (except for the TDM) which co-operate with organisations of non-Turkish migrants;
- cultural organisations predominantly co-operate with left-wing and other cultural organisations;
- right-wing organisations co-operate with other right-wing organisations and with mosques;
- the Turkish advisory council co-operates with almost all segments in the Turkish community (except with Kurds and commercial organisations); the TDM also co-operates with organisations of other non-Turkish migrants;
- all organisations work together with at least one Dutch organisation (political party, welfare organisations etc.);[11] if asked whether they were able to work with Dutch organisations all indicated that they are.

The organisations were given four options why they co-operate: to overcome inequality, to fight racism, to encourage Turkish culture or because they had existing links through a common foundation:

- left-wing organisations predominantly work together to overcome inequality or to fight racism;
- cultural organisations mention mainly 'stimulate culture' and overcoming inequality;
- the right wing oriented TFN mentioned all four categories;
- the Turkish advisory council mainly focused on overcoming inequality or fighting racism.

Asked for reasons why organisations do not co-operate with others, they all mentioned 'political/ideological differences'.

These results show that strong dividing lines in the Turkish community affect the way they mobilise themselves. The diverse streams have raised their own organisations which tend to work together with those who have the same ideological and religious backgrounds and avoid co-operation for political/ideological reasons. However, members of organisations can be pragmatic and work together for the common goal with those who have a different background. A clear example of this is the TDM in which various parties are linked to each other. Earlier in this chapter it was stated that the advisory council is one of the most important forms of participation. It is thus notable that almost all streams in the Turkish community are represented in this council. Some interviewed chairpersons stressed that a lot had changed compared to earlier days when dividing lines were much stronger and such co-operation structures could not have existed. Above results also show that all organisations do or are eager to work together with Dutch organisations and this way oriented on Dutch society. However, only left-wing organisations state to work with organisations of non-Turkish migrants.

Comparable research shall be conducted in the Moroccan, Surinamese, Antillean, Ghanese and Chinese community.

Political Variations at the District Level

In this section we analyse the interaction and the eventual mutual influence of political structures and policies and the participation and mobilisation of ethnic groups. Furthermore, by focusing on three districts within the city we show how there are important local variations within Amsterdam. These local variations are especially the result of the administrative decentralisation of the city in 1999. In this year the city was divided in 16 separate districts with their own elected councils and civil services, plus the Inner City as a co-ordinating and directing governmental body for the city as a whole.[12] Many of the municipal tasks were handed over to the sub-local level of the districts, including the greater part of the minorities policies, especially in policy fields of (primary) education and welfare (and the related policy of subsidies).

The Case of Bos en Lommer and Zeeburg[13]

Alink and Berger (1999) compare two city districts with respect to the policies towards minorities and the way minorities are organised. The two districts, Bos en Lommer and Zeeburg, are comparable with respect to the composition and social-economic position of their populations. There are two types of policy towards minorities; more specific policies focusing explicitly on ethnic groups and more general policies focusing predominantly on all citizens. In recent years the second type has become more dominant. 'Specific' policies include options for initiatives based on emancipation in the ethnic community itself and initiatives based on participation. When there is specific policy towards ethnic minorities with participation as central focus, the policy tries to involve ethnic minorities (and their organisations) in decision-making processes. When specific policies focus on emancipation in the ethnic community itself, Alink and Berger assume that organisations will not be encouraged to orientate themselves on society as a whole. When the policy towards migrants has a more general character there will be no opportunity for specific initiatives and the foundation of ethnic organisations shall not be stimulated.

Bos en Lommer is characterised by more specific policies. Ethnic organisations there play an important role and have representative, intermediate and advisory functions. Furthermore they are encouraged to co-operate with other ethnic or general welfare organisations and to join a so-called migrant committee. Immigrants are encouraged to become active in public life. In Zeeburg, however, a more general policy is adopted. There are no specific institutions for the consultation of ethnic organisations and no specific initiatives developed regarding ethnic minorities and their organisations. The budget for ethnic organisations has decreased and weakened their financial position, and has led to the grouping of organisations. There is no incentive from the local government of Zeeburg to involve ethnic organisations in decision making processes.

Differences between political opportunity structures within one city thus leads to different forms of mobilisation. In Bos en Lommer, ethnic organisations are seen as an important actor within the integration process and have orientated more towards Dutch society. Zeeburg on the other hand has marginalised ethnic organisations. As a result of the policy, ethnic organisations seem to focus solely on their own communities. Alink and Berger conclude that, without encouragement ethnic organisations may co-operate within their own communities but do not interact across ethnic boundaries.

The Case of Oost[14]

The politics of the city district Oost are evaluated by Van Heelsum and Penninx (1999). The research focuses on the achievement of the concrete objectives of policy and the role that is allocated to immigrant organisations. The authors show that after the new division of the city in 16 districts in 1990, Oost took the initiative to form a council of migrant organisations, named BOMO (Administrative Consultation Minority Organisations). All migrant organisations, irrespective of their primary aims – thus including four religious (mosque) organisations – were invited to join this bi-monthly meeting in which policy issues would be discussed.

The authors argue that this scheme has led to a mutual dependence between allied organisations and the City Administration. Immigrant organisations are dependent on the District Administration for financial subsidies and the districts are dependent on the organisations to legitimise its policies and to mobilise support for them. Van Heelsum and Penninx argue that the distribution of power within this framework of mutual dependence is not even however. The district authority starts from a position of power: it divides money and it asks for advice. It may consider comments of the immigrant organisations as 'not relevant or not useful'. It also has a kind of monopoly over information: immigrant organisations are less acquainted with rules and regulations or important developments within and outside the district. The professionals of the District Administration are in an advantageous position as compared to the (often less-educated) volunteers of the organisations.

With the exception of two, all of the 13 immigrant organisations continued their contact with BOMO through the years. When asked their opinion on BOMO, the organisations were positive about the opportunities it provided them to maintain and broaden their network of contacts. On the other hand, they criticise the way issues are prioritised on the agenda and the lack of results. From the point of view of the District Council, BOMO is a success; the fact that issues are discussed is an important step. The Council considers immigrant organisations as necessary partners in reducing the isolation of immigrants. It makes it easier for officials to identify partners with whom they may solve practical problems, such as celebrations of specific (religious) holidays. The opinion of the Council is, however, that immigrant organisations should not take over the work of professional public institutions in fields like childcare, youth-work, work for the elderly or language lessons. These public institutions should work for all inhabitants of the district. Immigrant organisations are supposed to inform their members and send clients to the public institutions.

Van Heelsum and Penninx conclude that BOMO is a consultative body at district level with no power or competence to enforce decisions. As to the (political) involvement of immigrants, district policies have been limited and open and active at the same time. They are limited mainly because political participation was actually narrowed down to the involvement of immigrant organisations as advisers. The actual impact of their involvement is also limited, as a consequence of the unequal balance of power between professionals of the administration and general institutions on the one hand and the (often – but not always – less educated) representatives of immigrant organisations on the other hand. The policies have also been open, in the sense that all immigrant organisations in the district were invited and there have been conscious efforts to keep them involved. District authorities have deliberately chosen to underwrite immigrant organisations financially and have urged them to participate in discussions on important matters. This is appreciated by immigrant organisations. The way this was done, however, has clear limitations: immigrant organisations are regarded as consultants and advisers. Implementation of policies to improve the disadvantaged position of immigrants is primarily the task of general, professional institutions in the district. Consultation of immigrant organisations by these institutions is regarded as very helpful, but the actual day-to-day work, such as language courses, should remain in the hands of these professional public institutions.

Both case studies show that district authorities in Amsterdam are very autonomous in constructing their policy towards ethnic minorities and migrant organisations. The position of migrant organisations depends on the chosen policy; specific or more general policies. Since migrant organisations are highly dependent on subsidies, the policy of a city district can be crucial. It further can influence their eventual orientation towards Dutch society as was shown in the case study of Alink and Berger.

There exists a tension between the claims and aspirations of migrant organisations on the one hand and both the district authorities and the general institutions on the other. The City Administration needs the support of the migrant organisations for their policies. This is especially the case in areas with a lot of ethnic minorities. At the same time it holds charge of financial means and takes the final decisions. The influence of the migrant organisations on the policy can be questioned. In all cases described above they have an advisory and representative function, but not a decisive one.

Summary

Following large immigration flows, family-reunification, the assumption from temporary to permanent presence and the disadvantaged social-economic position, government developed policies aimed at minorities. In the 1980s the focus was on ethnic and cultural differences and the maintaining of their cultural identity. In the beginning of the 1990s the accent moved towards integration into society. Now, in a new century, it seems that the disadvantaged position of ethnic groups were neither combated by the policy in the 1980s nor by the policies constructed in the beginning of the 1990s. Individual members of ethnic groups had been stigmatised and diversity of individuals had been neglected. A new policy is therefore needed according to the Municipality of Amsterdam. This so-called diversity policy is no longer focused on groups but on problems. The central aim of the diversity policy is the participation of all individuals in society and politics.

In the 1980s the foundation of migrant organisations was stimulated to function as intermediaries. They should construct a link between the new-comers and the governmental institutions. The current focus on problems instead of groups may affect group representing institutions like migrant organisations. The attention and efforts of the City Administration will be more focused on individual immigrants and less on migrant organisations. As was shown in the case in Zeeburg there was no incentive from the local government to involve the ethnic organisations in the development of politics and the budget to support migrant organisations had decreased since the installation of the new policy. Policy also influences the eventual orientation of organisations on Dutch society.

Resulting from the administrative division of the city in 1999 the various city districts have random freedom in the way they construct their policies. The mobilisation of ethnic minorities, the political opportunity structure and the way these interact are therefore not equal in every city district that makes it important to analyse local variations within the city.

In this chapter we have also shown that ethnic minorities still have several opportunities to influence policy in Amsterdam. Most important are the advisory councils. However, the role of the advisory council as well as other migrant organisations is restricted. They have no real power and are dependent on the city for financial support especially.

Notes

1   For figures on recent cycles of migration in Amsterdam see Kraal and Zorlu, 1998.
2   The total number of the population of non-Dutch origin includes another main category of immigrants, namely refugees (BSM-GA, 1996; O+S, 1994; Penninx et al., 1994).
3   Since 1999 the Central Bureau for Statistics applies a new definition to determine whether a person is 'allochtonous'. A person is called allochtonous if at least one of his parents is born outside the Netherlands (CBS, 2000).
4   In Amsterdam (Dutch) policy following groups are defined as ethnic groups and were target groups of the minorities policy: Surinamese, Antilleans, South-Europeans, Turks, Moroccan and people from non-industrialised countries.
5   For numbers on the first and second generation of the various ethnic groups in Amsterdam I refer to the City Template of Amsterdam (Kraal and Zorlu, 1998).

6   The unemployment rate among ethnic minorities is three-times higher than among native Dutch people.

7   This paragraph is based on Wolff (1999).

8   Amsterdam is governed by a City Council and a 'College' of Aldermen, each with her or his own portfolio of tasks and areas of responsibility. The Aldermen are elected councillors who have been selected by their party's representatives in the Council. They are chaired by the Mayor. The Aldermen remain members of the full Council and vote in its meetings.

9   More information of the research on mobilisation in the Turkish community can be found in Fennema and Tillie (1999) and Fennema et al. (2000).

10   In total Fennema and Tillie found a network of 106 organisations, including isolated organisations (see also Fennema and Tillie, 1999; Tillie and Fennema, 1997).

11   Papyrus indicated to work together with Dutch institutions which were not on our list.

12   Since the local elections of 1998 the number of city districts is reduced to 13.

13   This section is a summary of Alink and Berger (1999).

14   This section is a summary of Van Heelsum and Penninx (1999).

References

Alink, F. and Berger, M. (1999), 'Doors to Another World: A Research on the Influence of Local Policy on Turkish and Moroccan Organisations in Two Amsterdam Districts', Paper presented at the MPMC Workshop in Liège (Belgium), 30 October-2 November 1999, 12 pp.

Alink, F., Berger, M., Fennema, M. and Tillie, J. (1998), *Marokkaanse Organisaties in Amsterdam: Een Netwerkanalyse*, Het Spinhuis, Amsterdam.

Amersfoort, H. van and Cortie, C. (1996), 'Social Polarisation in a Welfare State? Immigrants in the Amsterdam Region', *New Community*, vol. 22, pp. 671-87.

Böcker, A. (1994), 'Op Weg naar een Beter Bestaan: De Ontwikkeling van de Maatschappelijke Positie van Turken in Nederland', in H. Vermeulen and R. Penninx (eds), *Het Democratisch Ongeduld: De Emancipatie en Integratie van Zes Doelgroepen van het Minderhedenbeleid*, Het Spinhuis, Amsterdam, pp. 145-76.

BSM-GA (1994 and 1996), *Etnische Groepen in Amsterdam*, O+S, Het Amsterdamse Bureau voor Onderzoek en Statistiek, Amsterdam.

CBS (1999), *Maandstatistiek van de Bevolking*, vol. 49, December, CBS, Heerlen/Voorburg.

CBS (2000), *Maandstatistiek van de Bevolking*, vol. 50, May, CBS, Heerlen/Voorburg.

Choenni, A. (1997), *Veelsoortig Assortiment: Allochtoon Ondernemerschap in Amsterdam als Incorparatietraject 1965-1995*, Het Spinhuis, Amsterdam.

Fennema, M. and Tillie, J. (1999), 'Political Participation and Political Trust in Amsterdam: Civic Communities and Ethnic Networks', *Journal of Ethnic and Migration Studies*, vol. 25, pp. 703-26.

Fennema, M., Tillie, J. and Kraal, K. (2000), 'Creating Turkish Networks in Amsterdam: Personal or Organizational Strategies', Paper prepared for the Workshop 'Associational Engagement and Democracy in Cities', CPR Joint Session of Workshops, Copenhagen 14-19 April 2000.

Gemeente Amsterdam (1996), *Sociale Kaart van Multicultureel Amsterdam*, Gemeente Amsterdam, Amsterdam.

Heelsum, A. van and Penninx, R. (1999), 'Evaluating Integration and Participation Policies for Immigrants and Minorities in an Amsterdam District: Oost', Paper presented at the MPMC Workshop in Liège (Belgium), 30 October-2 November 1999, 7 pp.

Heijs, E. (1995), *Van Vreemdeling tot Nederlander: De Verlening van het Nederlanderschap aan Vreemdelingen 1813-1992*, Het Spinhuis, Amsterdam.

Hoolt, J. and Scholten, D. (1996), *Etnische Groepen in Amsterdam: Jaarbericht 1996*, Bureau voor Strategisch Minderheidenbeleid Gemeente Amsterdam, Amsterdam.

Kloosterman, R.C. (1994), 'Amsterdamned: The Rise of Unemployment in Amsterdam in the 1980s', *Urban Studies* vol. 31, pp. 1325-44.

Kraal, K. and Zorlu, A. (1998), *City Template Amsterdam. Basic Information on Ethnic Minorities and their Participation: Report According to the Grid for City Templates of the MPMC Project*, IMES, Amsterdam.

Lucassen, J. and Penninx, R. (1997), *Newcomers: Immigrants and their Descendants in the Netherlands, 1550-1995*, Het Spinhuis, Amsterdam.

O+S (1990, 1994 and 1996), *Amsterdam in Cijfers: Jaarboek*, O+S, Het Amsterdamse Bureau voor Onderzoek en Statistiek, Amsterdam.

O+S (2000), *De Amsterdamse Bevolking*, http:www.Onderzoek-en-statistiek.amsterdam.nl, 25 October 2000.

Ostendorf, W. (1996), *Etnische Segregatie en Beleid: Een Internationale Vergelijking*, Amsterdam Study Centre for the Metropolitan Environment, Amsterdam.

Pennings, P. (1987), *Migrantenkiesrecht in Amsterdam: Een Onderzoek naar de Participatie en Mobilisatie van Etnische Groepen bij de Gemeenteraadverkiezingen van 19 Maart 1986*, Gemeenten Amsterdam, Amsterdam.

Penninx, R. (1979), *Ethnic Minorities: Towards an Overall Ethnic Minorities Policy*, Netherlands Scientific Council for Government Policy, The Hague.

Penninx, R., Schoorl, J. and Praag, C. van (1994), *The Impact of International Migration on Receiving Countries: The Case of the Netherlands*, Netherlands Interdisciplinary Demographic Institute, The Hague.

Rath, J. and Tillie, J. (1998), 'Etnische Minderheden en de Politiek', in R. Penninx, H. Münstermann and H. Entzinger (eds), *Etnische Minderheden en de Multiculturele Samenleving*, Wolters/Noordhoff, Groningen, pp. 451-74.

Tesser, P.T.M., Dugteren, F.A. van and Merens, A. (1996), *Rapportage Minderheden 1996: Bevolking, Arbeid, Onderwijs, Huisvesting*, Sociaal en Cultureel Planbureau, Rijswijk.

Tillie, J. (1994), *Kleurrijk Kiezen: Opkomst en Stemgedrag van Migranten tijdens de Gemeenteraadsverkiezingen van 2 Maart 1994*, Nederlands Centrum Buitenlanders, Utrecht.

Tillie, J. (2000), *De Etnische Stem: Opkomst en Stemgedrag van Migranten tijdens Gemeenteraadsverkiezingen, 1986-1998*, Forum, Utrecht.

Tillie, J. and Fennema, M. (1995), 'Multicultural and Political Integration in Amsterdam: Preliminary Results', Paper presented at the Warwick Workshop 'Multi-culturalism and Political integration in European Cities', 7-9 April 1995.

Tillie, J. and Fennema, M. (1997), *Turkse Organisaties in Amsterdam: Een Netwerkanalyse*, Het Spinhuis, Amsterdam.

Vlijmen, J. van (1996), *Ruimtelijke Segregatie in Amsterdam*, O+S, Het Amsterdamse Bureau voor Onderzoek en Statistiek, Amsterdam.

Wolff, R. (1999), 'Minorities Policy in the City of Amsterdam and the Amsterdam Districts', Paper presented at the MPMC Workshop in Liège (Belgium), 30 October-2 November 1999, 12 pp.

3 Ethnic Mobilisation in Athens: Steps and Initiatives towards Integration

MARINA PETRONOTI

Introduction

Greece was a country of mass emigration until the late 1960s. Its transformation to a society hosting immigrants has its roots in the 1970s and has until recently been highly informal: regularisation only occurred in 1998. The Greek authorities have adopted strict administrative control over immigrant flows, but do not systematically address the causes and consequences of their settlement. Nor have they taken any formal steps to establish regulations associated with the allocation of services to newcomers. Relevant laws simplify procedures of expulsion and grant judicial autonomy to local police. Since integration is not included among the state's objectives (Kourtovik, 1994, p. 192; Triandafyllidou, 1998), the idea behind existing measures is to defend the security and welfare of Greek citizens rather than set up an infrastructure for immigrants' benefit.

However, even though immigrants are confronted with insuperable obstacles, cannot seek assistance from their embassies, and national or local authorities do nothing to encourage their participation in the political domain, the number of ethnic associations is increasing. This paradox must be accounted for with reference to its social and historical context, the matrix of relationships it expresses and the ways immigrants and the indigenous population perceive these both. More specifically, ethnic mobilisation is full of ambiguities and contradictions. In spite of the fact that the Greek Constitution (art. 12, 1975/1986) allows all people living in the country to establish political associations, there are no policies to implement this article. The Greek society adheres to national culture and Greek identity is defined in terms of historical continuity and cultural homogeneity, thereby polarising the dichotomy between 'Us' and 'Others'.

This chapter focuses on the means with which immigrants improve their status and living conditions. The emphasis is placed on their interaction with local authorities and the nature of the associations they create. Ethnic bodies organise in ways that depend not only on their own requirements but also on existing structures and the values of the national majority. To put it in another way, the restrictions imposed by dominant institutions together with the inadequacy of immigrant policies urge us to look at the alternative (informal) mechanisms with which newcomers mobilise. I argue that, despite their minority status, the uncertainties they experience and their formal exclusion from decisions, which affect them, immigrants are actors who take advantage of the flexible organisation of the Greek society. The bodies they form and the activities that go with them have to be seen from a perspective that recognises both their lack of basic political resources and their engagement in competitive and dynamic struggle. What is more, whether as a collective or as an individual project, immigrants raise multiple claims and demands that are not exclusively ethnic or community-centred. Their goals as well as the ways in which they pursue them, leave traces in the social-economic and cultural life of the country and may also challenge asymmetrical power relationships (Petronoti, 1998).

A word about concepts: in speaking of 'immigrants' I refer to non-EU nationals regardless of whether they are legally or illegally present in Greece. At the time of the ethnographic research upon which this analysis is based was conducted (1997), the vast majority were unregistered. In addition, regularisation altered neither the content nor the outcome of their collective activities. Although in principle they can co-operate with state agents, in practice they do not do so, because the documents they have been issued with hardly affect institutional and ideological structures. As a corollary of these factors, I adopt Drury's (1994, p. 15) approach to mobilisation. I consider it as a multidimensional process whereby ethnic groups express oppositions that counterbalance each other through the negotiation of social and cultural symbols. What I regard as most essential however, is the notion of opposition between immigrants and the state apparatus. Direct or subtle confrontations are, of course, inevitable since there are no formal alternatives to immigrants' survival and mobility. Yet, I wish to argue that clear distinctions between the possession and lack of citizenship rights or participation and abstention from collective action at the national level conceal the great variety of immigrants' political choices and behaviour as well as the complex meanings of the relationships embracing them. To paraphrase Mahnig (1999), 'opportunity structures' include many more social forces than state authorities, local or national councils and institutions.

The research was carried out in Kypseli, a densely populated area of Athens, which is moreover inhabited by numerous ethnic groups. Contacts were made with policy makers, immigrants and representatives of two ethnic associations for purposes of comparison: Sudanese and Filipinos. Official data are inadequate because of discriminating institutions and the indifference of the Greek authorities. Analysts are forced to rely much more on their individual assessments.[1] Indeed, the available figures underestimate the actual number of immigrants by at least one-third (Fakiolas, 1994, p. 13). Hence, the picture is far from clear. Undocumented immigrant workers are sometimes said to amount to between 3.5 per cent to 4.3 per cent of the total population in Greece (PENED, 1997, p. 13). Other surveys give different figures, for example six to twelve per cent of the Greek labour force (SOPEMI, 1997, p. 112).[2] Finally, data deriving from immigrants' regularisation show that in 1998, 369,629 immigrants participated in this process, while the Greek labour force amounted to 4,294,408 workers (Cavounidi and Hatzaki, 1999).

Athens: A Pole for Immigrants and Ethnic Groups

Athens is a most appropriate site of investigation since it belongs to the 'new' immigration cities. Thirty per cent of the total population of Greece is settled there, and it attracts the majority of the country's urbanised immigrants. According to the 1981 Population Census they constitute 2.7 per cent of the capital's population (Statistical Yearbook of Greece, 1994-1995, p. 50). In fact, over two-fifths of registered immigrants in Greece (44.3 per cent) in 1998 were located in Greater Athens Area (Cavounidi and Hatzaki, 1999, p. 15). This concentration in Athens reflects a desire for urban lifestyles, the advantages of the anonymity of the city, the significance of major administrative and political agencies and the favourable structure of the urban labour market. Indeed, despite the transience and low pay dominating immigrants' work, there are many job opportunities as a result of the demand for unskilled labourers, the expansion of the service sector and construction enterprises (Emke-Poulopoulos, 1990, p. 23; Iosifides, 1997, p. 32). The Greek economy is not ethnically structured; immigrants are occupationally mobile and are not confined to specific kinds of employment. Moreover, because individuals with residence permits can only officially own firms, the number of ethnic enterprises is limited. Only those ethnic groups with more highly-skilled members show a wider range of economic activities and are adept at creating new niches of work (Iosifides, 1997, p. 48; Romaniszyn, 1997).

Table 3.1   Documented and undocumented immigrants in the Greater Athens Area (1996-1997)

Ethnic groups	Official data		Unofficial data
Albanians	2,810	86,292	100,000
Bangladeshis	139	2,894	2,000
Bulgarians	2,000	7,913	1,000
Egyptians	4,834	5,069	20,000
Eritreans	32	-	300
Ethiopians	1,114	919	3,000
Filipinos	5,254	4,989	1,000
Ghanaians	99	-	800
Indians	-	3,819	-
Iraqis	3,597	2,778	1,000
Kenyans	300	-	114
Nigerians	648	1,557	500
Pakistanis	-	10,063	-
Palestinians	27	-	200
Poles	3,323	7,329	40,000
Rumanians	-	7,319	-
Russians	7,169	1,482	-
Sierra Leonians	-	-	200
Sudanese	486	-	200
Turks	2,475	-	500
Total	34,307	142,423	170,814

Sources: 1st column Official data: data on Immigration, National Statistical Service of Greece (1997) and PENED (1997); 2nd column Official data: Cavounidi and Hatzaki (1999); Unofficial data: estimates by the representatives of ethnic associations.

There are a large number of immigrants and ethnic groups in Athens. In the late 1980s there was a massive influx from the Balkans. People arrived from former Yugoslavia, Bulgaria, Rumania and above all, Albania, which sends 52.7 per cent of all immigrants in the Greater Athens area (Cavounidi and Hatzaki, 1999, p. 10). Central Europe is mainly represented by Poles (2.3 per cent of the immigrant population) while Asians (especially Pakistanis, who first appeared in the 1970s) and Africans comprise smaller groups (see Table 3.1).

Unlike indigenous minorities and refugees of Greek origin, for whom the Greek government has made social and economic provisions (Polyzos et al., 1995, p. 165) immigrants accommodate themselves without any help from the state. Social exclusion is not so much expressed in spatial segregation, as in the kind of houses they inhabit, the high rents and the settlement in neighbourhoods abandoned by the indigenous population (Maloutas, 1990). Although ethnic groups develop their own residential strategies they are not highly concentrated in specific quarters but disperse around the city. In addition, since they have to cope with most of their problems themselves, they establish 'secret temples' (such as mosques) where they perform their religious practices and also set up ethnic shops and restaurants, which encourage their integration in the new environment.

Forms of Ethnic Mobilisation

As should be clear by now, immigrants do not implement policy. Despite discussions at the state level, the difficulties they encounter together with social services reforms, decentralisation and co-ordination of offices and councils, are still dealt with by ad hoc measures (Petrinioti, 1993, p. 16). New laws have not been consolidated and they face situations of great uncertainty. Trade unionists are unable to defend immigrant rights partly because, according to law 1264/1982, participation in trade unions is impossible without a work permit and partly as a result of immigrants' reluctance to seek union leadership and express themselves in public. Furthermore, their absence from national bodies is compounded by their concentration in the informal labour market. To meet the limitations generated by these factors, immigrants employ various strategies such as invoking symbols of cultural heritage and maintaining bonds with their home countries.

The discriminative logic of social institutions is consistent with the fact that only Greek citizens have access to the political domain. Neither birth in Greece nor marriage to Greeks automatically entitles a person to citizenship; so few immigrants have citizenship rights that they are analytically irrelevant.[3] It is not surprising that even those who have acquired such rights find themselves addressed to as 'lesser Greeks' for they are not automatically guaranteed social acceptance: national language, religion and cultural continuity are equally (or more) important prerequisites. Hence, Catholic Greeks are distinguished from Orthodox ones and repatriates are often seen as lacking essential bonds with the national culture.

With no institutions concerned with their survival, immigrants can only contact municipal offices in order to issue or renew work permits and perform civil marriages. Officials' advice about accommodation or jobs is made on a voluntary basis. Therefore, ethnic group mobilisation takes three main forms: the formation of social networks, the establishment of ethnic associations, as well as dependence on NGOs and anti-racist organisations.

Non-governmental Organisations

The lack of an adequate infrastructure dealing with immigrants' needs means that national and international non-governmental organisations (NGOs) are more likely to represent them while specific requests are primarily considered on humanitarian grounds (Mikrakis and Triandafyllidou, 1994; Petronoti, 1996). By delegating its duties towards newly settled populations to NGOs, the state promotes a system of clientelism and paternalism. Just as immigrants become dependent on NGOs rather than their own ethnic bodies, so these organisations turn to immigrants to sustain their roles and dominant institutions remain intact. Ethnic groups rely on numerous anti-racist organisations, which have a limited scope of activity, are unco-ordinated in terms of the assistance they offer and react to circumstances in an ad hoc fashion. These bodies are subsidised by donations and voluntary work, remain marginal to integration processes and do not provide immigrants with a place in political decision-making or collective forms of action. Their intermediary role is best illustrated by the case of regularisation; they exerted pressure on trade unions, which in turn influenced government authorities that eventually agreed to implement this process.

The most important NGOs are: the UNHCR, which issued blue cards (a type of residence permit) until recently; the Greek Council for Refugees, which offered money, counselling, food and shelter; CARITAS Hellas, which still sees to immigrants' settlement in other countries but also provides counselling, accommodation and material aid; Philallilia, which organises teaching courses, provides food and sends various items to immigrants' families; the Committee Against Racism and Xenophobia and Citizens' Mobilisation Against Racism, both of which defend immigrants' political and humanitarian rights; and the Catholic Church, which provides medical help, supplies letters of recommendation and maintains a strong assistance network.

The most active body concerned with minority rights is the Network of Social Support to Immigrants and Refugees. It developed outside the framework of state agencies. Its activities cover a wide spectrum of cultural events, political and social gatherings as well as meetings with various ethnic groups and institutions on a weekly basis. Its main task is to inform immigrants about ongoing discussions among the officials, as well as to pass on their claims to decision-makers at the national or municipal levels. In other words, collaboration with its representatives crosses the boundaries of ethnic communities and helps immigrants to create new forms of activity.

The Orthodox Church offers occasional assistance (food, money for rent, medicine, vaccination and courses in Greek) to Christian immigrants. The acceptance of donations brings comfort and a feeling of belonging to the religious community, but does not signify social integration. Thus, the Orthodox Church dominates national religious life while non-orthodox groups have unequal religious rights. Interestingly enough, Muslims take advantage of this priority and submit to the municipality of Athens for permission to carry out their ceremonies during the period of Ramadhan.

Networking

As a rule, immigrants turn to those of their own kind and form solidary relationships (Petronoti, 1993). Ethnic ties exist long before they settle in Athens and are rooted in complex arrangements for meeting essential needs and serving as sources of encouragement, comfort and accommodation to the new surroundings. Their operation depends on reciprocity, trust, commitment, loyalty and goodwill. In many respects inter-personal links prove stronger and more effective than immigrants' collective action. They are enhanced by the limitations imposed on their freedom of action and serve as a basis of empowerment (Friedman, 1995, p. 167). Though networking takes place mainly within the ethnic community it may also include members of other groups: these links are not geographically determined but extend far beyond Greece's borders. The connections retained with co-ethnics in other countries makes immigrants part of larger social formations rather than isolated and politically deprived individuals. Through them they organise burials in their homeland, finance political projects, send medicine and remittances to those left behind, keep alive family and community memories – all of which make their new life bearable and increase their self-esteem. Even in countries with well-organised migration policies, like Norway, collective power is based on social links, interaction and collaboration (Ranaweera, 2000).

Social and kinship bonds prove valuable in pursuing interests and are utilised when the occasion arises. Family members, friends and acquaintances are perceived as major and trustworthy means of protection and mobilise immigrants through emotive and moral symbols. Kinship combines with ethnicity to produce a relational basis on which ethnic groups' existence is perpetuated: their members plan alliances with their compatriots who are perceived as members of extended families.

There is also networking with the indigenous population but it rarely leads to stable and confidential bonds. Because of the sharp division between the rights accorded to citizens and non-citizens, immigrants often turn to the former for certain services. In particular, the interpersonal ties they sustain with employers or neighbours are evaluated in terms of ethnicity and gender. A relevant example concerns a female boss who used to offer small gifts and second-hand clothes to her domestic servant (a woman from Eritrea), visited her house to drink traditional coffee, established pseudo-kinship ties by becoming best-woman at her wedding, bought part of the food and drinks offered during this ceremony, shared with her crucial moments of motherhood and baptised her baby daughter.

Ethnic Organisations

In a list compiled by the Forum of Social Organisations and Youth, there are about 50 names of immigrant and refugee organisations, most of which are situated in Athens and have been founded since the 1990s (as far as I know only a few exist in Thessaloniki, Chania or other urban centres). They vary in terms of size (300 to 4,000 members) and differ in aims, composition and effectiveness in reaching their objectives. They perform many roles and functions, political and cultural, prepare training courses in the national language, set up links with the indigenous population, collect money in case of death, illness or accident and supply material aid to their home society. Political and ideological differences lead ethnic groups to create associations with contrasting goals, while others set up more than one body (i.e. Turks have about 10 organisations most of which are not officially registered). The multiplicity of their interests and targets further explains why ethnic associations retain links with political parties both in Greece and the home society; many seek to restore peace, freedom and democracy in the countries they left. In order to realise their goals they elect large executive boards (4-25 members) which are male-dominated and emphasise their members' educational and social qualifications, length of residence in Athens and competence in the Greek language. The effectiveness of their efforts is partly influenced by Greek external policy towards sending countries and the existence of bilateral agreements.

Although they are legalised, ethnic associations confront institutional discrimination and xenophobic attitudes. Hence, they do not express their requests systematically nor do they expect that these will be met. As a rule, they are self-sufficient and devote themselves to their own affairs. In spite of the variety of issues they deal with, their most visible manifestation is organising cultural festivities rather than political speeches. Such events often assume a folklorist dimension; cultural discourse provides the perspective through which ethnic inequalities are confirmed and cultural differences become reified. At the same time however, just as the majority group appeals to its ancient origins and western modes of consumption in order to justify its superiority, ethnic bodies reintroduce history as a mechanism with which they challenge their stigmatisation and defend their ethnic pride. Immigrants' identities have many more facets than those related to labour alone, while their existence is not reduced to the stereotypical categories employed by the host society. The elements of ethnicity they refer to do not merely denote a retreat into worlds of tradition or the simple regeneration of former lifestyles. The utilisation of symbols of the past serves both as a constraint and a resource through which they give new meanings to ethnic, cultural and political demands (Petronoti, 2000). To put it in another way, the potential immigrants have for integration is not only directed by national structures and ideologies, but is also determined by their cultural background and ethnic consciousness.

Besides, as evidence from other countries shows, social fragmentation and an inability to collaborate are symptoms frequently displayed by refugee populations (Zetter, 1994, p. 315). It is clear that the social and political dimensions of disempowerment, such as lack of state assistance, guide immigrants' collective organisation (Friedman, 1995, p. 164).[4]

As a consequence of the absence of institutionalised channels and central agencies dealing with immigrants, the accomplishments of ethnic associations can only be partial. Meetings with local authorities are described as 'fruitless discussions, full of un-materialised promises'. They seem more useful in terms of establishing inter-personal links. One is inclined to say that the durability of such links makes the creation of ethnic bodies appear redundant. Yet, these structures exist beyond and within such bodies; dense informal linkages are activated in order to cope with daily shortcomings or achieve ends, which cannot be met in formal ways.

Specific mention must be made of ethnic leaders. Ethnic mobilisation presupposes dynamic responses to specific circumstances and is invigorated by leading individuals who have the skill to represent immigrants to national centres of power. Realising their awkward position between restrictive laws and the community's needs, they try to maintain a delicate balance between ethnic groups and state officials or other Greeks and build carefully extended relationships as a primary resource of power. For instance, the Eritrean refugees' representative has family connections with, and is supported by, a Greek minister who was also his best man. Being key actors in community and religious issues these figures are seen as patriarchs whose consulting role makes up for the distance between the national majority and ethnic minorities. It seems reasonable to assume that the lack of beneficial legislation adds to their power of decision-making. However informal or indirect, their presence at the political stage implies that they get involved in public processes as well as that Greek authorities are not altogether indifferent to the demands raised by mass arrivals.

In spite of the higher standards they enjoy with respect to their co-ethnics, ethnic leaders are by no means immune to discrimination nor do they set their own agendas. They avoid direct opposition with officials and suggest conciliatory rather than confrontational action. Because few of their responsibilities are institutionalised, their social status and advancement originate from their ability to bridge communication gaps between the host society and immigrants. In short, we are dealing with a personalised type of leadership based on a web of duties and debts, kinship and social allegiances as well as patronage relationships. The management of community affairs serves as raw material in the competition for influence: in the name of demands for residence, jobs or medical care, activities related to regularisation and promotion of ethnic culture, ethnic representatives are oriented to the acquisition of symbolic goods and personal gain.

Case Study: Sudanese and Filipino Associations

Sudanese and Filipinos present contrasting cases in the relations maintained with Greeks, the ways they approach their goals and adjust to national culture. There are also differences within the two immigrant communities, since each has a wide range of intentions, varying according to gender, age, education, political orientation, history and so forth. According to a typology proposed by De Rudder et al. (1994) for immigrants' political activities, Filipinos may be classified as an example of 'dual mobilisation'. This involves sociability, active commitment to ethnic bodies, links with the homeland, competence in the national language and broad interaction with their compatriots, other immigrants and Greeks. The Sudanese, on the other hand, are best characterised by a model defined as 'resource to community'. This implies preference for members of their own group and the country of origin, reserved attitudes towards Greeks, relatively weak association ties but active mobilisation for the defence of political rights.

Nonetheless, despite the differences between Sudanese and Filipino cultures the elements they have in common are sufficient for comparative analysis. The bodies they form are by no means separatist or reactionary – as several Greeks perceive them. Such a view ignores the multiple interests these immigrant communities have in common, stress their internal fragmentation and undermine their potential for collective action. In fact, these ethnic bodies prove more efficient than those built by other immigrants. Sudanese and Filipinos use them as instruments of mobilisation, as approved means of fighting institutional and ideological constraints in Greece.

Neither of the associations investigated however, is solidary and tightly organised, nor is systematically directed towards the achievement of collective goals. The reality is more complicated than that. In the first place, voting and expressing views on community or national matters are not immigrants' main concerns. They expect a lot to be done for them by the state and they focus primarily on satisfying immediate requirements. Yet, the contradictions inherent in the social and political infrastructure leave room for counteraction so that Sudanese and Filipinos negotiate their marginalisation by introducing 'an ongoing debate on everything that seems problematic' (Rex and Josephides, 1987, p. 10). They acknowledge the need to place themselves in the wider social fabric rather than function as isolated ethnic enclaves. Since national and local government agents do not support them financially, they are subsidised by registration fees and money earned in festivities. Their orientations confirm the absence of co-ordination among state officials as well as the opportunities they have for manipulating them. Contacts with the authorities are made on an irregular basis and even then immigrants do not present a united front. Conversely, officials' behaviour towards immigrants tends to be 'promising but ultimately indifferent, disappointing, offensive, useless', as they use to say.

Sudanese and Filipino associations are subdivided into several smaller units ranging from spontaneously formed self-help organisations to legalised societies with several specialisations. Through the dynamics of their constitution and expression, these associations adopt immigrant discourse and represent decentralised movements. In particular, among the Asian group we find one major organisation, the KASAPI Hellas (an acronym for Filipino Migrant Workers in Greece), composed of about 750 members, as well as numerous informal bodies distinguished by religious, geographical or political affiliation. In contrast, the Sudanese originally established a small organisation consisting of University students, which later on expanded to include immigrants brought together on the basis of political goals. The Sudanese recently formed the Organisation of Sudanese Immigrants headed by the same individuals who initially participated in the Sudanese Community.

Immigrants' practices manifest their desire to establish micro-societies with distinct ideologies and objectives. None is concerned with building up powerful bodies as a corollary of the subordinate position they hold. By joining ethnic associations, individual Sudanese and Filipinos acquire a growing awareness of identity, aims, tactics and methods, seek to achieve equality of opportunity, ensure relatively peaceful relationships with officials and find help in practical matters such as filling in application forms, ask for knowledgeable lawyers and advice about how to combat exploitation. Unlike other immigrant organisations, which are often inactive and withdrawn, they strive to function as pressure groups and accomplish a number of goals. They construct a collective image, do their best to propagate their history through newsletters, and participate in demonstrations and TV programmes (the Sudanese even started a radio station in Athens). Above all, they voice claims within the host society and assert their own symbols of unity by delineating the boundaries between themselves and other immigrants in Greece.

Since the state makes no provisions for educating foreign immigrants, ethnic, religious and racial heterogeneity causes serious problems to their children.[5] They cannot receive grades unless they have residence permits or birth certificates, while their parents' lack of competence in Greek prevents contacts with the school staff. Immigrants however, attach great emphasis on children's schooling as a strategy of integration and social mobility. Hence, Filipinos send them to private schools and have established a nursery school that is supplied with food by the municipality. This is the only means with which local authorities contribute to the group's maintenance. The Sudanese seem less concerned with children's schooling, probably because the migrant community consists mostly of single men rather than of family units. Moreover, they meet rigorous resistance and ambivalence because of Greeks' opposition to their religious doctrine; the establishment of mosques is only permitted to Greek Muslims. To compensate for this discrimination, the Sudanese follow familiar ways of prayer, elect their own imam and set up informal places of worship. It is noteworthy that Filipinos also invited a Filipino priest from Italy in order to pray in their own language. In other words, religious faith endows immigrants with resilience and enables them to withstand misfortune.

One more significant point relates to the connection between gender and political commitment with reference to these ethnic organisations. Men predominate among the Sudanese as a corollary of strong patriarchal structures. This occurs despite the difficulty they have in finding work (they are mainly employed as petty-traders, night-watchmen or in construction and restaurants). By contrast, Filipino women outnumber their male counterparts in the bodies they set up (Fakiolas, 1997; Petrinioti, 1993). Their prevalence must be seen in relation to their ability to migrate independently and easily get jobs as baby sitters, domestic servants, nurses, and carers for the elderly (Minev et al., 1997; Romaniszyn, 1997). Their large numbers, together with their substantial contribution to the economy of their home country, distinguish them from Sudanese females, who abstain from community decision-making. Filipinos are very active in the executive board of their ethnic associations: they raise demands around economic and security benefits, are involved in various committees and attend to crucial aspects of community life. The remittances they send home to kin or for communal causes (mainly at times of crises or natural calamities rather than for progressive goals such as schools or hospitals) constitute highly symbolic acts that cut across geographical borders and ensure to them power and distinction.

Sudanese and Filipino immigrants further maintain their identity through their belief systems and by countering negative representations about Third World immigrants. Recreational activities, religious and ethnic festivals furnish occasions for organising large social gatherings. Many participate in these events even when they are not registered in ethnic associations. Their absence would denote that they do not consider themselves as part of the immigrant community and eventually they would not be regarded so by others. Cultural events bring immigrants together, cement their bonds, as well as provide opportunities for communication with the indigenous population and local authorities. They selectively adopt aspects of western culture, and combine them with their own – for instance dancing to both their own and European music. This helps us to understand why some immigrant women cooked lunch 'for everyone' at the offices of the

Network of Social Support to Immigrants and Refugees once a month. Getting the ingredients from 'home', then preparing and eating food throw light to the symbolic ties they retain both with their native soil and other immigrants in Athens.

It is difficult to explain the strength of Sudanese and Filipino organisations. I am inclined to suggest that dynamic involvement in ethnic bodies partly reflects political structures and conflicts born in the society of origin. It also relates with the causes of immigration, which sets the major parameters for their response to institutional discrimination in Greece. Thus, unlike the Sudanese who leave their native country because of political and religious factors, the Filipinos tend to immigrate for family reunion and are more eager to adapt to a Greek lifestyle. However that may be, immigrants' mobilisation further varies in accordance with the stage of their settlement in Athens: while initially they concentrated on explicit social-economic demands, they are gradually oriented towards ethnic and cultural processes.

To sum up, the investigation of Sudanese and Filipino associations reveals the influence of both the framework in which they are placed as well as the nature of their collective activities. Both associations offer alternatives for identity formation and serve as foci where immigrants question their image as unidentified Others, transmit community values and facilitate their adaptation to the host society through the circulation of material and symbolic goods. The constraints they experience in conjunction with the ambiguity of their legal status deprive them of trust in 'Greece as the country where democracy was born' and encourage them to live 'between cultures'. They keep one foot in the new social context and another in their homeland. Preservation of ethnic identity is not the only criterion for the creation of these bodies: they express multiple interests and play many roles. The most important of these concerns the fact that they bring together a large number of immigrants who use their services, attend cultural or other meetings and prepare the ground for a better future. Such procedures are possible because political opposition and claims appear in the costume of cultural difference. In this respect, Bastenier's (1994, p. 54) statement that ethnic self-assertion as a means with which ethnic minorities counteract stigmatisation 'will only take on open form where (...) particularly weakened groups are concerned' needs re-evaluation. Filipinos and Sudanese are not more disadvantaged than other displaced populations in Greece. Yet, they do set up festivities and even participate in events organised by NGOs. Resort to dominant institutions together with the promotion of ethnic specificities constitutes a 'dual discursive competence'

(Werbner, 1997, p. 18) which renders culture a primary element of their debate vis-à-vis state officials.

Concluding Remarks

How do local authorities interact with ethnic groups which, while becoming part and parcel of the economic life of Greece, remain in a precarious position as far as their political and juridical rights are concerned? The relevance of the Greek case lies in the discrepancies observed. On the one hand, despite immigrants' large numbers, there are no prospects for their political and social integration. Existing laws do not encourage their mobilisation, no initiatives are developed by the state regarding their self-determination, officials only provide ad hoc solutions and there is lack of institutional means for confronting ethnic demands. Hence, ethnic groups remain fragmented, self-referential and temporary, their interests are not directly incorporated in the mainstream political system, and they abstain from formal levels of the civic and social life and take no part in public discourse about political reform. On the other hand however, NGOs and welfare agencies operate as mediators between authorities and immigrants following procedures through which the latter survive and assert their cultural identity. In the absence of concrete immigrant policy the role of ethnic organisations is limited to informal collaboration with government agencies. Their welfare derives from voluntary help, maintenance of face-to-face communication, individual and community strategies with which they overcome obstacles and preserve their cultural values as initiatives towards integration.

Immigrants' activities do not correspond to the representations of the mainstream society. Nonetheless, since Greeks perceive themselves as a culturally homogeneous unit, they tend to think of arriving populations as undifferentiated Others with no potential for creative action and meagre chances of achieving social and political autonomy. Dominant stereotypes affect contacts across cultural boundaries: despite the widespread adoption of an anti-racist discourse in public, ethnic minorities are classified according to pre-existing images and distinctions are constantly drawn between 'Us' and 'Them'. It is perhaps interesting to stress that in daily usage references to heterogeneity do not necessarily focus on race; emphasis is placed on cultural differences and inequalities. In this sense, the scarcity of extreme manifestations of racism in verbal or non-verbal communication does not indicate absence of racial or other distinctions.

Instead, social and cultural distances are carefully preserved and Greeks adhere to institutionalised discriminations just as much they exhibit tolerance (rather than acceptance) of immigrant groups. This combination explains why discriminative policies alternate with rules of avoidance and humanitarian practices.

Consequently, although local authorities are notified by NGOs and social workers about the importance of setting up advisory committees, there are no reception centres or consultative bodies at the local level; few departments interact with ethnic groups in emergencies. In addition to the lack of clearly delineated jurisdictions or budgets to draw on, immigrants' dispersal in various districts of Athens as well as their mobility in getting jobs, meeting friends and performing religious practices restrict the power of local administrators. Effectively, neither ethnic associations nor Greek officials examine policy issues with respect to immigrants' residential area. The latter are activated at the neighbourhood level in times requiring immediate action but local government support is not economic nor does it consist in buildings that could serve as community centres. It is limited to informal services, counselling and, occasionally, permissions regarding cultural performances. A typical example of local authorities' attitudes is furnished by the Inter-party Committee for Foreigners and Minority Issues (consisting of members of political parties and the city board) which has announced several plans for 'the problem of immigration' but has not been actually concerned with it.

As long as immigrants and NGOs primarily deal ethnic interests, neither national nor municipal structures alter and the state retains the monopoly of power. To put it in another way, the mobilisation of these legal bodies is hindered by the lack of coherent measures. It seems reasonable to assume that the creation of ethnic associations does not only imply collective action with which immigrants satisfy vital needs, but also provides a basis for their manipulation by government authorities who practice a policy of laissez-faire (Lazaridis, 1996, p. 341). Immigrants negotiate their strength using available forms of organisation but have few and inadequate formal relationships with officials on which they can rely.

To the extent that their institutional and ideological exclusion is defined as social, its treatment is also conceived as social and the role of informal assistance is enhanced, distracting attention from the minimal allowances made by the government. Mobilisation along ethnic lines creates a kind of fragmented political stage with little or no dialogue with the state apparatus. The debate about Greece as a multicultural society conceals the political dimension of ethnicity and asymmetrical power relations (Petronoti, 1998,

p. 298). In this respect, it may well be that if ethnic groups find formal channels for political expression their attempts at cultural distinction will lose, some at least, of their current purpose and immigrants will no longer be seen as imposing threats on the integrity of the Greek nation.

In short, ethnic mobilisation cannot be approached as a process whereby immigrants organise in systematic ways and mark stable political or ethnic boundaries. They form transnational communities and wish to remain indispensable to their home countries as well as articulate with the country of settlement. Their collective activities are multifaceted and must be conceptualised as one aspect of relationships in which cultural variations and social inequalities are communicated. The analysis of their encounter with Greek authorities shows that their reactions are not altogether determined by discriminative institutions nor can all their problems be attributed to ethnocentric and racist attitudes. What is more, the nature of immigrants' practices does not stem from ethnic differences alone; cultural and social dimensions must be taken under consideration, too. Their arrival reflects wider social formations that prove flexible enough to leave room for manoeuvres and subtle, but important, transformations. The informal is intermingled with the official, the individual relates to the collective, deprivation of social capital increases involvement in immigrant communities without abolishing links with the indigenous population. Likewise, the local cannot be separated from the national; the attitude of the municipal government towards ethnic groups depends on the ways these are defined at the state level. Once very restrictive rules are institutionalised, variations in local administrators' decisions cannot be great.

Ethnic mobilisation is a two-way process whereby each side influences and is influenced by the other. In fact, it may be conceived as an inscription of interactive mechanisms aiming to increase power and prestige. Immigrants strive to convert their marginality into a site of resistance that in turn generates alternative perspectives and counter discourse. Though the Greek government is not committed to radical changes, bottom-up activities gradually open up space for rethinking attitudes towards cultural or other heterogeneity. The meanings and consequences of immigrants' presence are reconsidered; it becomes evident that the relationships between authorities, NGOs and ethnic associations encompass continuity and fractures, self-reliance and dependence. Despite the limitations they encounter, immigrant bodies are not merely subversive or directed towards self-defence. They function as social movements or rallying points for solidarity, avoid confrontations with the state or its ramifying institutions and liberate government agencies from inadequacies concerning their requirements.

Clearly, legitimised asymmetries provide the framework within which new representations are formed and alternative relationships take shape.

Notes

1   Until regularisation was initiated, the bulk of immigrants were unregistered. The UNHCR or other non-governmental organisations issued certain forms of documentation that prevented deportation but promised no political or social rights.

2   Data provided by the Ministry of Public Order in 1992 reveal the existence of 262,320 immigrants with residence permits in the country and at least 300,000 without any official documents. The Ministry of Foreign Affairs estimates that there are 400,000 unregistered foreigners while other sources consider that they reach 500,000 (PENED, 1997, p. 13). Likewise, Fakiolas (1995, p. 23) refers to 500,000, i.e. at least ten per cent more than the labour force holding work or residence permits.

3   According to law 1438/1984, regulations for naturalisation are very strict. Individuals married to Greek citizens have to wait five years before three Ministries (Fakiolas, 1994, p. 21) examine their applications. Authorities often issue such documents, but there are no data on rates of citizenship, the criteria of its acquisition or ethnic origin.

4   Immigrants' over-reliance on state support may have a numbing effect on their mobilisation since they are unlikely to turn against authorities. Yet, such a perspective cannot be explored in Greece since immigrant bodies are not subsidised by the government.

5   The emphasis official discourse places on multiculturalism in the sphere of education may be interpreted as a concern with representations of rather than the survival of ethnic heterogeneity in Greece. Co-existence of different immigrant groups is primarily affected by material and political factors disguised as ideologies and cultural symbols.

References

Bastenier, A. (1994), 'Immigration and the Ethnic Differentiation of Social Relations in Europe', in J. Rex and B. Drury (eds), *Ethnic Mobilisation in a Multi-cultural Europe*, Avebury, Aldershot, pp. 48-56.

Cavounidi, J. and Hatzaki, L. (1999), 'Foreigners who Submitted Application for Temporary Residence Permit: Ethnicity, Gender and Residence Area', National Institute for Labour, unpublished report (in Greek).

Drury, B. (1994), 'Ethnic Mobilisation: Some Theoretical Considerations', in J. Rex and B. Drury (eds), *Ethnic Mobilisation in a Multi-cultural Europe*, Avebury, Aldershot, pp. 13-22.

Emke-Poulopoulos, I. (1990), *Immigrants and Refugees in Greece, 1970-1990*, Eklogi, Athens (in Greek).

Fakiolas, R. (1994), 'Migration from and to Greece, OECD-SOPEMI', unpublished report.

Fakiolas, R. (1995), 'Preventing Racism at the Workplace: Greece', Working paper submitted to the European Foundation for the Improvement of Living and Working Conditions.

Fakiolas, R. (1997), *Migration and European Integration: Report for Greece*, Forschungs- institut der Deutschen Gesellschaft für Auswärtige Politik, Germany.

Friedman, J. (1995), 'Rethinking Poverty: Empowerment and Citizen Rights', *International Social Science Journal*, vol. 148, pp. 161-72.

Iosifides, Th. (1997), 'Immigrants in the Athens Labour Market: A Comparative Survey of Albanians, Egyptians and Filipinos', in R. King and R. Black (eds), *Southern Europe and the New Immigrations*, Academic Press, Sussex.

Kourtovik, I. (1994), 'The Legal Status of Immigrant Workers in Greece', in Chr. Theodoropoulos and Ath. Sykiotou (eds), *The Protection of Rights of Immigrant Workers and their Families: International and National Aspects*, Estia, Athens, pp. 182- 93.

Lazaridis, G. (1996), 'Immigration to Greece: A Critical Evaluation of Greek Policy', *New Community*, vol. 22, pp. 335-48.

Mahnig, H. (1999), 'Contradictions of Inclusion in a Direct Democracy: The Struggle for Political and Cultural Rights of Migrants in Zurich', Paper delivered in MPMC meeting in Liège, October 1999.

Maloutas, Th. (1990), *Athens, Residence, Family: Analysis of Post-war Residential Prac- tices*, Exandas: EKKE (in Greek).

Mikrakis, A. and Triandafyllidou, A. (1994), 'Greece: The "Others" Within', *Social Science Information*, vol. 33, pp. 787-805.

Minev, D., Zheliaskova M. et al. (1997), 'The Labour Migration from Bulgaria to Greece: Parameters, Factors, Consequences', Paper presented at the Conference on Non- military Aspects of Security in Southern Europe: Migration, Employment and Labour Market, Santorini.

PENED (1997), *The Perception of the 'Foreigner': Aspects of Xenophobia and Racism in Greece*, Contributors: Chr. Varouxi, A. Fragiskou et al., The National Centre for Social Research, Athens (in Greek).

Petrinioti, X. (1993), *Migration to Greece: A Preliminary Registration, Classification and Analysis*, Odysseas, Athens (in Greek).

Petronoti, M. (1993), 'Social Networks and Mobility Processes: The Case of Small-scale Entrepreneurs in Piraeus', in Z. Uherek (ed.), *Urban Anthropology and the Supra- national and Regional Networks of the Town*, Prague Occasional Papers in Ethnology, no. 2, pp. 130-47.

Petronoti, M. (1996), 'Greece as a Place for Refugees: An Anthropological Approach to Institutional Constraints Pertaining to Religious Practices', in R. Jambresic and M. Povrzanovic (eds), *War, Exile and Everyday Life*, Institute of Ethnology and Folklore Research, Zagreb, pp. 189-206.

Petronoti, M. (1998), *The Portrait of an Intercultural Relationship: Crystallizations, Frissures, Reconstructions* (with the contribution of K. Zarkia), UNESCO-EKKE- Plethron, Athens (in Greek).

Petronoti, M. (2000), 'Culture as Resistance: The Transformation of Eritrean Refugees' Rootlessness', in C. Vgenopoulos (ed.), *Population Movements and Development*, Papazissis, Athens, pp. 45-53.

Polyzos, I., Vlastos, Th. et al. (1995), *The Phenomenon of Marginalisation of Minorities in Attiki: The Characteristics of Gypsies in Urban Space*, Ethniko Metsovio Poly- technio, Athens, unpublished report (in Greek).

Ranaweera, A. (2000), 'Organizing Ethnic Minorities in Norway: A Mission Impossible?', in C. Vgenopoulos (ed.), *Population Movements and Development*, Papazissis, Athens, pp. 79-85.

Rex, J. and Josephides Th. (1987), 'Asian and Greek Cypriot Population in Britain', in J. Rex, D. Joly and C. Wilpert (eds), *Immigrant Associations in Europe*, Gower, Aldershot, pp. 11-41.

Romaniszyn, Kr. (1997), 'Clandestine Labour Migration from Poland to Greece, Italy and Spain in Light of Emerging Anthropological Perspectives', Paper presented at the Conference on Non-military Aspects of Security in Southern Europe: Migration, Employment and Labour Market, Santorini.

Rudder, V. de, Taboada, I. and Vourch, F. (1994), 'Immigrant Participation, Mobilisation and Integration Strategies in France: A Typology', in J. Rex and B. Drury (eds), *Ethnic Mobilisation in a Multi-cultural Europe*, Avebury, Aldershot, pp. 13-22.

SOPEMI (1997), *Annual Report on Greece*, by N. Petropoulos.

Triandafyllidou, A. (1998), 'Greek Immigration Policy: Fact and Fiction?', Paper presented at a Conference on the Contribution of a Changing Greece to the European Union: the Dynamics of a Complex Relationship, organised by the Hellenic Observatory of the London School of Economics.

Werbner, P. (1997), 'Introduction: The Dialectics of Cultural Hybridity', in P. Werbner and T. Modood (eds), *Debating Cultural Hybridity: Multi-cultural Identities and the Politics of Anti-racism*, Zed Books, London and New Jersey, pp. 1-28.

Zetter, R. (1994), 'The Greek-Cypriot Refugees: Perceptions of Return Under Conditions of Protracted Exile', *International Migration Review*, vol. 28, pp. 307-22.

4 Tuning the Channels: Local Government Policies and Immigrants' Participation in Barcelona[1]

RICARD MORÉN-ALEGRET

> Welcome everywhere you come from
> You'll lose your life or find home here
> Cause some do it right some do it wrong
> Some are talking wise some they're running their tongue
> Lot of soul in my block / from St. Pau to the Dock
> Are you ready to be hurt and shocked?
> Barrio Chino never fails to rock
> Los indios de Barcelona
> Son más indios que los de Arizona
> *Mano Negra*, 1988

Introduction

The significant features of Barcelona include its history of social mobilisation, its active and innovative City Government and its shift from being a city mainly attracting immigrants from the rest of Iberia to a cosmopolitan city where an increasing number of people from all continents reside.

The main aim of this chapter is to analyse the political participation of foreigners in Barcelona by taking into account the 'political opportunity structure', the nature of migrant associations, and how they interact. It will be shown how, on the one hand, a city government relatively active in fostering residents' political participation via advisory councils and, on the other hand, a diversity of big 'indigenous' NGOs, co-exist with a few cases of strong autonomous 'foreign' immigrants organisations.

Until recently people coming from other areas of the Iberian Peninsula or Europe mainly composed migrant communities in Barcelona. During the twentieth century, there have been two periods of rapid migration (Pascual

61

de Sans et al., 2000). Between 1916 to 1930 industrial expansion and public works needed workers that arrived from the geographically and, sometimes, also culturally closer areas to Catalonia. The estimated inflow was over 500,000 people. Then, between the 1950s and the early 1970s mass immigration into Barcelona was from more distant Spanish regions, where languages other than Catalan were spoken. The population increase due to immigration was around 1,400,000 people, largely to work in industry.

In the case of the European migrations, foreign immigration to Catalonia increased during the early industrial era (during the nineteenth century), when high-skilled workers, employers, and financial investors (and their families) arrived mainly in the Barcelona metropolitan region from Northern European countries. This group is still significant but is now a minority among the foreign population. In the last decades North Americans and Japanese high-skilled immigrants have joined this group (Solana and Pascual de Sans, 1995).

Table 4.1   Foreign residents in Barcelona by main nationality, 1991-1996

Nationality	1991	Nationality	1996
Argentina	2,170	Morocco	3,191
France	1,994	Peru	2,779
Germany	1,914	Philipinnes	1,784
Italy	1,777	France	1,707
Morocco	1,727	Italy	1,693
Philippines	1,253	Germany	1,589
		Agentina	1,173
Total foreigners	23,402		30,455
(% total pop.)	(1.4%)		(2.02%)

Source: Anuari Estadístic de la Ciutat de Barcelona 1996, Ajuntament de Barcelona, 1997.

However, during the last few decades an increasing number of people coming from other continents have influenced Barcelona's changing population. During the late 1960s and early 1970s African people stopped in the metropolitan area on their way to Northern Europe. This settlement before crossing the Pyrenees was due to the increasingly hostile immigration policies in North-western countries and the economic growth in Catalonia. They were the pioneers of later arrivals from Africa during the 1980s and 1990s, especially from Morocco, Senegal and Gambia.

Also during the 1960s students from some Latin American countries and Equatorial Guinea found schools and universities open to them in Barcelona. During the 1970s refugees from South America found a haven in the city creating the pillars of larger communities from Argentina, Chile and Uruguay when economic crisis in those countries during the 1980s and 1990s brought more people from the South American Cone (Domingo et al., 1995; Sepa Bonaba, 1993).

Furthermore, during the 1980s, inflows of Filipino women to domestic services, and Chinese immigrants to catering services took place. More recently, during the 1990s, domestic service has also drawn women from Peru, Ecuador and the Dominican Republic (in general through the contingents established annually by the Spanish government). Another recent significant group has been immigrants from Pakistan (some of them are owners of small food shops, while others work distributing gas cylinders).

Official statistics on foreign immigrants in Spain only allow general approaches to the real composition of the immigrant population, due to the existence of a significant number of 'dedocumented' immigrants.[2] However, in any case, foreign immigrant population in Barcelona is still small compared to other European cities.

Immigrants Political Opportunity Structure in Barcelona[3]

European, Spanish and Catalan government policies have a direct influence on the political opportunity structure for immigrants in Barcelona City. However, there are a number of ways initiated by the City Government on its own designed to foster political participation.

Foreigners do not have the right to vote in Spain, with the exception of those from European Union countries who can participate in local elections (plus some from a few countries with special agreements on this matter). In 1994 the number of naturalisations in Spain as a whole was 7,801, which is only 1.6 per cent of the documented foreign residents in Spain in 1993,[4] and in 1995 just 6,756 foreigners were naturalised, which represents 1.4 per cent of the foreign residents in 1994 (461,364 people). Thus, these data suggest that only small minorities of the immigrants from abroad are Spanish citizens with full rights. However, there are diverse situations, as

Latin Americans and Filipino immigrants can obtain nationality (and the right to vote) after two years of legal residence while most others need 10 years.

At the City Council level, the two most important authorities are the Ajuntament de Barcelona (City Government) and the ten administrative districts of the city (until recently they had just a few competencies, today they have a few more, but a possible reform of the internal city administration may foster district governments in the future). From the first local ballot after Franco dictatorship to the elections of June 1995 the Partit dels Socialistes de Catalunya (PSC) ran the City Government. They held the simple majority of votes, and needed the support of Iniciativa per Catalunya (IC), and Esquerra Republicana de Catalunya (ERC). However, in 1996, a fraction of ERC split to create the Partit per la Independència (PI) and the two councillors of that party became members of the latter. In June 1999, PSC won elections again and its candidate was elected Mayor with the support of IC.

In general terms, the key idea behind Barcelona City Government approach to foreign immigrants issues has been to consider them wherever possible just like any other resident and to channel their demands through the general administrative bodies. However, a few civil servants within the City Government have been specialised in 'foreigners issues', and among them Pere Novella (Social Affairs Area) and Josep Ignasi Urenda (Civil Rights Commissary) exemplify the two main visions that are influential in the local government immigration policies.

There has been a line of continuity between local policies that dealt with Spanish internal immigration during the 1960s and early 1970s and foreign immigration during the 1980s and 1990s, according to Pere Novella. Among the common themes, Novella emphasises an attitude that in general avoids a different treatment for groups based on diverse cultural or geographical backgrounds, denying the importance of a specific job called cultural 'mediator', instead everybody should mediate between different people. Following Novella, other aspects than just the country of origin have to be taken into account, such as rural and urban differences. A university student from Dakar may have more in common with a university student born in Barcelona, than the latter has with a peasant from a small Andalusian village, even if both are Spanish citizens.

However, Novella also recognises differences between both immigration waves. Among a significant number of the immigrants arrived in the second wave there is a lack of full citizens' rights (in the case of foreigners), there are difficulties in understanding and speaking local languages (when immigration was mainly from the rest of Spain almost everybody spoke Spanish) and, apparently, there is an higher refusal to welcome foreigners among local people. This lack of full citizenship rights together with some particular needs provided reasons for the creation of alternative ways of foreigners' participation beyond voting.

Advisory and Participatory Councils

One way of possible political participation is via advisory and participatory councils. In 1986, under new district organisation and citizens' participation rules, Barcelona City Council created advisory councils on social welfare, professional and employment training, voluntary associations, women, elderly people and so forth. Thus in the Social Welfare Area (Àmbit de Benestar Social) of Barcelona City Council there is an Advisory Board on foreign immigration and refugees. It has been working since the late 1980s, with the participation of representative members of political parties, trade unions (some of them foreign workers), NGOs, universities, civil servants from local, autonomic and central governments, and professional associations. However, between 1990 and 1996 foreigners' associations were not members of the Council (see Consell Municipal, 1990-1996). They only participated a few times as guests at meetings. These were the cases of a member of the Centro Filipino in the period 1991-1993 and of two members of the Federació de Collectius d'Immigrants a Catalunya (FCIC) in 1996. The contacts between local government members and foreign immigrant associations' members were, in general, informal.

In the light of this situation, on 24 October 1997 Barcelona City Council inaugurated the Consell Municipal d'Immigració de Barcelona. This initiative had the support of the European Commission programme on local integration (LIA). In the origins of this advisory council Pere Novella has been a key character, managing the relationship with a few selected immigrant's associations along the way (those more sympathetic with the local government visions), and discussing in advance the rules of the Immigration Municipal Council with them.

This suggests how a (local) government may 'use' some social organisations (which become institutionalised) in order to elaborate and legitimise policies, without giving more power to people, and how other organisations are excluded because they do not have the kind of incidence that the government considers as right. Thus Antonio Gramsci's (1971) inspired approach to the state, as the addition of government plus institutionalised civil society, is reflected here. However, not all social organisations play this game. Some members of organised civil society try to avoid institution-alisation processes, like Assemblea Papers per Tothom (Documents for Everybody Assembly), and try to perform in a more autonomous way.

Immigration Observatory

Beside the Social Welfare Area, in the Barcelona City Government, in early 1992, the then Mayor Pasqual Maragall (PSC) appointed Josep Ignasi Urenda as Mayor's Commissioner for Civil Rights. He was put in charge of monitoring the developments of ethnic and religious minorities in Barcelona City. In 1995, after the local elections, a new specific govern-ment body (Regidoria) of civil rights was created, and then the commis-sionner's main duties shifted to international relations (Barcelona Solidària), although immigration issues were kept as a minor but significant part of his activities. Among them, there was the development of an observatory on immigration in Barcelona City, which consists mainly of the compilation of various statistical data from official sources and from some NGOs. There was also a small budget for grants to those NGOs and trade unions that collaborate with the Commissary providing data on immigrants for the observatory (mainly, Caritas and the main trade unions: CITE-CCOO and AMIC-UGT). Thus the statistical control of immigrants is partially 'sub-contracted' (without a contract) to some NGOs, in a neo-liberal fashion.

There is not just one point of view within the Barcelona City Govern-ment in relation to immigration. A coalition of political parties is in power and there is disagreement within them as well. Pere Novella's visions contrast with Urenda's perceptions of what happens when a 'foreign immi-grant' from an impoverished country acquires Spanish nationality. For the latter, they are still a minority who needs special treatment and to be monitored, as exemplifies the creation of an immigration observatory. This contrast is more explicit when we discover what the 'theoretical' references of each are. Thus, while Pere Novella during the interviews is critical of the 'Anglo-Saxon' way of dealing with the 'ethnic minorities' issue, Ignasi Urenda's administrative body's name includes 'civil rights' because of an 'Anglo-Saxon' influence.

In any case, it has to be emphasised that both local administrative bodies share the core concern of the City Government's immigration policy, which is based on avoiding the creation of administrative bodies specific to 'foreign immigrants', unless it is really necessary, and an explicit rejection in their discourse of the concept of 'ghetto'.

Other Joint Forms of Participation

Other joint forms of participation between the City Government and other organisations have been implemented on immigration issues. Thus, there is an office that provides services for foreign immigrants and refugees, Servei d'Atenció a Immigrants Estrangers i Refugiats (SAIER) organised by five institutions and organisations: Barcelona City Council; the Centre d'Informació per a Treballadors Estrangers – CITE (this is the body of the trade union CCOO that deals with foreign workers' affairs); the Associació Catalana de Solidaritat i Ajuda als Refugiats (ACSAR); the Red Cross; and the College of Barristers. However, the City Government mainly funds it. In 1995, 2,350 cases were dealt with in the SAIER, among them 73.8 per cent were 'economic immigrants' and 26.2 per cent 'asylum seekers' (see Gerència Àmbit, 1995). In terms of immigrants' involvement, although one of the members of the office was an Equatorial Guinean immigrant naturalised Spanish (a member of CITE-CCOO), no 'foreign immigrant' associations participate in running this service. Thus it is an instance of collaboration between government and institutionalised civil society, and it shows how autonomous 'foreign immigrants' associations are excluded from the management of significant services directed at them.

Finally, the process of reaching an agreement to build a Muslim cemetery in Barcelona shows an informal joint form of participation. The 'distance' between the local City Government and the main Islamic associations based in the city was a difficulty in the negotiation process. Divisions among the Moroccan associations (the main Muslim 'national community' in Barcelona) also did not help. The role of a small Lebanese association was the key to reaching a compromise over a place for Muslim burials. One of the representative members of this association also participates in a trade union, and he was close to one of the political parties of the centre-left wing coalition that was in power in the Barcelona City Government. The fact he was not a member of a faction of the Moroccan community, and that he was not Muslim (thus he was not a member of any faction of the Islamic associations) but representative of an association with several Muslim members, were helpful points in reaching the agreement. Finally, this agreement was signed at the end of 1997 by Barcelona's City Council and the following associations: Associació de Catalunya Líban, Centre Islàmic, Associació Palestina, and Associació per a la Protecció dels Drets dels Pakistanesos. Thus the Moroccan associations did not participate in the signing, although some of them took part in the negotiations. In any case, the cemetery is open to all Muslim people, without discrimination according to origin, sex or nationality. It is located in the general cemetery of Collserola, covers 552 square metres, and has a capacity for one hundred tombs.

In summary, Barcelona City Government tries to channel all immigrants into mainstream services, while respecting cultural diversity. However, taking into account the limitation of rights among foreigners (e.g. lack of voting rights) and some special needs (e.g. language and legal support), there is a Municipal Council of Immigration and other joint forms of participation with social organisations on these issues. Thus the City Government is tuning a few other channels in order to provide some services to 'foreign' immigrants.

Migrant Organisations and Mobilisation

Apart from the opportunities for political involvement or the services offered by the City Government, there are other ways immigrants participate in local life. The world of organisations of 'foreign immigrants' in Barcelona is too diverse to be analysed properly here. However, this section will underline two key issues for understanding how migrant communities mobilise in European urban areas, with illustrations from Barcelona. Firstly, it examines the evolution from mainly protest organisations (i.e. associations for transforming society) to services associations (i.e. associations to manage society). Secondly, it discusses their geographical organisation over territory.

From Protesting to Providing Services?

From being mainly 'protest associations' created to overcome unjust situations caused by governments (such as 'dedocumentation') or by capital (labour exploitation), some associations have been transformed into 'service associations' that receive funding from the same government that oppresses the same people they aim to serve. This change happened between the mid-1970s and the 1990s. Furthermore, in this process the members of such associations often turn from comrades in struggle to 'co-users' of services. This process was still an exception among most immigrant associations in Barcelona, because the funding they have received has been small. But it applies much more to NGOs run by local-born people or among trade unions. In fact, it is the same neo-liberal model applied to other areas of Catalan society and in other European societies (Casey, 1996). According to this model the NGOs in general (and also QUANGOs) perform social tasks which, during the implementation of Keynesian policies may have corresponded to governments. What changes with neo-liberalism is that the government apparatus only performs the basic orientation of activities and the control of these tasks (an example is the management of professional training courses by Generalitat de Catalunya). The daily running of the activities is transferred to those social organisations willing to toe the government's line and which allow themselves to be monitored by the government. (In the case of professional training courses there is a wide range of NGOs that offer them to 'foreign immigrants' among other people.)

This complex balance between, on the one hand, obtaining funding for the provision of services and, on the other hand, the denunciation of unfair situations is one of the key worries for GRAMC, which is the acronym for Grups de Recerca i Actuació sobre Minories Culturals i Treballadors Estrangers. GRAMC was constituted from a group created around the Samba Kubali school (an inter-cultural school based in a Catalan town called Santa Coloma de Farners, near Girona) which was registered in 1989. There was no GRAMC local group (*assemblea local*) in Barcelona until 1994. This NGO, which in 1997 had a 700-strong membership, is unique in the context of Catalonia. GRAMC is defined as a network of over 12 grassroots local organisations and their main headquarters are located in Girona. Curiously, the Barcelona group is the smallest local assembly and, according to Carmen Murias, who is one of its members, it performs very specific tasks mainly related to spreading information.

The issue of funding has been discussed by GRAMC. As opposed to many NGOs and trade unions that have assumed uncritically that the only way to proceed is to become an organisation that provides services, within GRAMC there was a debate between two main positions. On one side were those members opposed to this 'services' option and, on the other, those members aiming to self-organise training activities for social and personal transformation.

Thus some GRAMC members commented that, in case of becoming a services association it was necessary to compete with other NGOs that provide services, such as the main trade unions, Caritas and SOS Racisme. The latter anti-racist association, after internal changes in 1994, adopted an organisational structure based on business management. In this sense SOS Racisme, from having just a part-time administrative secretary as a salaried worker in early 1992, according to Isidoro Barba (general manager of this NGO), in 1997 had seven full-time employees. At the same time it created a 'human resources' section dedicated to looking after the salaried staff and co-ordinating volunteers who were interested in participating in the association. Another new section was dedicated to internal management and new commissions for the 'control' of finance and personnel were set up. Furthermore, SOS Racisme fostered several remunerative services (such as merchandising, workshops, exhibitions) so their public funding amounts to only 55 per cent of their budget. In addition, the merchandising of the logo of this NGO has become another form of funding. In the issue published in February 1998 of the bulletin *Colors*, SOS Racisme announced the economic collaboration with the big clothes company Mango.

Diverse Ways of Geographical Organisation

From a political geographic point of view, GRAMC's territorial organisation has undergone interesting transformations due to their difficulties in co-ordinating local actions with actions at a higher territorial level.[5] This difficulty led them to experiment with the representation in the executive committee: from having one representative for each local group to having a representative for mid-level territorial areas composed of three or four local groups. The aim was to enhance collaboration between local groups following geographical criteria (basically, proximity). In most cases it did not work. Thus afterwards GRAMC re-adopted a direct representation of the local groups in the executive committee, except in cases where regional co-ordinations worked well. In other words, flexibility at the territorial organisation level can be a solution for the difficult balance between local direct participation and supra-local co-ordination.

In the case of SOS Racisme, its economic extension has been also accompanied by a territorial spread that has varied over time, with some groups appearing and disappearing. In early 1998, apart from the people who meet in the headquarters in Barcelona City centre, there were nine local groups distributed mainly in the Barcelona and Tarragona metropolitan areas.

In any case, the debates within GRAMC did not occur in SOS Racisme to the same extent owing to their lack of an organisational structure that could enable debate and the decision-making process from the bottom up as in GRAMC. The minor territorialisation of SOS Racisme in relation to GRAMC, while SOS Racisme possesses more resources and a higher budget than GRAMC,[6] confirms again SOS Racisme's lack of interest in reaching a horizontal grassroots development.

Following this debate over territorial organisation, but in contrast to these large associations with presence in several towns, a multi-organisational local project was set up. In 1993 some NGOs oriented mainly towards North-South co-operation initiated the 'Xenophilia project' (Projecte Xenofília) with the desire of becoming a local project, situated within Barcelona's Ciutat Vella district limits. It had its main site in Avinyó Street, There were thirty people working in the project, almost all of them volunteers. When they obtained enough funding[7] they employed somebody as a part-time and temporary worker (at some points there have been as many as three or four full-time employees, always in a semi-professional way). The areas in which they have performed have been the following: juridical (not a priority because other organisations already cover this area); women's issues (including a course on becoming community agents for immigrant women, and a training workshop on resources and environmental knowledge); mediation (including a Servei d'Atenció i Mediació Intercultural in order to mediate between immigrants and public administrations, social services, schools, etc.); housing (including a Servei de Suport al Lloguer d'Habitatges, where they give information on flats to rent and help in the search, give advice about contracts, produce statistics on housing conditions, and help to find resources to pay the rent or renovation); and training (including IT, hotel and restaurant jobs, legal advice, social facilities, introduction to media, and technical training courses on mediation for foreign immigrants). At this local level, the Xenophilia project saw results. Following police aggression against foreign neighbours a platform of organisations and neighbours was created to support the victims was immediately formed. However, recent public funding shortages put an end to this project in 1998, showing how the life of a project funded from institutions may depend on how long it gets money. Even if it is a socially successful project when participants get used to depend on money it is difficult to keep on working when money vanishes.

Self-organising versus Patronage

The situation at big NGOs, where members are mainly Spanish citizens or both immigrants and Spanish, is different than at most foreign immigrants associations. In general, the latter are small organisations either modestly funded or not funded at all. Thus it is interesting to see the efforts of the Federation of Immigrant Communities in Catalonia (Federació de Collectius Immigrants a Catalunya, FCIC) at co-ordinating several foreigners associations, mainly settled in Barcelona province. The FCIC assembled 26 immigrant associations and collectives of immigrants living in Catalonia. It brings together persons from different origins, such as the Maghreb, Latin America, Sub-Saharan Africa, Asia, and Europe. They have several working commissions, one of the most active of which addresses women's issues. It groups women from Latin America, the Maghreb, the Philippines, Gambia, and Equatorial Guinea.

FCIC was founded in 1990, with the announcement of foreign workers' regularisation. In 1991 during the Extraordinary Regularisation of Foreign Workers it began to consolidate itself. By then diverse NGOs, like SOS Racisme and Caritas, and trade unions, basically CCOO, had created a platform called Catalunya Solidària amb la Immigració (Catalonia Solidary with Immigration). It was in the framework of such a social organisations that the creation of a federation which grouped immigrants' associations was possible: 'a body that collected immigrants' demands which was run by immigrants themselves' in the words of Obam Micó, a member of the FCIC directory board. In this first phase there was a widespread response among the immigrants' collectives. There were meetings nearly every week in the framework of Catalunya Solidària: FCIC was being consolidated. But after the regularisation process there was a breakdown, the co-ordination between associations became very difficult (interview with Obam Micó).

The hardest period of the post-1991 Foreign Workers' Extraordinary Regularisation process coincided with the period when foreign immigrants' associations were over-shadowed by SOS Racisme. This anti-racist NGO became the *de facto* leader among social organisations dealing with immigration issues in Barcelona when a debate on foreigners in Catalonia came to the public's attention in 1992.

It is important to recognise that, to date, the influence of 'indigenous' NGOs (organisations of solidarity, trade unions, Christian charities, and so on) has been more significant in lobbying public authorities than the influence of foreigners organisations on their own. Some indigenous NGOs, like SOS Racisme, command a large amount of economic and human resources while, in general, foreigners associations precariously survive. Patronage is enemy of self-organisation.

An example of this is the organisation of the Festa de la Diversitat (Diversity Festival), an event organised every spring since 1993 in Barcelona City by SOS Racisme with economic support, almost every year, from the Barcelona City Council, the Generalitat de Catalunya, the Spanish Central Government, the EU, and private funding (apart from the funding, lately they receive also human help through the public bodies in charge of voluntary work). The budget is several million pesetas and it attracts over

50,000 people during a weekend. Some foreigners associations are invited to sell their products in stalls during the festival. In previous meetings they have been told by SOS Racisme what they should do until the festival and during the event: foreigners associations are not considered as equal partners of the organisation. SOS Racisme is in charge of the organisation while the foreigners associations offer 'exotic' drinks, food and music to mainly non-foreign people, in what becomes a fun fair.[8] Thus, in 1996, twenty foreigners associations and other solidarity NGOs distributed an open letter to the public, the press, the public authorities, and to SOS Racisme in order to uncover this unfair situation. It reported that they were paying the organisation between 30,000 and 60,000 pesetas to have a stall, while the organisation was receiving public funding. In focusing the festival on 'music stars' that received a lot of money, it was not fair that immigrants' music bands were playing a few metres away for free. This was not a new situation. Since the beginning of the festival in 1993 these and other issues (as the top-down relationship with the direction of SOS Racisme) were on the table. But until the fourth festival in 1996 things were not spread beyond the people directly involved in the its preparation. At the end of the open letter the associations underlined four points: 'we are not killjoy', 'we only wish SOS Racisme would reflect on it', 'we wish to be taken into account', and 'we want to open a dialogue with a clear will to reach an agreement.' However the result of that action, for some associations, was not as positive as it was expected. In 1997 they were not invited by SOS Racisme to attend the festival. This can be a problem for foreigners associations. The money they may collect during the Festa de la Diversitat weekend, in several cases, is the main source of funding for activities during the rest of the year. In 1999 most of these problems still remained.

However, SOS Racisme organises other activities apart from that festival that allow them to have good relationships with other foreigners associations (e.g. pedagogical activities, the report of racist attacks, training courses, information campaigns), even if the latter end up being dependant on the former. In fact, since the beginning of SOS Racisme, some foreigners associations' members have been present in several areas of work. But lately its position is becoming stronger because being 'friend' of SOS Racisme is a way of having better access to funding. SOS Racisme has even created a private Foundation to fund activities, re-enforcing its role as manager and distributor of money.

In summary, in order to understand the mobilisation of immigrants in Barcelona during the 1990s three aspects have been helpful:

- The extent to which protest or provision of services has been important among the activities done by organisations. This question is relevant in a decade that has seen the domestication of protests by the logic of the market and the new kinds of bureaucracy.
- The forms of territorial organisation have followed most associations. This question is relevant when, after the collapse of traditional forms, contradictory trends are taking place at the same time including groups characterised by grassroots flexible co-ordination, others inspired by neo-liberal business management, etc.
- The relations between 'indigenous' organisations' and 'foreign' immigrant associations. This is relevant because the existing divide partly created by big NGOs patronising immigrants and thus putting difficulties to 'foreign immigrants' self-organisation.

The Case of Moroccan Immigrants in Barcelona

People from Morocco are the main immigrant group in Barcelona if measured by nationality. In this section we will focus on associations mainly composed of Moroccans as a more detailed case study of the issues discussed above.

The presence of Moroccan people in Barcelona is not recent, and their arrival has not been a massive inflow concentrated in time. Instead a progressive settlement has been the pattern (Colectivo Ioé, 1994). There are three main periods of settlement since 1960, to which it is possible to add a fourth one corresponding to recent years. Such periods have also been characterised by different kinds of Moroccan immigrants' organisations and political participation.

1960-1975: Under Franco's Rule

During the 1960s, the age of 'desarrollismo' (development) under Franco, Moroccans settled temporally in some parts of Catalonia. They came looking for jobs, but when work was scarce they returned to Morocco or moved on to other European countries. The first Moroccans in Catalonia settled in Barcelona and the metropolitan area. They were single men who worked mainly in the foundry industry, and public works (roads and highways). In some cases, four or five years later their families arrived and then they stayed for a longer period. The lack of a 'foreigners policy' or rigorous controls made it possible for them to live without residence or work permits. There is therefore an underestimation of the number of Moroccans arriving in those years (in 1965 there were 129 Moroccan residents registered in the Barcelona province; in 1975 the number was 391).

Due to the political situation of dictatorship, political participation was limited to the fascist organisations of the regime and to cultural and leisure associations mainly linked to the Catholic Church. Of course, clandestine political organisations existed, but only a minority of people was active in them. The few Moroccan immigrants residing in Spain had little scope for political participation.

1975-1986: 'Democratic' Transition

This period started with the restriction on immigration in France and Germany, and ends when the Foreigners Law 7/1985 was passed in the Spanish Parliament, in Madrid. In the late 1970s and early 1980s, 'liberal democracy' began to filter through and the so-called State of Autonomies was installed in Spain. In local elections the centre-left-wing political parties obtained the power in the main urban city councils, and an economic crisis struck Spain's industrial areas, including Catalonia. At the same time, in Morocco the years of industrialisation through import substitution ended, and the IMF and World Bank 'adjustment' plans appeared.

The closed border of the Pyrenees since 1974 caused a concentration of Moroccans on its southern side. Thus a number settled in Catalonia, mainly in the Barcelona province. The available data show an increase in numbers of the Moroccan residents registered (from 263 people in 1970 in Barcelona province to 884 people in 1985), but the numbers of 'dedocumented' Moroccan immigrants also increased.

During the early years of this period, in the late 1970s, the arrival Moroccan immigrants coincided with the growing protest against Franco's regime and the first precarious 'democratic' government. With the legalisation of free trade unions in 1977 some immigrants managed to join those organisations. Thus in 1980, a group of Moroccan members of Comisiones Obreras (CCOO), after some basic training created the ephemeral Moroccan Emigrants' Association in Catalonia (AEMC) in the same headquarters that CCOO had in carrer Hospital, in the Raval neighbourhood (Roca et al., 1983).

In 1977, a few years before the creation of AEMC, the Arabic-Spanish cultural association Bayt Al Thaqafa already existed. It was formed by a group of young Arabian immigrants and local Barcelonan people. They began to run a Cultural Centre in a place offered by the Catholic community of Sta. Maria del Mar church. In this centre different people with Moroccan origin and from other Arabian countries had the chance to meet each other in their spare time to perform cultural activities and give lessons in Arabian and Spanish. This centre registered itself as the Spanish Association of Friendship with the Arabian People Bayt Al Thaqafa and over time they have been extending activities and services. The flat that this association has in Barcelona (there is another one in St. Vicenç dels Horts) is currently placed in Carrer Princesa, in the Ciutat Vella district. This centre was the first NGO exclusively dedicated to foreign immigrants in Barcelona. Ever since the early 1970s Caritas had already been helping impoverished foreign immigrants who knocked on its doors. But Bayt Al-Thaqafa was original because it was created to attend to the needs of a specific group of people: Muslim and Arabic immigrants. This association is also an instance of a service association appearing when protest movements were more prevalent. Thus, in some aspects, it was a pioneer of the kind of association that later became hegemonic. However, during this period, the influence of money in this and other associations was still limited.

1986-1992: Fortress Policies and Dependent Participation

After the entry in the European Community in 1986, a clearer and more restrictive foreign immigration policy appeared in Spain, alongside other European countries that signed the Schengen Agreement. In May 1990 the compulsory requirement of an entry visa for Moroccan citizens was passed, and in 1991 the second regularisation process was initiated. In Spain, this was a period of relative economic recovery and growth. In Morocco, the neo-liberal policy caused unemployment and social unrest.

The restrictive measures did not impede the entry into Spain of Moroccan citizens. Some arrived before 1990 as tourists or students, and settled down in Catalonia. Others arrived later crossing the Gibraltar strait in the so-called *pateras* (risky boats) putting their lives an danger (an unknown number of them have disappeared in the sea), buying passports from corrupt Spanish consulates in Morocco, or bribing frontier police agents to cross the border line. Thus in 1990 Moroccan residents numbered 3,181 in the Barcelona province, and 13,680 in April 1992, after the 1991 regularisation process.

The data of this regularisation reveal which sectors the Moroccans worked in Barcelona province. They were found mainly in services (73.2 per cent), followed by industry (14.5 per cent), fishery (5.8 per cent), construction (5 per cent) and agriculture (1.2 per cent). Among them, only the 30.7 per cent were women. The majority of the Moroccans arriving in this period were single migrants, mainly young men, but also single, divorced or widowed women. Furthermore, a few families arrived, once the family head had obtained a relative stable situation in terms of work, housing, and residence permits.

Among Moroccan immigrants associative participation was still weak during this period, for several reasons. The associations were recently created; the Moroccan Consulate controlled some; sometimes there was a mutual distrust between Berbers and Arabs; and there was also a general distrust for politics among immigrants due to political corruption in Morocco. Thus relationships within the community were not well organised, in most of the cases just the visit to the mosques, to the cultural centres and to specialised shops allow the communication among them (Colectivo Ioé, 1994; Domingo et al., 1995). Del Olmo (1996) has classified their associations into three groups: governmental (dependent on the Moroccan government), 'para-sindical' (linked to the Spanish trade unions) and Islamic associations (dependent on the mosques). This is an interesting classification that situates the general trends. However the local reality of Barcelona is a more complex one, as it is shown below.

Furthermore, during this period, a few Moroccan immigrants became involved in the process of creating special bodies in trade unions (e.g. in creating the Information Office for Foreign Workers, CITE, in Comisiones Obreras) and the foundation of NGOs like SOS Racisme.

1993-1999: New Challenges

The most recent years can be considered a fourth period of immigration and politics. After the 1992 Olympic Games, the Barcelona metropolitan region (as other Catalan and Spanish areas) suffered an economic crisis that deepened the de-industrialisation process, and increased the unemployment rate up to over 20 per cent of the active population. However, there was then a macroeconomic recovery, bringing with it increased insecurity for poorer members of society.

New associations with new characteristics were formed in this period, like those that mainly work on issues related to the children of immigrants, the so-called second generation. An example is the Associació Socio-

Cultural (ASC) Ibn Batuta, created in 1994 by several Moroccans who had been collaborating in Bayt-Al Thaqafa or SOS Racisme or other Moroccan associations. This association was created by Moroccan family men, who in a few cases have been living in Barcelona for more than 30 years. For Ahmed Yafou, an ASC Ibn Batuta member, obtaining a proper meeting place was an essential aspect of their first steps as an association, making explicit another aspect of organisational geography. Recently this association has started an extension overseas and a small group of members who went to Mallorca to work created a new group, conceived an auxiliary group on the island. However, one of the issues that this association wanted to resolve was children's lack of fluency in (or lack of knowledge of) Arabic.

The person who expresses this, Ahmed Yafou – a member of the executive of the association – is Berber who can speak the Berber language (*Amazigh*). But he believes that their children should be able to speak Arabic as well, because it is useful if they travel to Morocco. However, in the association there are no Berber language lessons. This is a complicated issue because Berber culture has been banned in northern Morocco for decades. In contrast, there are other Moroccan associations that prefer boosting the Berber culture, such as the Associació d'Immigrants Marroquins a Catalunya (AIMC), which has its main site in Mataró (a town near Barcelona) and is one of the most recently registered Moroccan associations.

Moroccan Immigrants' Autonomy versus Institutionalisation

Moroccan associations in Barcelona are characterised by diverse divisions. One of them is whether or not they are linked to the consulate. ASC Ibn Batuta has been accused many times of being linked to the consulate in some interviews. But Ahmed Yafou's response is that they only have two links with the consulate. In their first year they applied for funding from the Moroccan Minister of Emigration in order to buy Arabic textbooks. When they realised that it was only 50,000 pesetas per annum, and that they had to fill in a lot of forms and to celebrate 'national Moroccan' festivals in return, they decided not to apply for it. On another occasion they accepted the services of an Arabic language lecturer who is a Moroccan civil servant attached to the consulate. For Ahmed Yafou there is a big difference between collaborating with the consulate and being part of it.

A number of associations like ATIME, Centro Averroes or AIMC were opposed to differentiation. They shared a political opposition to the Moroccan Alauitan monarchy. They regard ASC Ibn Batuta, Nahda and Amical as the creations of the consulate. In particular, Mohamed Derdabi, ATIME's secretary, in an interview considered them as 'yellow associations' (sympathetic with power). Mohamed El-Bouhali, Centro Averroes' member noted a similarly critical point of view, but he took his criticism further. For him ASC Ibn Batuta, Nahda and Amical are instruments of control, folklorist, and created by the consulate in order to avoid consciousness among Moroccan immigrants and to impede them fighting to change their situation.

Protest Versus Provision of Services

Centro Averroes had its moment of greatest social leadership when in autumn 1992, a significant number of Moroccan people tried to cross the Gibraltar strait by *pateras* for the first time. Many of them died. The change of the Spanish visa policy (following the Schengen Agreement) and the impact of the global economic slump on Morocco liebehind these deaths. This global post-fordist economic re-structuring (also called 'crisis') encouraged thousands of Moroccans to a desperate emigration. As a protest against those deaths, Centro Averroes, with the support of dozens of other social organisations, launched a demonstration in the Parc de la Ciutadella in Barcelona on November 15, 1992.

However, all associations receive criticism. Thus ATIME-Catalunya is accused by other organisations of being not much more than a satellite branch of the association created with the same name in Madrid in 1989. However, the integration of ATIME-Catalunya in the countrywide organisation with the same name gives them a certain degree of autonomy. This allows them to have almost no relationship with AMIC, UGT-Catalunya's immigration branch, while in Madrid ATIME and UGT have close relations (in fact ATIME-Madrid was created from UGT). Despite all these differences, ATIME is a large and unique association with many local groups spread almost all over Spain. That critique is an instance of another general debate on the degree of autonomy of local branches in big organisations.

Another Moroccan association with a referent in Madrid is AIMC, whose members consider the Associación de Emigrantes Marroquies en España (AEME) members as comrades. However, they are two independent organisations with good relations, in the framework of a wider European network inspired by the leadership of the former political prisoner who was in jail for the longest period under the rule of Hassan II.[9] Abraham Serfati was released in 1991 after more than twenty years in prison; he currently lives in exile in Paris.[10] These Moroccan associations have as trade unions contacts in Spain with the left-wing critical sector of CCOO and the anarcho-syndicalist trade union called CGT, depending on the locality. In other words, organisational and political differences between AIMC and ATIME in Catalonia are quite clear in the degree of autonomy in relation to their counterparts in Madrid (AIMC is independent while ATIME is dependent from Madrid), and in the kind of relations with Spanish trade unions (AIMC is closer to the left of CCOO and CGT, and ATIME is closer to UGT and the official sector of CCOO).

An interesting instance of strategy, mobilisation and engaging with 'top-down' participatory frameworks is a project called Al-Wafâ. They are a group of Moroccan women that are walking towards their social and work insertion, they aim to create a co-operative company in order to spread in Catalan society their culture and to commercialise Arabic food. They organise workshops of Moroccan culture, Moroccan cuisine, henna artcraft, and Arabic pastries and tea for schools, highschools, adult schools, civic centres, and other places.

They are a group of 6-8 adult women, all over thirty years, and married and with children. Some of them hardly speak Spanish or Catalan. The origin of the group was in the Health Centre where some of them used to go. A social worker with the City Council contacted the doctors in charge of that centre (situated in Ciutat Vella) in order to find out which Moroccan women spoke better Spanish or Catalan. Thus a couple were selected to start a programme to spread health education among Moroccan women. After the success the programme and the good relations created among some of the Moroccan women involved, their self-confidence grew, and they started to think about creating a co-operative, and later an association. They had the support of a social worker, who helped them in their spare time. At first they held meetings in a NGO headquarters (SOS Racisme) and had the support of Caritas. But later they moved to Ca la Dona, a Women's House. This is a house managed by women, where several women's groups have meetings. In Ca la Dona they hold weekly meetings often with the presence of the social worker. They plan work-shops at the meetings. In May 1996 they published a book on Moroccan cuisine in the collection *Cocinas de Allí, Aquí* (*Cuisine from there, here*) of the Icaria editorial that had a second edition in April 1997.

So far, this approach to Moroccan immigrants' participation in political and social activities in Barcelona shows how diverse things can be within a collective composed by people of the same 'nationality'. Thus it questions the relevance of studying immigrant participation in European urban areas taking into account their 'nationality' or state of origin as the main criterion of definition. By the same token, this section also shows the relevance dualities like protest vs. provision of services, autonomy vs. links with institutions, and grassroots organisation vs. bureaucratic management.

Conclusions

Barcelona's local government has tried to minimise the number and diversity of 'multicultural policies', in the name of equality of all residents. However, since the mid-1980s the local government has also recognised 'foreign immigrants' specific needs, e.g. language(s) support and legal aid. Thus the City Government has been active and, to a certain extent, support-ive of some specific policies, which have been growing steadily. Often key civil servants were worrying about the possibilities of ghettoisation at the same time. This fear of social-cultural division was sometimes greater than the concerns for social-economic division. In the mid-1990s, after the local civil servants in charge of immigration issues realised of the weakness of the autonomous immigrants' organisations they started creating a local advisory council on immigration with the collaboration of a few 'foreign associations' (i.e. those associations that are more sympathetic with the local government).

This situation is coincident with a general transformation in Iberian societies of the main forms of participation from protesting to offering services and institutional participation. In brief, neo-liberal ideas mean funding cuts in public services and a delegation of some services in private hands, i.e. private companies, QUANGOs and NGOs. Once social bonds have been reduced after new economic forms of production and government policies, many associations can only contact people by offering services or showing that they can obtain 'things' from governments.

Offering services is also a way of getting funding from governments or private companies. Often these public authorities or companies control what kind of services have to be offered (plus when, where, and by who). Thus, for instance, many associations feel that to get funding, to offer services and to attract people they must have good relations with the local government. Thus they participate in forums as the municipal immigration advisory council. Money and a new kind of subtle bureaucracy are colonising the social world. However, in a more or less alternative way, some groups also have mutual help among members as basis for action. Their members are considered as equals, they do not have divisions between those who offer services and those who are clients.

These issues affect both associations composed mainly by immigrants and those mainly shaped by indigenous, but there is a divide between these two groups. So far, the influence of big 'indigenous' NGOs (organisations of solidarity, trade unions, Christian charities, and so on) has been more significant in lobbying public authorities than the influence of foreigners organisations on their own. Some indigenous NGOs, like SOS Racisme, command a huge amount of economic and human resources while, in general, foreigners associations survive precariously.

Barcelona has a long history of social and political mobilisation, including movements of immigrants from other Spanish areas (Huertas and Andreu, 1996). However, as it has been shown in this chapter, foreign immigrants have found more difficulties in participating in Barcelona local polity. Several features are helpful in understanding this situation:

- the hegemonic neo-liberal context of the 1990s is less open to participation than the context of the 1960s and 1970s, when most immigrants from the rest of Iberia arrived;
- those patronising policies implemented by public authorities and big 'indigenous' organisations create difficulties for foreign immigrants' self-organisation;
- the numbers of foreigners are small (both if compared to previous internal immigration waves and 'foreign immigration in other countries);
- most foreign immigrants are only recent arrivals;
- many immigrants are not fluent in Spanish or Catalan language (unlike previous immigration waves);
- most of them work long hours in precarious conditions, what makes social life very difficult.

The City Government, 'indigenous' NGOs, foreign immigrant associations, trade unions, charities, etc. have been tuning in order to find what channels are best for their interests in the local polity. Large 'indigenous' NGOs, Catholic charities and mainstream trade unions have occupied most frequencies of participation, making it difficult for immigrants to express themselves. However, a few instances of successful autonomous foreign immigrants' self-organisation may point to a change of who is in charge of tuning the main channels of participation in the future.

Notes

1   The information that made possible this paper was mainly gathered thanks to two Research Training Grants conceded under the TMR Programme of the European Commission (1996-1999) and a small research grant from Fundació Jaume Bofill (1996). I am thankful to Zig Layton-Henry, Àngels Pascual de Sans, John Rex, A. Miguel Solana, Steve Vertovec, Alisdair Rogers, and Charlotte van Tuyll for their comments on drafts of this chapter.

2   This concept avoids the negative implications of terms like 'illegal', 'clandestine', 'irregular', 'undocumented', etc. because it signals that their lack of documents is the responsibility of the states and not the immigrants.

3   This section is based mainly on original data from several tape-recorded interviews conducted with Pere Novella (official of the Social Affairs Area in charge of immigration issues, Ajuntament de Barcelona), and Josep Ignasi Urenda (Commissary for Civil Rights and International Solidarity, Ajuntament de Barcelona) in the framework of a larger research from 1996 until 1999.

4   The great majority of these naturalisations (4,355) were conceded to Latin Americans, and just a few to Africans (1,227) and Asians (1,086). This is because the legislation favours the nationals of most of the former Spanish colonies (Spanish speaking American countries, Ecuatorial Guineans, Philipineans) (see DGM, 1996).

5   Thus there are GRAMC local groups all along the Catalan coast and the North of País Valencià coast, from Costa Brava to Castelló.

6   From SOS Racisme it is said that they have 3,000 members in Catalonia, while GRAMC is said to have around 700 members.

7   They have received funding from the following organisations: Dirección General de Migraciones of Ministerio de Asuntos Sociales (which does not exist anymore), Àrea d'Afers Socials de l'Ajuntament de Barcelona, Districte de Ciutat Vella, Fundació de Serveis de Cultura Popular, Ministerio de Trabajo, European Union, and Mancomunitat de Municipis de l'Area Metropolitana de Barcelona (MMAMB). In contrast to SOS Racisme but in the same situation to FCIC, the Generalitat de Catalunya had not given them any funding.

8   Some of the foreigners' associations distribute leaflets, magazines and books. SOS Racisme also organise debates, but their importance in the festival is secondary.

9   Hassan II died in the summer of 1999, and was succeeded by his son Mohammed VI. It is still early to see if there will be significant changes in Morocco under the new ruler.

10   After a while he published in France a book called *Inside the king's prisons* (see Serfati, 1992).

References

Casey, J. (1996), 'El Papel de las ONGs en las Políticas Públicas: El Caso de la Integración de Inmigrantes Extranjeros en Catalunya', *Dossiers de Barcelona Associacions*, no. 20, Ajuntament de Barcelona.

Colectivo Ioé (1994), *Marroquins a Catalunya*, ICEM, Barcelona.

Consell Municipal de Benestar Social (1990-1996), *Barcelona som tots*, Ajuntament de Barcelona, Barcelona.

Del Olmo, N. (1996), 'Inmigración Marroquí y Asociacionismo', in B. López García (ed.), *Atlas de la Inmigración Magrebí en España*, Universidad Autónoma de Madrid-Ministerio de Asuntos Sociales, Madrid.

DGM (1996), *Anuario de Migraciones 1995*, Ministerio de Asuntos Sociales, Madrid.

Domingo, A. et al. (1995), *Condicions de Vida de la Població Immigrant d'Origen Africà i Latinoamericà a la Regió Metropolitana de Barcelona*, Barcelona, MMAMB-Diputació de Barcelona, IEMB.

Gerència Àmbit de Benestar Social (1995), *Catàleg de Serveis Personals*, Ajuntament de Barcelona, Barcelona.

Gramsci, A. (1971), 'State and Civil Society', in Q. Hoare and G.N. Smith (eds), *Selections from the Prison Notebooks of Antonio Gramsci*, Lawrence and Wishart, London.

Huertas, J.M. and Andreu, M. (1996), *Barcelona en Lluita: El Moviment Urbà 1965-1996*, FAVB, Barcelona.

Morén Alegret, R. (1999), 'Integration(s) and Resistance: Governments, Capital, Social Organisations and Movements, and the Arrival of "Foreign Immigrants" in Barcelona and Lisbon', unpublished PhD Thesis, Warwick University.

Oliver, J. (ed.) (1996), *Anuari Econòmic i Comarcal de Catalunya*, Caixa de Catalunya, Barcelona, Basingstoke.

Roca, M., Roger A. and Arranz, C. (1983), *Marroquins a Barcelona: Vint-i-dos Relats*, Laertes, Barcelona.

Serfati, A. (1992), *Dans les Prisons du Roi: Escrits de Kenitra sur le Maroc*, Messidor, París.

Sepa Bonaba, E. (1993), *Els Negres Catalans*, Altafulla/FSCP, Barcelona.

Solana, A.M. and Pascual de Sans, A. (1995), 'Mercado de Trabajo e Inmigración Extranjera en Cataluña: Situación Actual y Principales Tendencias', in *Habitar, Vivir, Prever: Actas del V Congreso de la Población Española*, Departament de Geografia and Centre de Estudis Demogràfics-Universitat Autònoma de Barcelona, Bellaterra.

5 Birmingham: Conventional Politics as the Main Channel for Political Incorporation

ROMAIN GARBAYE

Introduction

The situation of ethnic minorities in Birmingham is remarkable in two ways. First, the city's ethnic minority population is among the largest, most diverse, and most well established in Britain (with the exception of London). Second, Birmingham is arguably one of the cities in Europe where immigrant participation in local debates and local decision-making processes is the most successful, to the extent that one can speak of a real process of empowerment of ethnic minorities in the city. One must note at the outset, however, that there are important qualifications to this: ethnic minorities suffer from persistent disadvantage in the job market and are still plagued by numerous social problems (not least, relations between youths and the police, and drugs); racism is still rampant in party politics (as shown by the persistent failure of ethnic minority candidates for national parliamentary elections in the city), and several recent political developments in the city have underscored the fragility of ethnic minorities' political achievements.

Having taken note of these caveats, this chapter focuses on the comparatively successful participation of ethnic minorities in the affairs of the city. This success is linked to the historical evolution of the issue of ethnic minorities in British politics. Over the last forty years this has alternated through phases of strong xenophobia in elections and progressive policy making. On the whole, it has resulted in a policy framework that formulates the issue of immigrant populations in terms of relations between different races and ethnicities and encourages local authorities to fight against racial discrimination and to institutionalise ethnic minority groups (in particular the Third Race Relations Act of 1976).

At the local level in Birmingham itself, minorities' incorporation has taken three main forms:

- participation in the Labour Party and local electoral politics, with a large number of ethnic minority councillors entering the council;
- a high level of community organisation with around 300 local groups; and
- institutionalisation of ethnic groups within a consultative structure and through social services run by ethnic minorities.

These three phenomena are closely correlated and all started at approximately the same time, from the late 1970s onwards. All three have been instrumental in helping to articulate ethnic minorities' demands within the decision-making processes of the city. However, my main contention in this chapter is that this success is due mainly to two factors. Firstly, there is large ethnic minority population that has been settled in the city for a long time. Secondly, and most importantly, the Labour Party has acted as the central channel for participation, brought about the most opportunity for effective political participation, and enabled other forms of participation, such as community involvement and representation, to participate in the affairs of the city. I will therefore start with a brief description of the demographics of Birmingham's ethnic minorities. There follows a more detailed narrative of the historical process through which they have been increasingly able to defend their interest within the local party structure, and have thus created a favourable structure of opportunity for the development of community activity and social service provision.

A Large and Diverse Ethnic Minority Population

The City of Birmingham is the largest local authority in Great Britain, with a population of 960,970 (census 1991). It is governed by Birmingham City Council, which had a budget of around £1 billion in 1998, and employed a total of 25,727 people in 1996/1997. It lies in the middle of the Metropolitan Area of the West Midlands along with six other local authorities, Wolverhampton, Dudley, Coventry, Solihull, Walsall, and Sandwell. The total population of the area is 2,551,700, making it Britain's second largest urban area after London.

The West Midlands is a largely urbanised and industrialised region, situated about 180 kilometres (110 miles) north west of London. It was at the centre of the British metal and engineering industry since the beginning of the industrial revolution. Indeed, the development of Birmingham and its rise to the position of the first provincial British town occurred rapidly during the nineteenth century and are closely linked to the development of industry (Briggs, 1952). It is recovering from the economic crisis that affected industrial Britain in the 1970s and 1980s, with renewal based on services and commerce. The City Council is trying to diversify the city's industrial base by developing new, high value, high growth activities such as telecommunications, pharmaceuticals, and computer software/hardware services.[1] A number of flagship urban development schemes have also revived the decayed city centre, focusing on conferences and cultural industries.

Unlike British industrial ports such as Liverpool and Cardiff, which had black African populations as far back as the eighteenth century, Birmingham did not witness any significant immigration movement prior to the waves of post-colonial immigrants from the late 1940s onwards. There is one important exception, the long-established Irish community, which made up 5 per cent of the city's population in the 1960s (Woods, 1979). Most of Birmingham's current ethnic communities came from the New Commonwealth[2] and are largely typical of post-war immigration patterns to Britain. The economic boom of the 1950s, fuelled by the reconstruction effort, resulted in a shortage of labour. This attracted a flow of mostly young, single men who came to work in industries in and around Birmingham. It was facilitated by the extreme liberalism of British legislation on nationality and immigration, compared to other post-colonial European states. Any person born in Commonwealth territory (including newly independent countries that used to form part of the Empire) could enter British territory without restrictions. The largest populations came from the West Indies (Caribbean), then, starting a few years later, from Pakistan and India. Most were planning to return home after having worked and saved some money. As a process of chain migration developed, more and more men from the same villages and families arrived, as well as their wives and children.

In the late 1950s and early 1960s, a strong climate of racism and hostility towards immigrants developed in Britain (notably in Birmingham) and the government passed increasingly restrictive legislation with the 1962 and 1968 Commonwealth Immigration Acts. This prompted many immigrants to have their families join them in Britain while it was still possible, thus starting the diversification of the country's immigrant population. In 1971, a third act effectively halted all immigration from New Commonwealth countries, except for family reunification. The 'myth of return' (Anwar, 1979) faded away in the 1970s as it was becoming increasingly clear that this population was going to settle permanently. By that time, the immigrant population was rapidly diversifying, with many organisations and businesses. Since then, a second generation, born in Britain of parents of the New Commonwealth, has emerged.

Table 5.1   Birthplace of persons resident in Birmingham: 1951, 1961, 1971 (including percentage of total population)

	1951	*1961*	*1971*
United Kingdom	1,054,000	1,011,379	883,610
	(94.83)	(91.34)	(87.08)
Remainder of British Isles			
Irish Republic	26,568	44,798	39,565
	(2.39)	(4.05)	(3.90)
Ireland (part not stated)	1,530	2,784	5,300
	(0,14)	(0.25)	(0.52)
Old Commonwealth	1,581	1,339	1,330
(Australia, Canada, New Zealand)	(0.14)	(0.12)	(0.13)
New Commonwealth	5,057	29,369	68,325
	(0.45)	(2.65)	(6.73)
including:			
Europe	309	402	390
	(0.03)	(0.04)	(0.04)
Africa	336	666	4,925
	(0.03)	(0.06)	(0.49)
Jamaica (1)	345	12,017	19,385
Other American (2)	85	4,016	5,530
Sub-total (1) + (2)	493	16,298	25,365
	(0.04)	(1.47)	(2.50)
India	2,205	4,801	17,885
Pakistan	1,108	5,335	17,515
Other Asia (3) and Oceania (4)	606	1,796	2,250
Sub-total (3) and (4)	3,919	11,952	37,650
	(0.35)	(1.08)	(3.71)
Europe	7,342	8,019	7,390
	(0.66)	(0.72)	(0.73)
Others	15,477	8,852	8,150
	(1.39)	(0.80)	(0.90)
Total	1,112,361	1,107,187	1,014,670
	(100.0)	(100.0)	(100.0)

Source: Adapted form Ratcliffe (1981, pp. 5-6), based on data from the 1951, 1961, and 1971 census, Census County Reports for Warwickshire.

The history of immigration to Birmingham follows this general pattern. Much of it occurred between the early 1950s and 1971. If one considers the number of persons born in the New Commonwealth, the 1951 census showed a figure well under 500; by 1971, however, it had topped 68,000, moving from 0.44 per cent of the population to 6.73 per cent (see Table 5.1). The West Indian community started arriving first, from the early 1950s on, while immigrants from the Indian subcontinent came mostly during the 1960s.

Swelled by second- and then third-generations, the ethnic minority population of the city had reached 206,800 in 1991, or 21.5 per cent of total population, making it one of the largest ethnic minority community in both Britain and Europe. If one adds the more than 38,000 Irish-born people recorded in Birmingham in 1991, the figure for minority ethnic groups of all kinds reached around a quarter of a million. Subsequent to 1991, new influxes of immigrants and refugees from African and the Balkans have added to this population.

The residents of Birmingham who were enumerated as of ethnic minority background in 1991 were mainly 'Black' and 'Asian'[3] (see Table 5.2). There were nearly twice as many 'Asians' compared to 'Blacks', and Pakistanis formed the largest single ethnic/national minority group. These populations are chiefly characterised by economic disadvantage and spatial concentration in inner-city areas. First, the unemployment rate of ethnic minority men was almost twice the average unemployment rate for the city as a whole (14.3 per cent) in 1991. The highest rates of unemployment were amongst the Pakistanis and Bangladeshis: 35 per cent of Pakistani men and 45 per cent of Pakistani women, and 41.5 per cent of Bangladeshi men and 44 per cent of Bangladeshi women were unemployed. Second, in 1991, 57.3 per cent of Birmingham's ethnic minority population was to be found in seven of the city's 39 wards:[4] Handsworth, Soho, Sparkbrook, Sparkhill, Small Heath, Sandwell, and Aston, which are all inner-city, working-class areas. These all had more than half of their population made up of people from ethnic minority backgrounds, although within this concentration there were marked differences between the various groups. Nearly half of the African-Caribbean population lived in six wards: Handsworth, Soho, Aston, Ladywood, Sandwell and Sparkbrook. Indians had their high concentrations in Sandwell, Soho and Handsworth. By contrast, although there are large numbers of Pakistanis in Handsworth, the Pakistani group was more heavily concentrated in Small Heath, Sparkhill and Nechells. The highest proportion of Bangladeshis was in Aston and Sparkbrook. The concentration in selected wards within Birmingham was a major factor in the rapid and substantial integration of ethnic minorities into the city's formal political structure.

Table 5.2   Ethnic group of residents in Birmingham (1991)

Ethnic group	Number	%
White	754,274	78.5
Black	56,376	5.9
Black-Caribbean	44,770	4.7
Black-African	2,803	0.3
Black-Other	8,803	0.9
Asian	129,899	13.5
Indian	5,105	5.3
Pakistani	66,085	6.9
Bangladeshi	12,739	1.3
Chinese and others	20,492	2.1
Chinese	3,315	0.3
Other-Asian	5,653	0.3
Other-Other	11,524	1.2
Total	961,041	100.0

Source: Birmingham City Council, census 1991.

Mobilisation, Participation, and Policy: The Central Role of the Labour Party

As emphasised above, the Labour Party has been the main vehicle for the participation of ethnic minorities in Birmingham, through a gradual process of empowerment of ethnic minority activists within the Party structures. At the same time, ethnic community organisations multiplied in the city, and, encouraged by the Labour majority at the council which was increasingly influenced by its ethnic minority members, got increasingly involved with the City Council. Hence the development of various issues connected with ethnic minorities, and of ethnic minority groups.

The Labour Party as the Main Channel for Participation

The Labour Party has on the whole been sympathetic to ethnic minorities in all the major British cities, in return for strong electoral support from ethnic minority voters. In many cases this has enabled the Party to be dominant in inner city areas, where ethnic minorities are concentrated, at the expense of the other major parties, the Conservatives and the Liberal Democrats. Birmingham is a typical example. But, because the party happens to be overwhelmingly dominant in this city, more than in others, it has been able to provide ethnic minorities with an unusually wide avenue to representation and power. In keeping with the consensual and moderate culture that has characterised the politics of Birmingham for much of its history, the control of the City Council had kept moving from the Conservatives to the Labour with some regularity until the early 1980s. The Conservatives were in control of the council until 1982, lost it to the Labour Party for one year, then won it again in 1983, before losing it for good in 1984. This opened a long and unprecedented period of exclusive Labour control, during which the domination of Labour increased steadily to reach a majority of around 80 councillors, out of a total of 117, in the early 1990s. This increase has been won mainly over the Conservatives in middle-class, white wards. Indeed, in the same period, the Conservative group shrunk down to 20 councillors, while the Liberal Democrats have had highs and lows and was represented by 16 councillors in 1999.

This period of expansion is correlated with the steady rise of ethnic minority activists and councillors within the Labour Party and the Labour group. The position of ethnic minorities has moved from 'ethnic brokers' serving the interests of right-wing[5] Labour leaders to more left-wing 'race' activists and ethnic community leaders who now control parts of the Party and have acquired influence at the council. Within the Labour Party, it has taken the form of a coalition with the left wing of the local Party and some elements of the trade unions, and has fully benefited from the gradual growth of the latter at the expense of the right wing.

Ethnic minorities living in inner-city areas of British cities started receiving attention from politicians in the 1970s. This was in part due to a perceived rise in electoral participation on their part, predominantly in favour of Labour.[6] In Birmingham, the Labour Party was indeed dominant in inner-city areas and had been enjoying the electoral support of large sections of the ethnic minority population for some time already. From the late 1970s onwards, this support appeared to become crucial for the overall control of the inner cities. A major explanation for this was the internal power struggle between the then dominant right wing of the Party and left-wing activists over control of inner-city Party branches. This was happening in the context of declining membership; hence, right-wing leaders such as Roy Hattersley in Sparkbrook (once deputy leader of the national Labour Party), Brian Walden in Ladywood, and Denis Howell in Small Heath, sought the support of Black and Asian community leaders to help them fill in ranks and counter the left, whose influence was then rising (Back and Solomos, 1995, p. 68). They would typically propose services for the community in return, such as help with immigration papers or dealings with social services of the council. This process amplified a movement of rising numbers and influence of ethnic minority members in Labour local political branches, as well as the emergence of a first generation of Black community leaders such as James Hunte, a popular African-Caribbean community leader in Handsworth. But it always confined them to the limited role of ethnic brokers.

The Conservatives, by contrast, had few links with ethnic minority organisations and as a rule did not try to encourage ethnic minority individuals to join their ranks or to stand for elections as Conservative candidates. This was true both nationally and in Birmingham but there were some exceptions. For instance, an Indian-born woman, Pamela Le Hunte, stood as the Conservative candidate for the 1983 general elections in the Birmingham inner-city area of Ladywood (and only got 3.2 per cent of the vote). In addition, it was the Conservatives who, just before losing power in 1983, introduced the very first policy in favour of racial equality to the council, in the form of an attempt to monitor ethnicity within the council's workforce. But the Conservatives were never very successful in recruiting ethnic minorities as activists and potential candidates, and this limited policy effort was started just before the Party lost power for good and started spiralling down. The now marginal Conservative group at the council still advocates a tough stance against ethnic minorities, calling for the dismantling of the City Council's programmes for them.

Against the right of the Labour Party, the left wing was also lining up its own supporters of ethnic minority background. From the early 1980s onwards, they were to gain the ascendancy, and break through the patron/client relationship of ethnic brokers. By the mid 1980s, ethnic minorities were becoming increasingly powerful in the inner-city Labour organisations, to the point where many ward organisations elected ethnic minority chairmen and secretaries. The number of ethnic minority activists increased steadily, also fuelled by the trade union movement.[7] By 1986, there were nine Labour councillors of ethnic minority background, and the Party fielded 18 more in that year's election. This led minority activists to question more and more openly the traditional patterns of patronage of Black and Asian leaders by prominent Labour figures such as Roy Hattersley.

This was not an effortless, linear evolution; it took place in the face of considerable resistance from traditional moderate leaders of the local Party. The debate over the 'Black sections' in the Party epitomises this. As early as 1984, there had been proposals by left-wing members of the Party (among them Clare Short, already the Member of Parliament (MP) for Ladywood) to support the creation of Black sections. These were sub-groups within the local Party consisting only of Black and Asians members. It was argued that they were a necessary step to further claims specific to ethnic minorities within the Party's policy-making structure and to entrench the notion that there was an issue of race within the Party. Important forces within the Party, among which right-wing MPs such as Roy Hattersley and Jeff Rooker, opposed them on the grounds that it amounted to *de facto* discrimination. Two years later, Roy Hattersley reacted to a new proposal for a Black section in his Sparkbrook parliamentary constituency by calling it a 'racist and divisive move', and the supporters of the sections were expelled from the Labour Party. This was a crucial episode because it pitted some activists and councillors against their former mentor, Hattersley. In particular, a Sparkbrook Pakistani councillor, Amir Khan, who had worked closely with Hattersley until then, and an Irish left-wing activist, Kevin Scally, were both expelled. They simultaneously accused Hattersley of trying to fix the vote for his re-selection as MP by mobilising fictitious ethnic minority voters. The conflict ended with the creation, albeit short-lived, of a Birmingham-wide Black section, and the re-instatement of expelled councillors.[8] Although the Black section eventually disappeared, this episode marked the rising influence of rebellions against the traditional white leaders of the Party in Black-dominated, inner-city Birmingham.

In addition, there were attempts by ethnic minorities to create break-away parties, which threatened to compete with Labour in inner-city wards. For instance, many proponents of Black sections threatened to join the ranks of a Democratic Party, which was created by a minority councillor (Mohammad Queshri) who had left Labour in protest against Labour's 'milking of the ethnic vote' (*Birmingham Post*, February 19, 1986). Regarding such parties, however, it must also be noted that they also reflected divisions within ethnic minorities and can in certain contexts diminish their chances of getting elected.

At the same time, the balance of power within the Labour group kept on changing in favour of the Left. In 1993, Theresa Stewart, a long-standing left-wing councillor, became leader of the Council, which comforted further the position of race activists. For instance, Philip Murphy, an African-Caribbean activist close to Theresa Stewart, became one of the most respected figures on the City Council. The number of ethnic minority councillors also increased in the early 1990s to around twenty.

However, old-style patronage did not disappear from Birmingham that easily. In particular, minorities reproduced traditional patterns. In 1995, the regional and national Labour Party suspended several inner-city branches because of irregularities in voting for the selection of candidates. These branches had been taken over by Pakistani activists who had encouraged other Pakistanis to join the Party just to participate in the selection process. When Roy Hattersley retired as Member of Parliament, attempts by minority councillors to replace him were defeated by a white candidate who manipulated the rules presiding over the participation of trade unions in the candidate selection process (Back and Solomos, 1994). There are also very deep divisions among minorities. At the time of the Black sections debate, many Blacks and Asians opposed them and trusted the existing Party structure to bring political incorporation. When minority parties such as the Democratic Party in 1986 appeared, they also triggered opposition on the part of Labour loyalists. In the 1998 and 1999 City Council elections, independent candidates successfully challenged Pakistani Labour candidates in Sparkbrook.

What had definitely changed by the 1990s is that minorities were now real actors in the political process. Ethnic minorities are now close to, although not entirely part of, the inner circles of power. After the 1999 local elections, there were 21 ethnic minority councillors on the Birmingham City Council. Eighteen were members of the Labour group and three were independents. Most were elected in inner-city wards, but a few represent middle-class, predominantly white British wards. A large majority was of Pakistani background: in 1999, 12 out of 21 were of Pakistani background, which makes the community over-represented on the City Council. African-Caribbeans were also rather well represented, with five councillors.

In 1998, two ethnic minority councillors were elected chairmen of committees (Transportation and General Purposes Committees), and four were committee vice-chairs (Commercial Services, Equalities, Personnel, and Urban Renewal). All were activists in the Labour Party before serving as councillors; and many came to the Labour Party through trade unionism.

Several of these, notably the chair of personnel and the chair of general purposes, are long serving members of the Council and have gained prominence through their expertise and dedication.

Community Group Mobilisation: A Spectacular Development in the 1980s

After mobilisation within the Labour Party, community organisation is the second most important style of participation in local affairs for Birmingham's ethnic minorities. Indeed, it is closely related to mobilisation within the Party, as many councillors of ethnic minority background are also actively involved in cultural, religious and charitable work in their wards.

A landmark study on the politics of community organisations in the late 1960s and early 1970s showed a high level of community activity among the population of the city, with over 4,000 groups recorded at the time (Newton, 1976, p. 31). This covered all types of community organisations, sports clubs, churches, welfare groups, etc. Newton showed that on the whole they were integrated within a stable and dense network of connections with the Council, through contacts with councillors and the acquisition of grants. This web of relations between the groups and the Council was seldom if ever politicised, but it did exclude certain interests, including the ethnic minority population. In fact, most councillors, when interviewed, displayed a spectacular ignorance of the specifics and needs of the ethnic minority population (Newton, 1976, p. 208).

The situation started changing in the 1970s, with the development of a few Community Centres either concerned with the interests of ethnic minorities – the Sparkbrook Housing Association described by Rex and Moore (1967) – or run by ethnic minorities community activists, such as Harambee House or the Asian Resource Centre (Rex and Tomlinson, 1979).

The 1980s then witnessed an explosion of ethnic minority community activity, which has probably caught up with the level of organisation of other communities, if not overtaken them. Hundreds of religious groups, welfare associations and cultural groups sprang up. To take the example of the Pakistani community, which is the largest and has been studied more closely than the others (Joly, 1987), only 22 per cent of the existing associations in 1988 had been created between 1960 and 1969, but 38 per cent had been created between 1979 and 1984.

Table 5.3   Main Black and ethnic minority organisations in Birmingham (1995)

Group	Number	Main organisations
African-Caribbean	45	African and Caribbean People's Movement, African Caribbean Day Centre, African-Caribbean Resource Centre, Harambee House Youth Project.
Bangladeshi	57	Asian Hindu Cultural Association, Bangladesh Community Development, Bangladesh Islamic and Social Organisation, Federation of Bangladeshi Organisations, Handsworth Bangladeshi Association, Handsworth Mosque and Islamic Centre; Jalalabad Mosque and Islamic Centre.
Pakistani	68	All Pakistan Women's Association, Council of British Pakistanis, Handsworth Islamic Youth Employment Centre, Jama Mosque and Madrasa, Madrasia Islamia Mosque, Pakistan Community Centre, Pakistan Forum, Pakistan Workers Association, Pakistan Muslim League UK.
Indian	39	Birmingham Pragati Mandal (Krishna temple), Gujarati (Hindu Association), Guru Nanak Gurdwara, Hindu Bengali Association, Punjabi Community Centre, Ramgharia Sikh temple, Urdu Forum (UK) Birmingham.
Sikh Gurdwaras	8	The Council of Sikh Gurdwaras of Birmingham, Guru Nanak Gurdwaras, and Punjabi Language Development Board.
Irish	7	Birmingham Cork Association, Birmingham Irish Community Forum, Irish Welfare and Information Centre Longford County Association.
Vietnamese	4	Chinese and Vietnamese Cultural School, Midlands Buddhist Association, Midlands Vietnamese Community Association.
Chinese	9	Birmingham Chinatown Lions Club, Birmingham Chinese Elders Concern Group, Birmingham Chinese Society, and Chinese Community Centre.
Youth	198	African Community Association, Asian Girl's and Young Women's Group, Balsall Heath Church Centre, Bangali Tenants Association, Coventry Road Community and Islamic Centre; East Birmingham Family Service Unit, Golden Hillock Employment and Training Centre, Indian Parents Association, Irish Welfare and Information Centre, Pakistan Business Forum, Sparkhill Irish Women's Group, UK Asian Women's Centre, Shree Geeta Bhawan, Shree Birmingham Brahm Samaj.

In an attempt to classify these organisations, the City Council's Race Relations Unit published a Directory of Black and Minority Ethnic voluntary organisations in 1991, updated in 1995 under the title *Directory of Black and Ethnic Minority Organisations in Birmingham*. I give here a listing of the main organisations mentioned in the guide (see Table 5.3).

Many of these community groups have sought to engage in relations with the City Council. They have done so over all kinds of issues but religious issues, particularly concerning Islam, are especially salient. The Indian community is organised in around 40 more or less institutionalised castes, and also has several Sikh temples (or Gurdwaras). The African-Caribbean community is also largely organised along religious lines with several Black churches. The Pakistani community is characterised by a high level of religious institutionalisation, with 55 mosques in 1987, and undoubtedly many more now (Joly, 1987), representing all brands of Pakistani Islam in the UK, mainly Deobandi and Barelvi. After a difficult period in the 1970s when permission for the construction of mosques was seldom granted, the climate became more tolerant in the early 1980s (Joly, 1987, p. 26).

Indeed, by that time, Pakistani and other ethnic minority groups were engaging in more and more relationships with the City Council over various issues, especially religious. In addition to the construction of Mosques, there was the problem of education, with the issue of *Halal* food in schools, religious education, compulsory sports for girls, and single-sex schools. The Muslim community organised in 1987 to negotiate with the Council on these issues. At the same time, the Council was taking important, innovative measures in response.

The Development of 'Race-Relations' Policies

The gradual strengthening of the minorities' influence on the City Council during the 1980s enabled their specific claims (e.g. the recognition of cultural difference in various policy areas and the struggle against racial discrimination) to gain wider acceptance within the Council at large. The spectacular expansion of ethnic minority community activity also compelled the Council to listen to ethnic minorities' demands. At the same time, several pieces of national legislation, especially the 1976 Race Relations Act, formulated the issue of immigrant populations in terms of relations between 'races' and in terms of racial discrimination, and placed the responsibility for these on local authorities. The combination of these three factors led to the creation of a new department within the Council, the Race

Relations Unit (with several name changes throughout the years). This has had a profound impact on the Council departments responsible for delivering services through its monitoring activities. In addition, it has supervised the development of the ad hoc structure for participation of the city, the Standing Consultative Forum (SCF).

In July 1983, the Conservative-led City Council adopted formalised goals in the field of equality of employment within the Council's workforce; however, Labour made the real breakthrough when it gained control of the Council in 1984. The development of race relation policies was also encouraged by section 71 of the 1976 Race Relations Act, which attributes responsibility for 'equality of opportunity' and 'good relations between people of different races' to local government. It has taken two main directions: the creation of a Race Relations Unit and the creation of a consultative structure for ethnic groups, the Standing Consultative Forum.

The first structure created within the Council was the Race Relations Committee, together with an Equal Opportunities and Women's Committee. Then came the Race Relations Unit in 1984, which initially reported through the structure of the Race Relations Committee, and was placed by Labour at the heart of the Council's policy-making.

In 1987, however, it lost that central place. Both the Race Relations and the Equal Opportunities and Women's Committees were merged with the Personnel Committee to form the Personnel and Equal Opportunities Committee. This meant that the Race Relations Unit would from then on be part of the personnel department and would therefore lose its central place in the administration. This was due to a poor performance by the Labour Party in the previous year's elections, which prompted it to distance itself from more radical councils in an attempt to retain support among white voters. This shows how fragile the gains made by ethnic minority activists were in the city at that time. In spite of their increasing numbers in the council and despite the salience of the issue nation-wide, they still were not able to counterbalance those who viewed them as a political liability.

Finally, there were more changes in 1995, when the policy remit of Equalities, including the Race Relations Unit, was removed from the Personnel Committee and handed to a new sub-committee of Personnel, the Equalities Committee. In 1997, the Race Relations Unit was suppressed and replaced by a new Equalities Unit, which deals with issues of women's rights, handicapped persons as well as racial discrimination and consultation of ethnic groups. This new division remains powerful, and employs around 50 people with a budget of £1.6 million; but, on the whole, its creation was clearly intended to downplay the issue of ethnic minorities, as shows the evolution of the SCF that was closely linked to this (see below). In fact, these recent changes are part of a wider, ongoing trend in the handling of race relations by local authorities whereby the emphasis is put increasingly on 'issue based policies' and less on 'community based policies'. As we will see, this was to have an important impact on the experiments concerning the involvement of ethnic community groups with the Standing Consultative Forum.

The Institutionalisation of Ethnic Minority Welfare Groups

Over the years many large ethnic minority organisations have become actively associated with the City Council's various urban regeneration programmes. Most notably, many are closely associated with the Council through the Employment Resource Centres (ERCs) set up by the Economic Development Department (EDD) of the Council from the 1980s onwards. The EDD's aim was to provide an alternative to the central government-run job agencies in the city by helping 'local communities' (in their own terms) run advice services for the unemployed. There are 23 such centres, based in all sorts of pre-existing community groups, from a centre for the deaf to an estate project. Five of them are ethnic minority organisations: the UK Asian Women's Centre, the Islamic Resource Centre, the Bangladesh Women's Association, the Afro-Caribbean Resource Centre, and the Sikh Community and Youth Service. All receive funding from the Council to employ permanent staff and rent premises. This, however, is often far from being their sole source of revenue, nor their sole activity. For instance, the Islamic Resource Centre is also the headquarters of an international Muslim network which runs many educational, social and religious projects both in the United Kingdom and abroad. The Asian Resource Centre was originally founded by a group close to the Indian Workers Association (IWA) and has now many ties with left-wing activists in the Labour Party, as well as with Labour councillors.[9]

The various central government-led urban regeneration programmes also involve many ethnic minority groups. At present, there are two large programmes funded by the Single Regeneration Budget (SRB): the Saltley and Small Heath programme, and the Sparkbrook, Sparkhill and Tyseley initiative. Several ethnic minority councillors sit on the boards of these schemes, alongside leaders of ethnic organisations and local community organisations, including the Birmingham Asian Business Association (BABA).

The SCF: A Tentative Association of Ethnic Groups to the City Council's Policies

The third policy development that came from the Council in the 1980s was the creation of formal structures for the participation of ethnic minorities groups in the Council's work. This was designed to address the surge in ethnic minority activity mentioned above, and was immediately triggered by the Handsworth Riots in 1985, in which two Asian shopkeepers were killed and which caused a great shock both locally and nationally. It was also the result of lobbying by ethnic minority councillors (Back and Solomos, 1995, p. 176).

However, the institutionalisation of these groups was by no means a straightforward process. It only happened in the face of considerable reticence on the part of the Council. Labour Party activists managed to include a pledge to associate local community groups with the Council in the Party's manifesto for the 1984 local election. But, after the Handsworth Riots, the Council was under pressure to do something more for the city's minorities. It started working towards the establishment of a structure that would ensure that ethnic groups had an official channel to voice concerns and issues. A first attempt, called the Birmingham Community Advisory Liaison Committee, failed in 1985 in part because of conflicts between some groups – some Indian representatives blamed the two deaths during the riots on African-Caribbean rioters, and the African-Caribbean representatives refused to apologise (Back and Solomos, 1995). Eventually, the Council decided in 1988 to create an innovative democratic framework designed to encourage the participation of ethnic minority groups. This was to be based on the creation of self-organised groups that would emerge from the community groups of the city. In turn these were to be grouped in umbrella groups which would each cover an ethnic/religious affiliation. By 1993, there were nine such umbrella groups: the Black-led Churches Liaison Committee, the African-Caribbean peoples movement, the Bangladeshi Islamic Projects Consultative Council, the Chinese Consultative Council, the Council of Sikh Gurdwaras, the Hindu Council, the Pakistan Forum, the Irish Forum, and the Vietnamese Forum. These eventually included more than 300 organisations of all kinds. In 1990, a formal structure, the Standing Consultative Forum, was established, in an attempt to link all umbrella groups together. In effect it was to function as a 'super' umbrella group. Each of the 'sub-groups' was to send three representatives to the SCF.

In 1992, in the face of discontent of group leaders who doubted the Council's commitment to race equality, it decided to fund one full-time post for each sub-group. These new community officers were placed directly under the authority of the Council's Race Relations Unit (Smith, 1999, p. 20). In addition, a formal calendar of meetings with chief officers of various departments was set up: these meetings were to serve as opportunities for the representatives to express their views on the Council's race policy and to monitor, in conjunction with the service delivery departments, the introduction of race equality targets. The community officers were to help the representatives with the work at policy level that was new to many of them.

This organisation functioned for a period of time and enabled the participating groups to obtain some policy results. Notably, the Council recognised the Pakistani and Indian Independence Day celebrations, allowing the communities to stage large-scale celebrations in city parks. The Council also perceived the SCF as an efficient way of managing tensions within the ethnic minority community, as seems to have demonstrated the efficiency of calls to calm in the Asian community when the Ayoda Mosque was burnt down in India (Smith et al., 1999, p. 21). It did not completely suppress, however, important tensions between Indians and Pakistanis in the city at that time (*Birmingham Post*, December 9, 1992). However, in spite of the successes mentioned earlier, vocal critics of the SCF started to emerge. There were accusations on all sides of patronage within the sub-umbrella groups and destructive competition between ethnic groups. Several actors also pointed to the inefficiency of the structure, the incompetence of the representatives (in spite of the help of the community officers), and their poor representation of the wider community due to the absence of any selection procedures. As a result, the Council decided in 1998 to replace the structure by a new project, the Race Equality Partnership (REP), which was being set up in the first semester of 1999. This was also due to wider developments in the policy orientations of the Council, namely the replacement of the Race Relations Unit with the Equalities Unit mentioned earlier. This coincided with a shift in focus of policy, from a 'community-based' approach to a more nuanced 'issue-based' approach, i.e. one that balances specifically racial issues with matters common to all disadvantaged groups (as expressed by policy documents, Birmingham City Council, 1999a and 1999b). From the point of view of the Equalities Unit, the SCF was not addressing directly enough the most pressing issues faced by the ethnic minority communities: health and education. The participation of ethnic minorities could be channelled through the Local Involvement and

Local Action programme (LILA), a new decentralisation initiative of the Council that consists in holding council meetings in all the wards of the city to encourage local participation.

The Race Equality Partnership (REP) will be an independent body, run by representatives of the City Council, the Health Authority, the Birmingham and Solihull Training and Enterprise Council (TEC), and some representatives of ethnic groups. It will be organised by Community Action Forums (CAFs), with each Forum being focused on one issue, e.g. education, health, housing, etc., and being made up of representatives of the local community. Each of these CAFs will elect 12 community auditors, who will choose two among them to represent their CAF on the board of the REP. It will produce recommendations on the best practice for the implementation of race conscious policies in the city.

It is too soon to assess the REP's development, or judge whether it is serving its function better than the SCF. But it is clear at the outset that it is designed to be purely consultative. Because it is not attached to the Council, but rather is an independent structure co-organised by various bodies, it will not have any say in policy decisions. This has been immediately noticed and criticised by representatives of the SCF, which were present at a meeting organised by the Council's Equalities Unit to launch the new body.

The Success of the Muslim Liaison Committee

The failure of the SCF does not necessarily mean, however, that all attempts to create direct links between the Council and minority groups are doomed to failure. An example of success is the Muslim Liaison Committee (MLC), founded in the 1980s over the issue of Islam in local schools. In 1987, at a time when the SCF was being established, this issue was becoming very prominent. But one of the problems encountered by the Muslim community in Birmingham is that it is very divided along religious and regional cleavages. Because of this, it is difficult for it to stand united in negotiations with local authorities. For example, in the midst of the debate in the 1970s about planning permissions for mosques, one leader of the Islamic mission (representing the Jamaat-i-Islami) promised that all mosques would from then on apply for permission. In reality, he was not able to give any guarantee on this (Joly, 1987, p. 5).

Faced with the growing concern of Muslim parents for the education of their children, the community organised itself in the form of the Muslim Liaison Committee, which by 1983 brought together more than 50 Muslim organisations. By 1987, there were around 65 organisations affiliated to it. It sought to address the typical issues faced by Muslims across the country regarding education, partly by playing an advisory role with Muslim parents, but also by negotiating with the City Council a series of measures regarding Muslim children in schools within the Birmingham education authority. These included: facilities for prayer, proper Muslim dress and diet, respect of Muslim perspectives in the school curriculum, particularly in Religious Education, drama, music, and sex education (Nielsen, 1995, p. 58).

The interesting thing with the Muslim Liaison Committee, compared to other similar instances in Leicester or Bradford, is that it decided at the beginning not to try to push too many demands, and especially not to demand the creation of Muslim voluntarily-aided schools (i.e. Muslim schools funded by the state). It focused instead on demands affecting all Muslim children within the remit of the Local Education Authority (in this instance the Birmingham City Council). It was thus easier for the Council to accept the less controversial points made by the Committee, and, in addition, these measures affected all Muslim children. Trying to establish special schools would only have benefited a portion of them. The City Council also adopted a conciliatory attitude. Rather than responding by opening negotiations on a political level, the Council set up a joint working party composed of seven Muslim Liaison Committee representatives, five head-teachers from inner city areas and five persons of the City Council Department of Education (Joly, 1987, p. 20). This successful negotiation was also made easier by the fact that Birmingham had retained six secondary girls' schools before, mainly in response to previous demands by Muslim and other minorities. Thus there was a lesser need than elsewhere for the Muslim groups to ask for single sex schools, which is another important issue for Muslims (Nielsen, 1995, p. 59).

Conclusion

The ethnic minority populations that have established themselves in Birmingham for the last forty years have already had a rich history of participation in the city's politics. This was achieved against the odds to begin with, in the face of strong xenophobic movements in local politics in the 1950s and a marked racist vote. In spite of this, there has been a dramatic increase in the participation of ethnic minority activists in the local Labour Party since the early 1980s, in the level of organisation of the ethnic minority community, and their involvement with the local authority. In particular, participation in the Labour Party has enabled ethnic minorities to obtain significant representation at the City Council, because the Labour Party has been overwhelmingly dominant in the city since the early 1980s. This has been instrumental in facilitating the participation of ethnic community groups in local public life, particularly through the Standing Consultative Forum (SCF), created after violent riots in 1985 shook the Council into action, and through groups and institutions such as the Muslim Liaison Committee in 1983, or various social services run by ethnic minority groups.

As noted in the introduction, this process of the empowerment of minorities in Birmingham has been partly triggered by national trends, which have encouraged local authorities to take an interest in ethnic minority populations and to tackle racial discrimination. In the same way, recent changes noted in this chapter in the approach of the City Council to its Equalities policy, shifting from an approach based on race relations and ethnicity to a one grounded more in terms of equality, are correlated with the emergence in national politics of New Labour, which advocates a similar shift in the national policy discourse on ethnic minorities. Interestingly, the other European country which formulated the issue of ethnic minorities at policy level at an early stage, the Netherlands, is now experiencing a similar policy shift, both at national and local level, at least if one considers the case of Amsterdam (noted for the national level by Koopmans and Duyvené de Wit, 1999; and for Amsterdam by Wolf, 1999, p. 30). If the example of these two models of relatively early formulation of ad hoc policies is any benchmark to go by, this ebb and flow of institutionalisation of ethnic minority groups, and return to more 'issue-based' policies, may become a recurring pattern in other European cities.

Notes

1   According to the Economic Development Programme 1997/1998, Birmingham City Council.

2   In the 1948 British Nationality Act The 'New Commonwealth' designates British colonies, later to become independent states who remained part of the Commonwealth, whose citizens were granted free acess to British territory and British citizenship, until restrictions started being introduced with the 1962 Immigrants Act and subsequent acts in 1968, 1971, and 1983. The Old Commonwealth consisted of white settler societies such as Australia, Canada and New Zealand. The New Commonwealth referred mainly to African, Caribbean and Asian countries.

3   'Black' and 'Asians' are categories which have been commonly used in Britain to refer to ethnic minorities since the 1960s. 'Blacks' refers to populations originating from the West Indies and Africa, and tends to be increasingly replaced by the terms 'African-Carribeans' or 'Black African'. 'Asians' refers to people from Pakistan, India, and Bangladesh, rather than Japan or Malaysia for instance.

4   Wards are the smallest territorial division of the city and serve as the basis for representation at the City Council. There are at present 39 wards in Birmingham.

5   The left wing of the Party encompasses several political trends whose influence within the Party grew during the 1970s: mainly Marxist 'militant' activists, or middle-class 'new urban left' activists. By contrast, the term 'right wing' is usually used to characterise more traditional elements of the Party, more often close to trade unions.

6   A survey by the Race Relations Board on the 1974 general election concluded that there was an important rise of ethnic minority electoral participation, to the extent that they were becoming a marginal electorate for some seats. The validity of these conclusions was later questioned, but what is important is that they did prompt increased interest from mainstream politicians at the time.

7   A large proportion of Labour councillors or ethnic minority background came to the Labour Party through activities in trade unions.

8   Interview Khan, June 26, 1999.

9   Interview Mohammed Idrich, May 19, 1999.

References

Anwar, M. (1979), *The Myth of Return: Pakistanis in Britain*, Heineman, London.

Back, L. and Solomos, J. (1994), 'Labour and Racism: Trade Unions and the Selection of Parliamentary Candidates', *The Sociological Review*, vol. 42, pp. 165-201.

Back, L. and Solomos, J. (1995), *Race, Politics and Social Change*, Routledge, London and New York.

Birmingham City Council (1999a), *A New Deal for Communities: Race Equality in Birmingham*, Policy Guidelines, January.

Birmingham City Council (1999b), *Review and Development of the Standing Consultative Forum*, Report of the Head of Equalities, Equalities Committee, January 26.

Briggs, A. (1952), *History of Birmingham*, vol. 3, Oxford University Press, Oxford.

Gaffney, J. (1987), 'Interpretations of Violence: The Handsworth Riots of 1985', Policy Paper in Ethnic Relations no. 10, Centre for Research in Ethnic Relations, University of Warwick, Coventry.

Joly, D. (1987), 'Making a Place for Islam in British Society: Muslims in Birmingham', Research Paper in Ethnic Relations no. 4, Centre for Research in Ethnic Relations, University of Warwick, Coventry.

Koopmans, R. and Duyvené de Wit, T. (1999), 'New Pillars in the Polder: Ethnic Minority Claims-Making in the Netherlands', Paper presented at the Joint Sessions of workshops of the European Consortium for Political Research, Mannheim, 26-31 March.

Newton, K. (1976), *Second City Politics, Democratic Processes and Decision-Making Processes in Birmingham*, Clarendon Press, Oxford.

Nielsen, J. (1995), *Muslims in Western Europe*, 2nd Edition, Edinburgh University Press, Edinburgh.

Ratcliffe, P. (1981), *Racism and Reaction: A Study of Handsworth*, Routledge and Kegan Paul, London.

Rex, J. and Moore, R. (1967), *Race, Community, and Conflict: A Study of Sparkbrook*, Oxford University Press, London.

Rex, J. and Tomlinson, S. (1979), *Colonial Immigrants in a British City: A Class Analysis*, Routledge and Kegan Paul, London.

Smith, G. et al. (1999), 'Social Capital and Urban Governance: Adding a More Contextualised "Top-Down" Perspective', Unpublished paper.

Wolf, R. (1999), 'Minorities Policy in the City of Amsterdam and the Amsterdam Districts', Paper presented at the MPMC Workshop in Liège, Belgium, 30 October-2 November.

Woods, R. (1979), 'Ethnic Segregation in Birmingham in the 1960s and 1970s', *Ethnic and Racial Studies*, vol. 2, pp. 455-76.

6 Immigrants in a Multinational Political Sphere: The Case of Brussels[1]

DIRK JACOBS

Introduction

In Brussels, issues of the integration of immigrants, and especially their political participation, are very closely related to the dominant political cleavage along linguistic lines. The power struggle between the two national communities (the Flemish and the Francophones) both enables and frustrates political incorporation of ethnic minority groups. The stakes are especially high for the Flemish community: the political incorporation of the foreign population could put into question their demands for group differentiated rights but could arguably also lead to a strengthening of their position. Due to fears within the Flemish community, non-EU non-nationals have so far remained disenfranchised. Within one and the same territory, Flemish and Francophone policy-makers use different frameworks for incorporation of immigrants. The Flemish mainly adhere to Anglo-Saxon and Dutch ideas of group-based multiculturalism. The Francophones are mainly influenced by the individualist republican model of France. The multigovernance situation, with which Brussels is confronted, thus causes very diffuse political opportunity structures for participation of ethnic minority groups.

Brussels, a Hybrid Region in a Multination State

Belgium was formally a pure unitary state until 1970. The constitutional reforms of 1970, 1980 and 1988, however, gradually gave rise to a more diversified political system, containing several sub-national institutional levels (i.e. regions and communities). The most recent phase of this development was found in the 1993 constitutional reform in which Belgium was officially transformed into a federal state. The new Belgian Constitution recognises that the constitutive nation is not a homogeneous entity. The constitutive nation of the Belgian state is instead seen to be the sum of national (autochthonous) sub-groups with (or which strive towards) an own cultural identity. The process of state reform and devolution has placed recognition of cultural-linguistic diversity in the foreground as the guiding principle for Belgian political life. The (new) Constitution, indeed, clearly departs from the postulate of a multination state (Kymlicka, 1995) and recognises the rights of (partial) self-determination of those groups which are seen to be the constitutive elements of the Belgian nation (Martiniello, 1997, p. 71). The Constitution states that the Francophone, Germanophone and Flemish groups are the fundamental cultural communities of Belgium. This postulate then serves as the basis for organisation of the entire Belgian political field. The Flemish-Francophone divide, however, clearly constitutes the central political axis.

The Region of Brussels-Capital, an enclave within the Flemish Region, is an officially bilingual (Dutch- and French-speaking) region. Both the Flemish and the Francophone communities have jurisdiction in the Region of Brussels-Capital. It contains 19 autonomous municipalities. Together these 19 autonomous municipalities are usually referred to as the 'City of Brussels'. This could (and often does) create some confusion. The Region of Brussels-Capital is not a city in exact legal terms and has no city government as a whole, but it is a region and has its own regional government and representative body alongside 19 municipal councils. Only one of those municipalities is officially named 'the City of Brussels' ('Brussel' in Dutch, 'Bruxelles' in French) and it contains the historical (and touristic) centre. We will be dealing with the entire Region of Brussels-Capital here.

According to population statistics, the Region of Brussels-Capital had 953,175 inhabitants on 1 January 1998, of which 279,810 (29.4 per cent) were non-Belgian residents. Of the 673,365 Belgian inhabitants (71.4 per cent of the total population), approximately 15-20 per cent has Dutch (Flemish) and 80-85 per cent has French as the mother tongue. These are unavoidably only rough estimates and it should be noted that there are quite some perfectly bilingual people in Brussels. There is no possibility of knowing the exact proportions, because since 1961 it has been forbidden to ask language affiliation in the census in order to avoid political tensions.

Although the Flemish are clearly in a minority position in Brussels, Dutch is in principle used alongside French as a fully-fledged official language. The exact procedures to ensure this are the result of over three decades of difficult negotiations and complex reforms (for further reading in English see Fitzmaurice, 1996; Murphy, 1988; Roessingh, 1996). Due to a set of specific procedures to institutionalise bilingualism in Brussels, the Flemish are usually slightly over-represented in administrations. It is also fair to say that the Flemish have more political power than could be expected on the basis of their demographic importance. One example is the guaranteed representation of the Flemish in the regional government. This advantageous situation for the Flemish in Brussels is balanced by an advantageous situation of the Francophones at the national level. Although the Francophones are demographically in a minority position in Belgium, they have been granted the right to an equal amount of ministers in the federal government. There is also an 'alarm bell' procedure on the federal level in which both language groups can block decisions if they judge them to be detrimental for their own position.

It will come as no surprise that this system of 'parities' is vulnerable. In the run-up to the 1999 elections, all the Flemish parties (except the ecologist party) argued for a minimal guaranteed political representation for the Flemish in Brussels, while some Francophone parties (in particular the Francophone party Front Démocratique des Francophones (FDF) and the right-liberal PRL) campaigned strongly to get rid of the special protections for the Flemish in the Region of Brussels-Capital.

Brussels As a Town of Immigrants

The Region of Brussels-Capital hosts a rather substantial number of foreign residents: in 1998 no less than 279,810 persons were non-nationals (29.4 per cent of the total population). Half of these foreigners are EU citizens (139,898 foreign residents), the other half are third country nationals (139,912 foreign residents). Of the latter, 50 per cent is Moroccan.

The striking importance of foreigners in the total population of Brussels, is a phenomenon that has to be understood in the light of social and economic developments in the last three decades. From the 1960s onwards the Region of Brussels-Capital experienced strong economic growth, a process which led to a disrupted demand-supply situation on the labour market and the housing market. On the one hand the city had a large demand for cheap low-skilled labourers, but on the other hand the enriched middle classes moved to better and more modern neighbourhoods which had been built on the periphery of the city in the 1950s. Due to a mortality and emigration surplus of Belgians, a lot of houses in the nineteenth century inner-city neighbourhoods of Brussels became vacant. Demand in the labour and housing markets was subsequently filled by immigrants.

Brussels increasingly attracted relatively large numbers of foreigners, while the original Belgian inhabitants started moving out of the city. The growth of the immigrant population in Brussels was at first largely due to low-skilled foreign workers (predominantly from Italy and Spain, and later from Morocco and Turkey). The growth of the foreign population was later caused by highly-educated foreigners working for international organisations (and associated bodies) such as the European Communities and NATO (Van der Haegen et al., 1995, p. 4). In contrast to the low-skilled foreign labourers, these richer foreigners did predominantly look for housing in the periphery. Large numbers of Belgian inhabitants started moving out of Brussels to the suburbs (later joined by rich foreign residents) and young Belgians no longer moved into Brussels at the same rate as earlier. This process led to a deterioration of the quality of housing in significant parts of the inner city. As a result, the total number of inhabitants in the city dropped below a million (Van der Haegen et al., 1995, p. 5). At the same time foreign workers moved into the impoverished parts of the city. Between 1963 and 1995 the number of Belgian inhabitants in Brussels dropped from approximately 950,000 to approximately 666,000, while the foreign population (people not holding a Belgian passport) grew from approximately 90,000 to approximately 286,000 (Van der Haegen et al., 1995, p. 5). As a result, the foreign population in 1999 accounted for nearly 30 per cent of the total number of inhabitants.

It is not known precisely how many children of foreign residents in Brussels acquired Belgian nationality due to the gradual introduction of *ius soli* in 1985 and 1991. It is obvious that, while the population of foreign residents makes up 30 per cent of the total population of the Region of Brussels-Capital, the proportion of people of foreign descent must be well over one third. The exact size of the immigrant community cannot be established exactly. There have never been any attempts – or the data were at least never published – by official administrations to chart the ethnic groups of the city (the only data available are based on the criterion of nationality). We *do* know that in the Census of 1991, almost 54,000 Belgian persons did not have Belgian nationality at the time of birth. As a result we know that *at least* 34.1 per cent of the inhabitants of Brussels were of foreign origin in 1991. One can estimate that today approximately 38-40 per cent of the inhabitants of Brussels is of immigrant origin, i.e. including second generation.

Integration Policy or Policies?

Immigration policy (regulation of access to the territory and residence) has always clearly been a national prerogative. Integration policy, on the other hand, is in principle a policy competence of the Communities since 1980 (see Hubeau and Van Put, 1990). However, depending on the policy field in question (labour, education, housing, urban renewal, fight against poverty, etc.) or the geographic region (Flanders, Wallonia or Brussels), in practice all political levels have some sort of policies directly or indirectly related to immigrants and ethnic and cultural minorities. In spite of this multilevel governance situation (Favell and Martiniello, 1998), it should be stressed that the overall framework for any policy regarding immigrants in Belgium – whatever institutional level it is stemming from – has clearly been set in 1989 by the Royal Commissariat for Migrant Policies (RCMP). This semi-official government body, attached to the Prime Minister's administration, was set up in order to develop and monitor policy related to the integration of foreigners and ethnic minorities. In 1993, the Commissariat was replaced by a permanent institute, the Centre for Equal Opportunities and the Fight against Racism (CEOFR), still attached to the administration of the Prime Minister. The creation of the institute should be seen as the direct result of the electoral success of the extreme right-wing and racist party Vlaams Blok in the municipal elections of 1988 in the city of Antwerp.

Of particular importance is the definition of 'integration' the Royal Commissariat introduced as the pivotal concept for government policies on migrants and ethnic minorities. On the one hand integration is seen to be insertion of migrants into the Belgian society according to three guiding principles:

1. assimilation where the "public order" demands this;
2. consequent promotion of the best possible fitting in according to the orientating social principles which support the culture of the host country and which are related to "modernity", "emancipation" and "true pluralism" – as understood by a modern western state; and
3. unambiguous respect for the cultural diversity-as-mutual-enrichment in all other areas (RCMP, 1989, pp. 38-9).

On the other hand integration entails 'promotion of structural involvement of minorities in activities and aims of the government' (RCMP, 1989, p. 39).

This definition of integration was said to be the result of efforts to find a compromise between the theoretical options of assimilation and segregation for an immigrant policy (RCMP, 1993, p. 51). It should be noted that the definition clearly excluded demands stemming from the political extremes on the immigrant issue. On the one hand, the far-right idea of sending immigrants back to their countries of origin was rejected explicitly; while on the other hand the (left-wing) idea of enfranchising foreign residents was also made impossible (Jacobs, 1998, p. 177). The definition of integration introduced by the Commissariat in 1989 has, from 1990 onwards, functioned as the official reference point for government policy regarding to immigrants and ethnic minorities.

The Flemish, Francophone, Walloon and Brussels' policies towards immigrants and ethnic minorities have all taken over the integration framework of the RCM and CEOFR as guidelines for their own policy efforts. They have, however, put the stress on other dimensions. The Flemish government has had a clear preference for supporting migrants' own organisations which are willing to co-operate in federations and are co-ordinated by QUANGOs. In addition, it has financially supported local initiatives aimed at urban renewal and integration of deprived groups in disfavoured neighbourhoods. In 1998, the Flemish government adopted a new overarching policy framework based on the recognition of ethnic-cultural groups and including both (settled legal) migrants and refugees and groups with nomadic lifestyles ('gypsies') as its target groups. The Flemish government has therefore based its model of integration of immigrants in line with Anglo-Saxon and Dutch ideas of group-based multiculturalism.

Intellectually influenced by the individualist republican model of France, the Francophone and Walloon governments have not been willing to recognise ethnic-cultural groups as specific entities in its policies towards immigrants. Furthermore, although in practice often primarily directed towards immigrant groups, initiatives were often framed in such a way that immigrants were not specifically defined as target groups. The same can be said of several measures taken by the Region of Brussels-Capital. The large numbers of foreign residents and the *de facto* residential concentration of ethnic minorities have nevertheless forced officials in Brussels towards a more multicultural stance. The Brussels parliament, the Common Community Commission (GGC), the Flemish Community Commission (VGC) and the Francophone Community Commission (COCOF) have thus put forward a special Charter, the *Charte des devoirs et des droits pour une cohabitation harmonieuse des populations bruxelloises*, stipulating the ground rules for co-existence of the different groups in Brussels. In addition, a 'mixed' consultative commission on immigrant issues in Brussels was created in 1991 and installed in 1992. It is mixed in that it contains equal numbers of elected politicians and representatives of immigrant groups. This commission possessed a consultative power in issues particularly relevant and/or important to the immigrant communities, i.e. employment, housing, living conditions, education, relations with the police, problems associated to non-implementation of laws, teaching of Islam religion, local political participation, the rights and the position of women in society and refugees. It is worth noting that instead of starting its second term in 1995, the mixed commission was split up into a separate Francophone mixed commission and a Flemish mixed commission.

Competing Flemish-Francophone Approaches towards Immigrants

Both the Flemish Community Commission (VGC) as the Flemish community subsidise migrant self-organisations in Brussels. To be eligible for funding an organisation has to be oriented towards emancipation, education and integration has to function as a meeting point and has to fulfil a cultural purpose. In addition, the organisation has to operate using (also) the Dutch language – if not always, then at least at the executive level. It should be emphasised that the creation and functioning of 'Flemish' migrant self-organisations is very actively stimulated by the VGC and that this has given an important boost to immigrant associational life in Brussels. In the second half of the 1990s, the VGC gave the organisation Intercultureel Centrum voor Migranten vzw (ICCM) the task of co-ordinating and supporting the 'Flemish' migrant self-organisations. Since its creation on 31 March 1993, the ICCM has already supported a significant number of migrant associations in Brussels (Agrupacion Cultural Sur, Alhambra vzw, Bawasa vzw, Blanco y Negro, Centro Gallego, EATA, Evrites vzw, Matalumbo vzw, Meervoud, Koerdisch Bureau, Koerdisch Instituut, Touba vzw, Ghanaba, Euro-Afrikaanse Fondatie, Mezcla vzw, N'Imagighen vzw and Pachamama vzw). There is a special collaboration with the Moroccan federation FMDO and the African federation RVDAGE focusing on activities in Brussels.

There were substantial efforts to ensure good contacts with these and other immigrant associations. For example, the Flemish mixed commission invited all interested spokespersons of immigrant associations to extraordinary sessions in parliament in November and December 1998. In addition, the mixed commission organised the well-advertised 'Day of Dialogue' in March 1999 – with concerts, free food and drinks – to promote the Flemish community among immigrant associations. It is reasonable to conclude that these (and other) activities are – at least partially – strategic attempts by the Flemish government in Brussels to incorporate immigrant (often Francophone) self-organisations into its policy networks. In so doing it hopes to strengthen the sphere of influence of the Flemish community within the Region of Brussels-Capital. Immigrant associations, of course, welcome these efforts as interesting new possibilities for funding and lobbying. In earlier years, the lack of governmental financial support of immigrant organisations had frustrated the creation of strong immigrant associations and had stimulated incorporation of immigrants into existing (Belgian) religious and syndical organisations (Layton-Henry, 1990). The recent financial support by the (Flemish) government has, in contrast, given impetus to immigrant associational life.

On Francophone side, the Flemish efforts are regarded with some suspicion. Indeed, most Francophones claim a totally different policy should prevail. The militant Francophone party FDF, one of the partners in the regional government and an important political force in almost all municipalities of the Region, claims assimilation of immigrants into French culture is the only solution in Brussels:

> La culture française est le creuset des solidarités entre habitants de Bruxelles. La dualisation sociale que subissent des populations précarisées à Bruxelles aurait des conséquences plus graves encore si les autorisés bruxelloises, influencées par les revendications des responsables politiques flamands, se laissaient guider par le discours en faveur du multiculturalisme, qui n'est que le discours de l'indifférence culturelle et de la ghettoïsation des communautés d'origine étranger. A Bruxelles, la participation de toutes les populations au rayonnement de la culture française est un des plus puissants leviers de leur intération à la vie sociale (FDF, Congres doctrinal du 25 Octobre 1997, Bruxelles).[2]

Favell and Martiniello (1998) correctly pointed out that the multilevelled governance situation in Brussels enables and encourages new types of immigrant opportunities and political voice. To give one example, immigrant associations can now 'shop around' for funding and influence in either the Flemish or Francophone community. Favell and Martiniello (1998), however, also stress that the institutional structures may eventually lead to pathological forms of political activity and expression among marginalised ethnic minority groups. The observation that political attention – and in its wake not only temporary harsher police control but also funding opportunities, renovation programs, youth centres – increases after urban violence, does not seem to be a good incentive for more constructive political and social forms of integration. Of course, urban violence by immigrant youngsters has not been a premeditated form of political activism.

Figure 6.1   **Scatterplot of percentage of unemployed and percentage of Moroccan and Turkish nationals on neighbourhood level in the Capitol Region of Brussels**

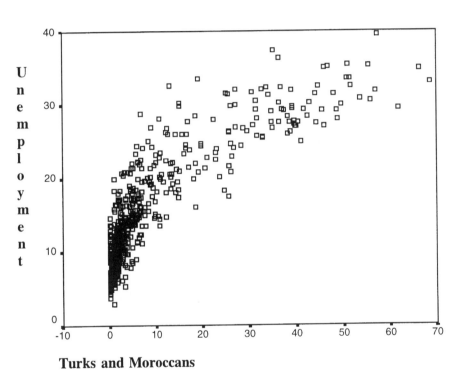

Turks and Moroccans

Source: Census data 1991, treatment by IPSoM.

However, it should be pointed out that, for instance, the extreme leftist organisation PTB-PvdA systematically tries to cash in on local problems and exaggerates every incident involving immigrants and the police. Nearly every major incident is followed by anti-police demonstrations, which, as a 'safe' recipe for conflict between police and youngsters, often lead to violent outbursts. In addition, a significant element among Moroccan and Turkish youth is increasingly questioning the credibility and legitimacy of (immigrant) social workers, welfare organisations and official channels for political demands and instead prefers to opt for confrontation with local authorities and violent infrapolitics (and/or involvement in criminal activities). Without doubt, a structural reason for this is the residential concentration of Moroccan and Turkish youth in disadvantaged neighbourhoods with high unemployment figures and little hope for short term social-economic revival (see Figure 6.1 for the link between unemployment and residential concentration of Moroccans and Turks).

In order to tackle this problem, both Flemish as Francophone authorities support initiatives aimed at sustaining the (re)development of disadvantaged neighbourhoods. These programmes, however, lead to major improvements only slowly. The situation in the worst-off neighbourhoods, where often 40 per cent or more of the inhabitants is disenfranchised because they are foreign residents, has been one of the main reasons for anti-racist lobbying in favour of enfranchisement of non-nationals.

Enfranchisement?

In very different ways, the Flemish-Francophone struggle has had 'positive' effects on possibilities for political participation of immigrants. One example is the setting up of municipal advisory committees in the 1970s. The radical Francophone political party Front Démocratique des Francophones (FDF) had demanded the creation of advisory committees in Brussels in 1971. Given that the municipalities in which advisory committees were created were generally the richer ones, it becomes evident that the aim was not merely to increase the political participation of immigrant workers as such, but of all foreigners – particularly those working in large multinational firms and international organisations – and thus indirectly strengthen the position of the French language in the city and its periphery. For comparable strategic reasons, the Flemish authorities now support immigrant associations and stimulate (controlled) ethnic mobilisation in order to diminish Francophone influences and strengthen the Flemish position. The Flemish-Francophone struggle has, however, not only been beneficial for political incorporation of immigrants. Indeed, it has strongly inhibited formal enfranchisement of foreign residents.

As I have highlighted in earlier work (Jacobs, 1998, 1999 and 2000), Belgian politicians have been remarkably reluctant to enfranchise foreign residents. This was, as I have argued, mainly due to polarisation and electoral struggle over the anti-immigrant vote in the 1980s and early 1990s and to the disruptive effect of the Flemish-Francophone cleavage in the second half of the 1990s. It was not until early 1999 that Belgium finally enfranchised EU citizens in compliance with the Maastricht Treaty and the derived European directive. They will be able to participate in the next local elections, which will take place in October 2000. Non-Europeans, however, might only be allowed to vote in local elections in 2006 (municipal elections are held every six years). To assure this, the former Socialist-Christian Democrat government included a special clause in the Constitution that the electoral laws could only be modified in order to enfranchise third country nationals in the year 2001.

Particularly politicians of the Flemish community were reluctant to enfranchise all foreign residents, fearing that the foreign vote would immediately benefit French-speaking political parties and that the electoral position of Flemish parties in Brussels would be weakened even more. It is a public secret that Francophone politicians shared these views and regarded maximal extension of the local electorate, although presented as a sacred universal principle, as a weapon in the conflict between the two communities. The debate over local enfranchisement of EU and non-EU citizens has thus become an issue in the power struggle between the two linguistic communities.

It may be questioned how founded the Flemish fears are about imminent electoral success of the Francophones, in case of enfranchisement of foreign residents. Estimates by Bousetta and Swyngedouw (1999, pp. 120-7) have shown that the effect of EU enfranchisement will probably be very diverse and local. In addition, no more than 8.5 per cent of all EU citizens registered to vote in the October 2000 municipal elections. Undoubtedly the overall majority of foreigners in Brussels will vote for Francophone parties. French is, after all, the lingua franca and the most likely language foreigners would (decide to) pick up. Since the overall majority of the Belgian electorate votes Francophone as well, it is however hardly certain that the political presence of the Flemish in Brussels would automatically be affected negatively. In municipalities where 85 per cent of Belgian inhabitants now vote for Francophone lists, a situation in which only 75 per cent of the foreign residents would vote Francophone, could even improve the situation of the Flemish (Jacobs, 1998, p. 248). Positive campaigning by the Flemish within foreign communities could help them strengthen their positions. It could well be, however, that the negative position the Flemish have taken in the debate will turn their fear into a self fulfilling prophecy; foreign voters will not vote for political parties which have tried to keep them disenfranchised (Jacobs, 1998, p. 244). In any event, whatever the electoral scores of the Flemish on the municipal level may be, there will be no direct consequences for the rights of the Dutch-speaking in Brussels, since these are protected in the Constitution. The Flemish, however, fear the Francophones will increasingly question these special minority rights if the political presence of the Flemish decreases. Flemish resistance to the enfranchisement of foreigners boils down to defending the power and positions of the Dutch-speaking. Enfranchisement is said to disrupt the existing system of checks and balances between Flemish and Francophones, which ultimately is the basis for the federal structure of the country. Bousetta and Swyngedouw (1999, p. 115) point out that it is striking that the same arguments have not been put forward explicitly in debates over acquisition of state citizenship.

It is nevertheless clear that, especially in Brussels, there will be an increasing importance of the so-called 'new Belgians' (people of foreign origin who acquired citizenship through ius soli, option or naturalisation) among the electorate. Martiniello (1998, p. 138) has estimated that there were about 35,500 Belgian voters of foreign non-EU origin in Brussels in 1996, thus constituting 6.6 per cent of the electorate. It is equally clear that a large majority of these new Belgians are likely to be Francophone voters (Martiniello, p. 115). To explain why the debates over acquisition of state citizenship in the 1980s and early 1990s did nevertheless not become an issue in the power struggle between the two linguistic communities, Bousetta and Swyngedouw (1999) have advanced some plausible reasons. They have put forward an interesting institutional explanation, observing that only once Belgium had become a federal state, did it made sense to see the idea of group differentiated rights as a stake (Bousetta and Swyngedouw, 1999, p. 118). In addition, they have indicated the importance of the difference in salience and social impact of enfranchisement on the one hand and acquisition of nationality on the other hand. The former is a measure immediately affecting a large group; the latter is a more gradual measure that apparently is judged to be less threatening.

In any event, in the wake of the ardent debates between Flemish and Francophones over enfranchisement in the late 1990s, both groups increasingly became aware of the increasing electoral importance, especially in Brussels, of the new Belgians in the upcoming 1999 national and regional elections. As mentioned before, the Flemish community (Commission) in

Brussels began making substantial efforts to incorporate immigrant communities into its policy schemes and from the end of 1998 openly wooed immigrant organisations. On the Francophone side, the right-liberal party PRL, which had before clearly been a party with moderate anti-immigrant positions, in March 1998 attracted Mostafa Ouezekhti, a well-known former Ecology Party politician of Moroccan descent, to its party. In addition, the PRL radically transformed its positions on enfranchisement of non-EU residents and on acquisition of nationality, which they would now ardently defend.

The new 1999 'purple-green' government Verhofstadt, a coalition of socialists, right-liberals and ecologists, promised in its government agreement to further liberalise nationality acquisition rather than enfranchise foreign residents. Although socialists, ecologists and the Francophone right-liberals supported enfranchisement, the Flemish right-liberals were able to veto change in this matter. It seems the other coalition partners are willing to drop the issue in exchange for new (and – in international comparison – very open) procedures for nationality acquisition. Whatever the outcome of the debate over enfranchisement might be, there is no doubt that the issue of political incorporation of immigrants will remain closely tied to the Flemish-Francophone divide for years to come and that the political importance of the ethnic minority groups will unavoidably increase (given the importance of nationality acquisition). It remains an open question what the effect of the immigrant voices will be on the linguistic struggle in Brussels.

Conclusion

Brussels is confronted with multilevelled governance. In this context it should be noted that there is an important difference in the approaches of the Flemish authorities and the Francophone authorities towards immigrants and ethnic minorities. The Flemish encourage collective mobilisation and support self-organisation of ethnic minorities. The Francophones opt for an individual assimilationist approach and want to insert immigrants – and their (political) mobilisation – into existing structures, organisations and networks. As a result of the Francophone approach, many immigrants are active within the structures of existing social organisations (e.g. trade unions) and anti-racist organisations. The fact that migrant associations are treated as legitimate partners for discussion by the Flemish authorities, has, however, also enhanced the creation of self-organisations and processes of ethnic mobilisation. The immigrant associations thus gain funding, while the Flemish authorities hope to gain influence. Overall, the (seemingly) contradictory policy schemes of the Flemish and Francophone authorities create all kinds of inhibitions and possibilities for immigrant mobilisation. The positions and actions of the Flemish and Francophones concerning the issue of political incorporation of immigrants should be seen in relation to their power struggle. Indeed, the possibility that foreigners can disrupt the existing power balance between the two linguistic communities in either direction motivates the different political strategies and visions related to political participation of immigrants and ethnic minority groups. What the ultimate effects of the immigrant political voices will be on the Flemish-Francophone power balance in Brussels, however, remains to be seen.

Notes

1   With many thanks to Hassan Bousetta, Adrian Favell, Marc Swyngedouw, Andrea Rea, Marco Martiniello, Nadia Ben Mohamed and Mylène Nys, who assisted in the research in preparation of this paper. Special thanks is due to Andrea Rea and Mylène Nys with whom I collaborated in preparing the first draft of the Brussels city template. The research in preparation of this paper was made possible by funding of the Region of Brussels-Capital. Met de steun van de Vlaamse minister voor Cultuur, Jeugd, Brusselse Aangelegenheden en Ontwikkelingssamenwerking.

2   'The French culture is the cradle of solidarities among the inhabitants of Brussels. The social dualisation which is endured by the disfavoured populations of Brussels would have even worser consequences if the authorities of Brussels, pressured by the demands of Flemish politicians, would adopt a discourse in favour of multiculturalism. Such a discourse is only a discourse of cultural indifference and of ghettoisation of immigrant communities. In Brussels, the participation of all groups into the French culture is one of the most potent levers to assure their integration to the social life.'

References

Bousetta, H. and Swyngedouw, M. (1999), *La Citoyenneté de l'Union Européenne et l'Enjeu de Bruxelles: Le Droit Supranational Européen Confronté aux Réalités d'une Société Multiethnique et Multinational Divisée*, Courrier Hebdomadaire du CRISP no. 1,636.

Favell, A. and Martiniello, M. (1998), 'Multinational, Multicultural and Multilevelled: Post-National Politics in Brussels, Capital of Europe', Paper presented at the ECPR Joint Sessions, Warwick University, March 1998.

Fitzmaurice, J. (1996), *The Politics of Belgium: A Unique Federalism*, Hurst, London.

Haegen H. van der, Juchtmans G. and Kesteloot C. (1995), *Multicultureel Brussel*, Brussels Hoofdstedelijk Gewest, Brussel.

Hubeau, B. and Put, R. van (1990), 'Les Compétences des Communautés en Matière d'Immigration', *Revue du Droit des étrangers*, vol. 58, pp. 71-80.

Jacobs, D. (1998), *Nieuwkomers in de Politiek*, Academia Press, Gent.

Jacobs, D. (1999), 'The Debate Over Enfranchisement of Foreign Residents in Belgium', *Journal of Ethnic and Migration Studies*, vol. 25, pp. 649-63.

Jacobs, D. (2000), 'Multinational and Polyethnic Politics Entwined: Minority Representation in the Region of Brussels-Capital', *Journal of Ethnic and Migration Studies*, vol. 26, pp. 289-304.

Kymlicka, W. (1995), *Multicultural Citizenship*, Clarendon Press, Oxford.

Layton-Henry, Z. (1990), 'Immigrant Associations', in Z. Layton-Henry (ed.), *The Political Rights of Migrants in Western Europe*, Sage, London.

Martiniello, M. (1997), *Sortir des Ghettos Culturels*, Presses de Sciences Po., Paris.

Martiniello, M. (1998), 'Les Élus d'Origine Étrangère à Bruxelles: Une Nouvelle Étape de la Participation Politique des Populations d'Origine Immigrée', *Revue Européenne des Migrations Internationales*, vol. 14, pp. 123-50.

Murphy, A. (1988), 'The Regional Dynamics of Language Differentiation in Belgium', Geography Research Paper no. 227, University of Chicago, Chicago.

RCMP (Koninklijk Commissariaat voor Migrantenbeleid) (1989), *Integratie(beleid): Een Werk van Lange Adem*, Inbel, Brussel.

RCMP (Koninklijk Commissariaat voor Migrantenbeleid) (1993), *Tekenen voor Gelijkwaardigheid*, Eindrapport, Inbel, Brussel.

Roessingh, M. (1996), *Ethnonationalism and Political Systems in Europe: A State of Tension*, Amsterdam University Press, Amsterdam.

7 Marseille: Institutional Links with Ethnic Minorities and the French Republican Model

DAMIAN MOORE

Introduction

The situation of ethnic minorities in Marseille cannot be analysed without taking into account the debate on immigration that has been occupying the foreground of the French political scene since the 1970s. This debate has recently changed its nature. Questions about the economic utility of immigrants and the social costs linked to their presence have gradually given way to questions related to French national identity, which is elsewhere challenged by European integration. This development, and the anxiety that it generates, is apparent within public debates on immigration: the images of the immigrant worker, stigmatised as scrounging from French society or of oversized immigrant families attacked as useless for the national economy, have now been replaced by the theme of immigrants as alternative and potentially threatening groups in French society. Debates over the construction of mosques have replaced the cultural theme of incompatibility of ways of life.

At the same time as this shift in representations, one can observe a change in urban questions linked to immigration. Debates over cohabitation and neighbourhood relations between French and immigrants have given way to the problem of inner cities, not as areas of division between French and immigrants, but as areas of social-ethnic segregation giving birth to a new category of urban actors.

This hardening of social representations and urban tensions linked to immigration is happening at the same time as a reassertion of the French integration model, by political leaders and many research workers, based on a supposed indivisible link between the cultural and legal aspects of the naturalisation of foreigners (Poutignat and Streiff-Fenart, 1995; Schnapper, 1994). In contrast to British or American societies that accord an official status to ethnic and racial differences, the French tradition, in conformity with the French Constitution, does not distinguish citizens on the basis of race, ethnic origin or religion. The social distance between French and foreigners is widely perceived as stubborn, if not growing. The legal categories of 'French' and 'foreigners', the only legitimate ones in official classifications, do not correspond with the operating categories influencing social relationships. There exists discrimination towards those who are considered, whatever their nationality, as being racially or ethnically different on the basis of these social categories.

This tension between the legal categories of 'French' and 'foreigners', from which public policies are elaborated, and the operating categories that concern ethnic minorities is a constant theme our fieldwork carried out in Marseille.

Some French authors have however, contributed to the rise of a concept of *ethnicité à la française*. Vincent Geisser (1997), after having observed links between the local sections of the French Socialist Party and North African minorities, explains that the debate on ethnicity cannot be reduced to the assimilation-integration alternative. An approval of the republican ideal and an attachment to the classical conception of the nation state does not exclude, in France, an aspiration for the emergence of a mode of representation that could reconcile political pluralism and cultural pluralism. Therefore, according to Geisser, there is room for a debate on different forms of production of ethnicity. Jocelyne Césari (1994) insists on the fact that, for the younger generations, ethnicity is rooted inside the experience of difference: post-colonial racism linked to a gradual loss of the parents' culture. The forms of mobilisation of these generations (associations rather than political parties) and their various requirements (housing, training and so forth) advance a civil conception of citizenship. This civil conception is marked by the fact that nowadays, mediation between different groups is privileged by these social actors rather than having recourse to classical political institutions (political parties, unions). In this context, the North African population of Marseille is not different from the Jewish, Armenian or Black African populations. The specificity of the North Africans lies in the separation of demands addressed to local authorities; i.e. religious demands are separate from social demands.

Our research on Marseille is based on a theoretical framework that advances the concept of *ethnicité à la française*. This chapter, based on fieldwork carried out on a local level, enables us to show that, in France, as in Greece or in Portugal, behind a formal discourse that ignores cultural and ethnic differences, both political and administrative institutions produce ethnicity and invent informal modes of mediation with ethnic minorities.

It is important to recognise that the North African minority settled in Marseille in a context of both economic and identity crisis and did not benefit from a process of integration into the city by joining the working class. The paths of integration that used to characterise the working class (unions and the French Communist Party) have today imploded. This is why the cleavage inside the territory of Marseille does take place between the working class and the 'bourgeoisie' but between the French and the North African immigrants that have settled, mainly for economic reasons, in the northern areas of the city.

Inside these northern areas the occupation of common territories by groups considered as ethnically different becomes conflictual, functions as a source of insecurity and also contributes to creating gaps between ethnic groups that share the same economic and social conditions. Nevertheless, one must insist on the fact that, in some cases, there are also reasonable and sociable relations between people belonging to these ethnic groups. These representations that can lead to conflicts are now being questioned by new generations of North Africans. Therefore, according to Césari (1994), unlike the British situation, *ethnicité à la française* does not consist in the official recognition of the existence of ethnic groups inside the urban territory. This concept can be defined as alternative identities built by individuals in reaction to racism based on physical appearance, ethnic origin or religion.

This chapter focuses on modes of mobilisation of minorities originating mainly from North Africa having settled in Marseille. For these actors, ethnicity is constructed in order to code a situation of social exclusion by borrowing norms and values both from the host society and from a family past revisited and redefined in terms of community. References to an Arab origin or to Islam therefore make sense in day-to-day interactions and allows these actors to build what could be defined as a 'provocative identity' in order to anticipate forms of racial discrimination. My main contention in this chapter is that, at the beginning of the 1980s, when the local authorities launched urban regeneration policies in Marseille's northern districts, a group of individuals emerged and acted as mediators between the North African minority and public institutions by referring both to a situation of social exclusion and to an Arab origin. These mediators gradually pushed the local authorities into creating formal or informal political and institutional opportunity structures for the North African minority and for other ethnic minorities settled in the city. I will begin this chapter with a brief narrative of the historical process of migrations in Marseille and also with a description of the city's ethnic minorities today. There follows an analysis of the emergence of interactions between local public authorities and ethnic minorities through which they have gradually been able to defend their interest, mainly since urban regeneration policies were launched at the end of the 1980s in the northern areas of Marseille. These interactions induced both formal and informal management of ethnicity by local public authorities.

Marseille, a City of Migrations

Marseille is a Mediterranean port city, located in the Department of Bouches-du-Rhône in the Region of Provence-Alpes-Côte d'Azur in southeast France. It is the third largest city of France and is the administrative capital of both the Region and the Department. The population of the city itself is 797,700, out of 1,832,848 in the Department as a whole (1999 census, provisional results INSEE). But the urbanised area around Marseilles extends beyond the city's boundaries to include industrial districts and smaller settlements such as Fos, Berre, Vitrolles and Aix-en-Provence. The Marseille-Aix-en-Provence urban unit covers only part of the Department and is not itself an administrative territory. Furthermore, whereas many of the inland settlements are thriving as part of a 'neocalifornian economy' (Viard, 1995), Marseille has experienced severe economic and social problems. For instance, since 1990 the city's population has declined by 2,000, with many professionals and well-qualified people leaving for other places within the Region. Therefore, Marseille is a problem area with-in the generally buoyant Euro-Mediterranean economic arc, which stretches from Valencia in Spain to northeast Italy. The city's crisis is defined by the intersection of its status within this arc and its exchange with North Africa.

Partly because of its geographical location, Marseille has always experienced the comings and goings of foreigners. In some ways this makes it distinct from most French cities. At the beginning of the nineteenth century it became the staging post for long distance migrations, towards America Algeria, and the rest of Africa. Later in the century, more of these migrants stayed and settled – in 1914 a quarter of the population were Italians.

After the First World War came a turning point. The labour surplus that had marked Southern Europe began to weaken as the population aged. Marseille became a port of entry for young workers entering both France and Europe. Among them were refugees, including 60,000 Armenians who arrived in 1915 following the genocide. A third of them stayed in Bouches-du-Rhône, 14,000 in Marseille itself. Other communities, admittedly less important ones, went unnoticed: 20,000 Greeks, for example, of whom more than 10 per cent stayed in the city.

The end of the French-Algerian war in 1962 was marked by the arrival of the *pieds-noirs*, French settlers fleeing from newly independent Algeria. Around 150,000 settled in Marseille, which was a considerable number for a big city already going through an economic crisis. Moreover, it has been estimated that about two million people came to France, through Marseille, from North Africa, in particular Algerians, during the 1960s and the 1970s. The arrival of the people from North Africa, in particular the Algerians, during the 1960s was like closing the 'fourth city' (Temime, 1990-1991) opened by the Italian migration in the middle of the nineteenth century.

More precisely, from 1962 to 1974, Marseille was the hub for the influx of an immigrant work force to France. The Belsunce area in the city centre illustrated this function. Until 1988, this area played the role of an 'economic lung' for Algeria: the income of immigrants who worked in France was turned into consumer goods that were exported towards Algeria. At that time, the 'Belsunce business' was equivalent to the transfer that took place towards Portugal. In the 1980s, Algerians crossed the Mediterranean to shop in Marseille with the remittances from family members settled there: it is estimated that one million francs per year was recycled this way. This was the equivalent to 35,000 Algerians spending 7,000 FF each per week on consumer goods.

In 1990 at least 56,102 foreign immigrants were resident in Marseille (INSEE, 1990). They constituted 7 per cent of the city's population of 799,849. In addition, cross-tabulated statistics indicate that there were 45,000 Comorians (who have French nationality) in Marseille. A high percentage of the foreign immigrants living in Marseille are North Africans (see Table 7.1). There are a growing number of individuals of North African background or heritage who possess French nationality, by automatic acquisition for the younger generations, or by naturalisation. This accounts for a further 30,000 individuals. Finally, cross-tabulated statistics show that about 4,000 *Harkis* of Algerian descent live in Marseille.

The majority of North African immigrants are concentrated in one region within Marseille. This region takes the form of a 'triangle of poverty'. The base of the triangle lies to the north of the built-up area, stretching between La Rose and l'Estaque. The point of the triangle is located south of the Canebière, between the Cours Julien and the *préfecture*.

Table 7.1   **The foreign population in the city of Marseille and the Marseille-Aix-en-Provence urban unit**

Population	Marseille City	Aix-en-Provence Urban Unit
French	743,747	1,149,789
Total Foreigners	56,102	80,282
	(7.0%)	(6.5%)
European Union	8,932	15,554
Algerian	24,546	32,945
Moroccan	3,640	5,142
Tunisian	7,251	10,839
Turkish	916	1,500

Source: INSEE, 1990 census.

This triangle points into the heart of the city centre. More than a third of the *marseillais* live inside it, nearly 310,000 inhabitants. All the following problems are concentrated there: unhealthy housing and large blocks of flats, poverty, large families and unemployment. The triangle includes 42,000 people who are unemployed (32 per cent of adults), as well as a higher proportion of children and large families than the rest of the city. Almost two-thirds of households pay no tax. No other place in France has such a high proportion living in poverty.

Therefore, in Marseille, unlike most cities in France, the main social-spatial divide is not between the centre and the suburbs, but between the old industrial city and the seaside resort. The Canebière is the no man's land.

The main cleavage inside the territory of the city of Marseille is less along the lines of class and more between the French citizens one the one hand, and the North African immigrants on the other (Césari, 1994). The ideologically constructed figure of the 'North African' has become the Other of white *marseillais*. This 'othering', furthermore, has a spatial correlate. The binary oppositions of French and foreign, citizen and immigrant, white and black have become mapped onto representation of urban space, separating south from north. The social differentiation between the north and the south of the city is therefore becoming an ethnic differentiation leading to the following equation: northern areas = immigrants =

North Africans. This social differentiation affects the way that ethnic minorities relate to political institutions.

Interactions between Ethnic Minorities and Local Public Institutions

Except for EU immigrants, foreigners do not have the right to vote in national or local elections. In 1990, the number of naturalisations in France as a whole totalled 34,899, around 1 per cent of the documented foreign residents in France the same year. In 1994, the number of naturalisations in France as a whole was 49,449.

Foreigners are allowed to take part in assemblies and demonstrations and to form their own associations. The claim for the foreign immigrants' right to vote in the local elections has been one of the usual demands in the solidarity campaigns with the foreign population. It has also been the subject of a strong debate inside the French left-wing political parties for many years. The foreign immigrants' right to vote in the local elections was part of François Mitterrand's political programme in 1981. President Mitterrand never put this measure into practice and argued that 'French society was not ready'. Since 1981, associations like SOS Racisme, the left wing of the Socialist Party and the French Communist Party have always defended the foreign immigrants right to vote in the local elections.

The question of local voting rights has taken on a new dimension since December 1999 and the *proposition de loi constitutionnelle* made by Noël Mamère (Green Party Member of Parliament, representing the Department of Gironde). According to Mamère (who proposed to complete Article 3 of the French Constitution and also to cut out Article 88-3 on the right to vote and to be elected for foreign residents at local elections) the time has come to debate this crucial issue of French democracy with serenity. He recalled that since the Maastricht Treaty, EU citizens residing in France are entitled to vote and to be elected for municipal elections. Mamère goes further and explains that citizenship today in France functions according to a cast system: full citizenship for the French, rebated citizenship for EU citizens and privation of citizenship for all foreigners. Therefore, according to him, because they pay local tax and because the number of local councillors is based on the population of cities (including foreign inhabitants) and not on the number of electors, the question of the right to vote for foreigners should be reconsidered. It should be reviewed in light of the republican equality principle in order to find solutions for the four million foreigners residing in France (7 per cent of the French population). This question, which is crucial for the 56,102 foreigners living in Marseille, has now to be debated by the senators.

There are three main levels of government in France, the region, department and municipality (*commune*). In general, reforms since 1982-1983 have resulted in decentralisation towards lower levels of government. But in addition, there are various 'horizontal' administrative arrangements. The key one regarding Marseille's foreign community is the Contrat de Ville de Marseille. Its most recent version was a five-year co-operation agreement between state, region and municipality begun in 1994. Its aim was the urban regeneration of northern Marseille. The Fonds d'Action Sociale pour les travailleurs immigrés et leurs famille (FAS) is also associated with it.

With the first Contrat de Ville de Marseille in 1983, a social group emerged and still functions as an intermediary between the institutions and the ethnic minorities. Until 1983, social workers assumed this function, which was mainly based on housing and learning French.

This group is comprised of men of North African origin, today aged between 40 and 45 years old. They have all grown up in the northern areas of Marseille. These mediators have been able to push the local political institutions to move from a 'social services' vision of foreign immigrants to a more 'cultural and ethnic' vision (social services in France do not take ethnicity into account for delivering services). This evolution is not only due to ethnic minorities creating their own associations, but also to the growing difficulties of social workers faced with social violence in the northern districts. The informal institutional recognition of these mediators has enabled North African immigrants to be gradually considered as an ethnic minority. The mediators are only concerned with the aspect of the ethnic minorities' life in Marseille that is taken into account by urban social regeneration policies, not the religious aspect.

The religious aspect of the ethnic minorities' life in is given expression through different associations and mediators. In 1989, the socialist Mayor of Marseille decided to institutionalise relations with ethnic minorities by naming a local civil servant officially responsible for them. Marseille is the only city in France to have chosen this type of organisation. This decision was not questioned after the 1995 local elections (The current Mayor of Marseille, Mr Jean-Claude Gaudin, belongs to the national opposition to the socialist government.) The Marseille Esperance structure, which now answers to the Department managed by this civil servant (*service de relations avec les communautés*), groups all the religious minorities that have settled in the city of Marseille. It can be defined as a municipal 'confessional' commission. The Mayor created it after an attack on the Jewish cemetery in Carpentras. This commission, called Marseille Espérance, enables the Mayor to debate with the different local religious leaders. But they do not take part in decisions concerning the management of the city. Therefore, Marseille Espérance allows the Mayor to diffuse a message of tolerance and anti-racism, but does not have a direct effect on the situation of the ethnic minorities settled in the city.

Three main places of worship today function as mosques in Marseille. They are well frequented on Fridays, but are hardly visible elements of the urban landscape (they are mainly located in the cellars of blocks of flats). They have not received official recognition as mosques.

There has been a long-running controversy on mosques involving the local authorities, leaders of Islamic organisations and representatives of migrants' homeland governments. The first official statement of the Mayor of Marseille on this issue dates back to September 1989. He declared that he was in favour of the construction of a mosque in the city under two conditions: the management of the place of worship would have to be assumed by a Muslim with French nationality, and the funds from foreign countries would have to be diversified. He added that the mosque would be 'a place of worship and nothing else'. The local political deal is therefore based on two main goals: the control of the religious activities that take place in the city, and the will to recognise the presence of a population that represents an important electoral potential (a growing number of foreign immigrants have French nationality).

The Muslim community in Marseille reacted strongly against the idea of the mosque being 'a place of worship and nothing else'. Cultural issues seem to have been as important for them as religious ones. This political offer also stirred up the rivalries among local Islamic leadership. In order to gain independence from the Muslims' former states, and mainly from the Algerian government, some religious leaders put forward the idea that either the state or the municipality could finance this project. This proposal was incompatible with the 1905 Act, according to which '*l'Etat ne reconnaît, ne salarie, ni ne subventionne aucun culte*'.

In 1990, the Mayor explained that he would not go forward on this project as long as the local Muslim community was not united. Although the situation is still paralysed, this issue, for the first time in local political history, created a proper debate between ethnic minorities and local government. Nevertheless, since the 1980s, both the emergence of mediators and the debate on the mosque have given way to an institutionalisation of the relations between local authorities and the North African minority.

As noted above, in 1989, the Mayor of Marseille officially named a local civil servant in charge of relations between the local authority and ethnic communities. This function, named *service des relations avec les communautés*, still exists today. This civil servant works with the associations created by different ethnic minorities: Jewish, Armenian, Comorian, North African, Afro-Caribbean, Asian and also solidarity and anti-racist associations. The innovative aspect of this new function is the systematic following up of the ethnic minorities this civil servant is in charge of. The result is that the local authority funds community activities managed by these associations: for instance, cultural or sports events can be funded. Or the local authority can provide these associations with premises inside which cultural or religious activities can be organised.

This gradual institutionalisation of the relations between the local authority and ethnic minorities can also take other forms inside which the Mayor of Marseille remains the main actor: inauguration of symbolical monuments, trips to countries the ethnic minorities originate from (Israel, North Africa, Armenia). The Mayor also meets representatives from ethnic minorities for ritual ceremonies: Yom Kippour or Aïd-El-Kebir. For instance, he systematically visits a Muslim family at the end of the Ramadan month.

This policy towards ethnic minorities, developed by the Mayor in relation with Marseille Espérance, certainly contributed to the legitimisation of the presence of cultural minorities in the city of Marseille. Marseille Espérance therefore functions as a place of legitimisation for leaders of associations willing to be representative of the Muslims of Marseille. At the same time, this institutionalisation of relations with leaders from the Muslim community enables the local authority to control the activities of this social group. All the demands emanating from ethnic minorities are analysed by the civil servant named by the Mayor of Marseille and are therefore formulated according to the constraints of the local political and institutional system.

The main consequence of this institutionalisation of relations with ethnic minorities, via a civil servant appointed by Marseille Espérance and the Mayor, resides in an implicit definition of the North African minority which excludes the leaders of the younger generations who active in urban and social regeneration actions. According to us, this formal institutionalisation of relations with ethnic minorities is mainly symbolic and centred on the political activity of the Mayor. The everyday needs of the ethnic minorities (social needs, education, housing etc.) are taken into account neither by the civil servant nor by the commission.

According to the Marseille local authorities, ethnic minorities do not develop specific social, educational or housing needs. These demands have to be taken into account by colour-blind urban social regeneration policies. This policy developed by the Marseille local authority corresponds to the French tradition that, as noted above, does not distinguish citizens on the basis of race or ethnic origin. This tradition leads to colour-blind social and educational public policies. Nevertheless, since 1983, social urban regeneration policies developed with the Contrat de Ville de Marseille have led to the creation, by the younger generations, of associations acting in the urban and social policies field. As noted above, a small group of individuals have emerged from these associations, and are today informally considered as mediators between local institutions and ethnic minorities for educational, housing and social issues. Although these informal mediators have been able to push the local public social services to move from a 'social' vision of foreign immigrants to a more 'cultural and ethnic' vision, this evolution has not led to the elaboration of specific social public policies directed towards ethnic minorities. Therefore, the local public authorities use these mediators in order to manage ethnicity on an informal basis in social urban policies field.

An interesting example of this informal management of ethnicity is the Espace Jeunes project in the Saint-Mauront area of Marseille. In July 1995, a group of youngsters of Algerian origin physically assaulted social workers in Saint-Mauront. They explained that they had committed these acts of violence in order to attract the local authorities' attention to the fact that they were neglected and unemployed. They also wanted the local authorities to provide them with a place where they could develop leisure activities.

After several meetings with the youngsters and the social workers, the Ville de Marseille decided to give agree to these demands, and to provide them with an *espace jeunes* ('space for the young'). For the local authorities, the key point was to find the right person able to manage the Espace Jeunes. Furthermore, the state and the Ville de Marseille agreed on the fact that the person in charge of the Espace Jeunes would have to come from another area of the city, but would also have to able to understand the cultural and identity problems put forward by the youngsters.

At that point, as in many other cases, the local authorities decided to recruit someone who can be described as being a mediator as we have defined them above. This person was a young Algerian man, aged 35 years old. He had been in charge of several different associations since the urban regeneration policies were launched in northern Marseille in 1983. Therefore, he had developed a good knowledge of social policies, and his ethnicity enabled him to understand the cultural problems voiced by the Saint-Mauront youngsters.

This example illustrates the fact that behind a formal discourse that ignores cultural and ethnic differences, the public authorities in charge of social urban policies in Marseille manage ethnicity on an informal basis. Furthermore, although top-down initiatives in the field of social urban policies ignore cultural and ethnic issues, ethnicity is managed on an informal basis via bottom-up initiatives like the Espace Jeunes project. In order to go further in this analysis of interactions between ethnic minorities and local institutions in Marseille, we now turn to the different community associations and the modes of mobilisation of ethnic groups.

The Community Associations

In Marseille, there are two main types of foreigners' associations: the inner-city (*quartier*) associations, and the associations with a clear ethnic and cultural reference. There are also religious associations. As noted above, the separation between the inner-city associations and the religious associations can be explained by the mode of institutionalisation of relations with ethnic minorities developed by local authorities in Marseille.

In most of the *quartiers* situated inside the city's poverty triangle there are youth associations, generally named for the area itself. In fact, these associations are mainly composed of youngsters of North African origin, usually males aged between 16 and 25. Most of these associations were created by a group of friends or are linked to a group activity, such as music, sport or dance. The authorities often ask youths to create an association in order to obtain funds or premises for their leisure activities.

For the authorities, the association is a way of regulating social life inside a difficult area of the city. It also allows youngsters to take initiatives outside the family circle. The association is also a way of obtaining material and symbolic goods from the authorities, and therefore tackling social exclusion. They are also important centres of socialisation for young North African males within their local environment. Finally, they are often organised as a way of gaining independence from social workers, who are accused of having an outdated approach to immigrants.

These associations do not have any official political reference. The youngsters who run them generally suspect national political organisations of wanting to take them over. Therefore, they did not take part in the *marches des beurs* between 1983 and 1985.

These inner-city associations are modestly funded by the Ville de Marseille, the Fonds d'Action Sociale (FAS), or the Conseil Général des Bouches-du-Rhône. The funding is decided inside the *politique de la ville* configuration, where the local authorities and the state work in partnership.

The second kind of organisation has a clear ethnic or cultural reference. Two approaches generally structure their activities: either they work exclusively on behalf of one ethnic minority on an exclusive basis, or they try and situate this minority inside the total ethnic mosaic of the city of Marseille.

The first approach can be understood as a reaction against both the inner-city associations and national initiatives like SOS Racisme or France Plus. In Marseille, the Centre d'Information et de Documentation sur le Maghreb (CIDIM) works according to this guideline. Ex-militants from the Arab Workers Movement and social workers created this association in March 1980. The goal was to bring together individuals with the same cultural background and to run a resource centre on the Arab world. The Ville de Marseille and the FAS fund the cultural events organised by the CIDIM. The Mouvement des jeunes Arabes, created in 1984, defends values such as *arabité* and Islam, and acts strongly against the assimilationist policies developed by the public authorities.

There is a multicultural radio in Marseille, called Radio Gazelle, and run by the Rencontre et Amitié association. This structure works according to the second approach, by legitimising the presence of the North African community inside the local civil society as a whole. Radio Gazelle allows all the ethnic minorities that have settled in Marseille to express themselves, even though North Africans mainly run it.

Finally, in Marseille, foreign immigrants also tend to form religious associations. The demand for prayer rooms appeared significantly in the middle of the 1970s, at the same time as strikes in workers' hostels. It corresponded to a time when the immigrant workers considered their migration as being temporary. Also, their full-time jobs did not allow them to practise the Muslim religion on a regular basis. In Marseille 24 official places of worship now exist, either as a result of religious groups creating their own associations (under legislation passed in 1901), or as a result of an official decision taken by the local authorities. If one takes into account the unofficial worship places like garages, cellars etc., their number goes up to about 50. The first one of these places of worship was declared an association in 1975.

Later, a law passed by the French parliament in 1981 (October 9) allowed associations created by foreigners to function under the general regime defined by the 1901 Act. After this decision, the number of Islamic associations grew considerably. The worshippers started direct negotiations with institutional partners and created cultural associations in order to manage the worship rooms they were responsible for. Nevertheless, none of the Marseille worship rooms are ruled by the 1905 Act. The Muslim community itself tends not to be aware of this Act. The social workers, which are generally reluctant to refer to the idea of cultural difference, do not really inform the Muslim leaders about this legal regime.

The governments of the Muslims' states of origin tend to try to carry on influencing them. They do their best to organise the Muslim minority in France. Their aim is to create arguments for a general negotiation on Islam in France with the French state. In Marseille, the Algerian minority is the most active in this respect. From 1982 onwards, the Paris mosque (the Algerian government's key institution in the religious field) tried to assert a federal role over the different streams of French Islam in order to appear as the legitimate intermediary between Muslims and the French state and its local authorities. Before he died, Cheik Abbas tried to launch the idea of regional federations of Islamic associations for the south of France. This structure has 147 associations from the Provence-Alpes-Côte d'Azur, 23 of which are based in Marseille. In spite of these initiatives, there is no single religious leader accepted by all the Muslim minorities in Marseille, or by local authorities.

From Social Exclusion to Mobilisation

In Marseille, the different forms of mobilisation developed by the ethnic minorities younger generations generally take place in the northern areas of the city, which correspond to the old working class areas. This geographical specification is linked not only to the history of the North African migration inside the urban territory, but also to the social differentiation based on exclusion and marginality that concern all the inhabitants of this area of the city. Within this context of social decomposition, the younger generations elaborate modalities of collective action based on a moral reaction against racial discrimination. These modalities contribute to differentiate them with the white inhabitants of the inner-city areas who share the same social and economical conditions. I would therefore like to stress that, unlike what is often claimed by journalists and local political leaders, the younger generations do not mobilise on the basis of a conflict which would oppose their culture to norms or values of the host society.

What could, in some cases, be considered as a deviant behaviour of some members of the younger generations can be analysed as the result of a process of acculturation that takes place in a context of social disintegration (disintegration of traditional integration vectors: work, political parties and unions). In Marseille, just as in other large French cities, these new generations are confronted to the same difficulties as the whites that share the same social and economical conditions. These difficulties are linked to the weakening of the institutions that carry the central norms and values for the republic: schools, political parties and unions. This weakening is stronger in ex-'red areas' (*banlieues rouges*) like the northern areas of Marseille. Today, disorganisation and weakening of protest action combine and place younger generations in a situation of social exclusion. This leads to the loss of the idea of belonging to a social class: identification to the city via a sense of belonging to a social class no longer exists in the northern areas of Marseille, in the way that it did in the post-war period. The younger generations are not familiar with the industrial culture and the working-class world. They consider political parties, unionists, judges and police forces as being the expression of violence and domination. This can lead to episodes of violence like in the Saint-Mauront area in the summer of 1995. In this context, the mobilisation of ethnic minorities' younger generations is based on a reaction against a situation of social exclusion.

Nevertheless, they are more active than the white younger generations in organising collective action mainly because, for them, this situation of social exclusion is made worse by racial discrimination. A good example of collective mobilisation linked to the experience of racial discrimination is the Ganache association. This structure was created in the Flamants Area, in the north of Marseille, after, the young Lahouari Ben Mohamed was killed by the police. The young North Africans who manage this association wanted to make sure the citizens of Marseille never forgot this event.

The Algerian Minority in Marseille

It is estimated that during the 1960s and 1970s about two million people came from North Africa, in particular the Algerians. More precisely, between 1962 and 1974, Marseille was the hub for an influx of immigrant workers arriving in France. Today, 24,600 Algerians live in Marseille.

In fact the first Algerians to come to Marseille were 'imported' in 1907 in order to break strikes organised by Italian workers. After 1947, the government encouraged the Algerians to settle: post-war France needed a low-cost labour force. This demand became more important in Marseille in 1964, when the industrialisation of Fos-sur-Mer started. As we have noted above, Marseille is a magnet that faces a destabilised North Africa. Migration is important not only for the economy of Marseille, but also for the economy of Algeria.

Algerians were considered, and are still considered by the indigenous population, more as Arabs and Muslims than Algerians. This attitude is linked to the colonial history of Algeria. Therefore the question of the Muslim religion is fundamental to study the situation of the Algerians in Marseille.

In 1975, four Algerian shopkeepers decided to bring Muslim religion into the open by creating an association named Er Rahmaniyyà. This name is linked to a brotherhood based in Algeria, although this link no longer exists in the activities of the association. Their mosque was named the Bon Pasteur, which is the name of the street where it is based. With a capacity of about a thousand places, this is now the main mosque in Marseille. After the creation of the Er Rahmaniyyà association, groups of Algerians living in different areas of the city decided to create places of worship. Generally these social groups were composed of fathers aged over 35 years old. These individuals tend to get together on an ethnic basis, with links with the former states. The demand for places of worship provoked contacts between the Algerian immigrants and the local public institutions.

For example, in 1977, the Algerian immigrants settled in the Fonvert Area asked the Council Housing Authority for a place of worship in the neighbourhood. The social workers acted as mediators during the negotiations between the leaders of the Algerian minority and the local authorities. Finally, the Algerian minority created an association and obtained a small flat from the Council Housing Authority and was able to open a worship place. These types of negotiations happened in different areas of Marseille during the 1970s and the early 1980s. These places also served as community centres for the Algerian community.

The development of these associations and places of worship is evidence of the adaptation of the Algerian immigrants to the immediate environment. The organisation of religious activities in a context of 'transplanted Islam' belongs to the Algerian minority itself. The Algerian state, or the Amicale des Algériens does not take part in the creation process, but generally tries to control these associations once they are created.

The Algerian immigrants gradually acquired the main characteristics of an ethnic minority settled throughout Marseille. The common referent of this ethnic minority tends to be Islam more than Algeria. The demand for places of worship appears when the project of going back to Algeria is gradually abandoned by the first generation of immigrants. Therefore, they can be analysed as a sign of adaptation of the first generation to the French society.

The mobilisation of the second generation is not linked to the places of worship. Since 1983, Algerian youth has taken advantage of the urban regeneration policies (the Contrat de Ville de Marseille) in order to create their own associations. This process allowed the emergence of mediators from the Algerian ethnic minority. These second-generation mediators tend to act inside the social workers' field. Algerian immigrants and the second generation have both entered into a process of institutionalisation of their relations with the local authorities. The first generation has gained recognition from the local political class by allowing the Muslim religion to become visible in the urban space. Today, the leaders in charge of the associations that run the places of worship are taking part in the debate with the Mayor of Marseille on the 'official mosque' issue, and are members of Marseille Espérance.

The mediators who have emerged from the second generation take part in an informal management of ethnicity by the local social urban regeneration policies. Some of them have become full time social workers and are employed by the Conseil Général des Bouches-du-Rhône or the Ville de Marseille, while others have professionalised their associations in order to become institutional actors in the urban regeneration policies. It must be stressed that the trajectories of members of the second generation are more individual than group trajectories.

The key actors in the religious field are the leaders of the associations who manage places of worship. By doing fieldwork in Marseille, we have discovered the following associations: Association islamique de la cité Bellevue; Centre culturel maghrébin de la Solidarité; Association islamique pour la mosquée des créneaux; and Association culturelle islamique Er Rahmaniyyà.

The Muslims' former states tend to try to carry on influencing them. They also do their best to organise the Muslim minority in France. From 1982, the Paris mosque, the Algerian government's key player in the religious field, tried to assert its federative role for the different streams of French Islam in order to appear as the legitimate partner for the French state and the local authorities. In 1995, Sohieb Bencheik was named *Mufti* of Marseille by the *recteur* of the Paris mosque. Soheib Bencheik was born in 1962 and qualified in religious sciences in Paris. In 1988 he published a book on Islam in France entitled *Marianne et le Prophète: l'Islam dans la France Laïque*. However, Bencheik is not fully accepted as a religious leader by the Algerian minority in Marseille.

The different forms of mobilisation of the Algerian minority (the association rather than the political party) and the themes of demands aimed at public authorities (reaction against racial discrimination, housing, training etc.) advance, as noted above, a civil conception of citizenship.

This conception of citizenship is illustrated by the fact that mediation between different groups has now replaced participation in political parties or workers unions. In this respect, the Algerian minority in Marseille is comparable to the Armenian or Black African minorities. The distinctive feature of the Algerian minority is the separation between social demands aimed at local authorities and religious demands (Islam). This separation is linked to a sociological difference in modes of identification between generations, and also the modalities of institutionalisation of the links with ethnic minorities launched by the local authority. This explains the fact that the inner-city associations and the associations with a clear ethnic and cultural reference (that are managed by the second generation) do not really interact with the religious associations (that are managed by the first generation).

A new form of mobilisation is emerging inside the second generation of the Algerian minority in Marseille. This form of mobilisation is gradually linking civil and social mobilisation to Islam. The Association Entraide et Initiative Eugène Pottier et Environs, created in 1993 in the Saint-Mauront area, is a good example of this new form of mobilisation. This Association develops the following activities: welcoming people belonging to the Algerian minority going through social difficulties, racial discrimination, and cultural and educational activities. The Muslim religion structures the general management of this Association. All the activities are based on a Muslim approach to life. Therefore, the Association Entraide et Initiative Eugène Pottier et Environs, by mixing collective action against racial discrimination and social exclusion with religious activities, is creating a link between two forms of mobilisation which, until now, have remained separate. Recent fieldwork carried out by Jocelyne Césari (1998) shows that such associations are developing in other main cities in France.

Conclusion: Towards an Evolution of the French Republican Integration Model?

Until recently, the emphasis in France has been placed on the risks inherent in the adoption of an approach in terms of ethnic minorities. According to Catherine Neveu (1993), both research workers and policy-makers can not ignore these dangers. The main danger would be that an ethnic terminology could reinforce and increase differences. More precisely, the hypothesis of ethnicity, in the French context of historically established 'universalism' which tends to consider differences as sources of inequality, is problematic. Nevertheless, our research in northern Marseille enables us to assert that, as noted in the introduction, a growing gap can be observed between the legal categories of 'French' and 'foreigners', the only legitimate ones in official classifications and public policies, and the operating categories influencing social relationships, on the basis of which there exists discrimination towards those who are considered, whatever their nationality is, as being racially or ethnically different. This growing gap pushes local authorities in Marseille to manage their relations with ethnic minorities via formal or informal actions that do not always correspond to the official model of French republican integration.

References

Césari, J. (1994), *Etre Musulman en France: Associations, Militants, Mosquées*, Karthala-IREMAM, Paris.

Césari, J. (1998), *Musulmans et Républicains: Les Jeunes, l'Islam et la France*, Edition Complexe, Paris.

Geisser, V. (1997), *Ethnicité Républicaine: Les Élites d'Origine Maghrébine dans le Système Politique Français*, Presses de Science-Po, Paris.

Neveu, C. (1993), *Communauté, Nationalité et Citoyenneté. De l'autre Côté du Miroir: Les Bangladeshis de Londres*, Karthala, Paris.

Poutignat, P. and Streiff-Fenart, J. (1995), *Théories de l'Ethnicité*, PUF, Le Sociologue, Paris.

Schnapper, D. (1994), *La Communauté des Citoyens: Sur l'Idée Moderne de Nation*, Gallimard, Paris.

Temime, E. (ed.) (1990-1991), *Migrance: Histoire des Migrations à Marseille*, Edisud, Aix-en-Provence.

Viard, J. (1995), *Marseille: Une Ville Impossible*, Payot et Rivages.

8 Politics, Welfare and the Rise of Immigrant Participation in a Portuguese Suburban Context: Oeiras during the 1990s[1]

M. MARGARIDA MARQUES AND RUI SANTOS

Introduction

Portugal only recently became a receiving country for sizeable immigration flows (Machado, 1997), while at the same time retaining the features of a sending country with a large number of citizens living abroad (Baganha and Peixoto, 1997). Besides the shorter longevity and the smaller demographic dimension of the phenomenon, as compared to older receiving countries, it also lacks the corporatist articulation of interests and strong welfare state generally found in Northern Europe (Esping-Andersen, 1993; Lucena, 1982, 1985). The processes leading to immigrants' representation in the political sphere mirror these contextual differences, and contrast with the more formalised and hierarchical arrangements underlying the assumptions of the comparative framework of the MPMC project. The experiences of older receiving countries in dealing with immigrants' incorporation, however, have obviously informed Portuguese policies on these matters. Different political perspectives are in play, cutting across established political party divides and affecting policy-making at different institutional levels.

The diversity of political representation and participation of immigrants at the local (city) level is enhanced by the relative autonomy of municipal institutions in policy definition and implementation. The Lisbon Metropolitan Area (LMA), where some two thirds of immigrants to Portugal are settled, encompasses eighteen municipalities, without any effective co-ordinating structure. Each municipality thus shapes its own guidelines for dealing with the increasingly visible issue of immigrants' and ethnic minorities' incorporation in (local) civil society, depending on the political party in office and its local leadership's beliefs, and on the outcome of previous processes. Thus, for instance, some municipalities developed a mode of formal political representation of minorities through consultative councils. Indeed, the pioneering step taken in that direction by the Socialist-led municipal government of Lisbon in 1993 was emulated by the national government after the Socialist Party won the 1995 elections, steering Portuguese official policy toward a corporatist system of collective interest articulation. But this model is far from being universally adopted. In Oeiras, our case study, the centre-right political leadership of the Social Democratic Party has actively opposed this mode, holding instead the 'liberal neutrality' view (Penninx, 2000) that immigrants and members of ethnic minorities should be treated as any other citizens, dealing directly with the local administration without crystallising differences in any kind of intermediate body.

Being autonomous, however, is not the same as being immune to external processes. We intend to show in this case study that, while no policy homogeneity should be assumed at metropolitan level, local political structures and dynamics do not sufficiently account for the reshaping of political opportunity structures for immigrants and ethnic minorities. The city level of analysis has to be opened to higher level processes if we are to understand the – often unintended – consequences of local policies. Conversely, local level policies influence the ways in which participation opportunities created at higher levels are appropriated, namely by the selection of local actors. We aim to explore local policies and processes, namely:

- the refusal to recognise minorities' representation through formal mediators that goes hand in hand with the availability to support specific associations' activities;
- the ongoing effects of the massive public re-housing of previous shanty town dwellers conducted by the Town Hall;
- the local development project carried out by the Town Hall under the URBAN European Programme;
- their combined effect in the local associative field.

We establish how they interact with policy definitions and developments at higher levels, namely:

- the two significant periods of the regularisation of undocumented immigrants in 1992-1993 and 1996;

- the creation of a High Commissioner for Immigrants and Ethnic Minorities (HCIEM) at government level in 1996, advised by a Consultative Council gathering representatives of national immigrants' associations;
- the granting of voting rights in local elections to immigrants in 1996;
- the local development philosophy imposed by the EU on the URBAN programme, centred on partnership with local actors, participation and self-representation by local populations.

This will allow us to show that, whereas the top-down approach to partnership building and participation taken by the URBAN team had little effect on the associative field and on formal participation, the welfare redistribution through re-housing and its associated spatial reorganisation did have major outcomes in the structure and scope of associations representing immigrants' interests at the local level. Combined with the active roles taken by some immigrants' associations both during the two periods of regularisation and the campaign for immigrant electoral enrolment, and the newly granted voting rights first exercised in the 1997 local elections, these processes may enhance the political 'voice' (Hirschman, 1970) of immigrants in the local polity.

We shall begin by presenting an overview of recent immigration trends to Portugal, and particularly to the LMA. We shall then move on to describe the evolution of relevant national level policies for immigrant and ethnic minorities' inclusion, and the main types of organisations dealing with these issues. The Oeiras case study will be presented next, concentrating on local government's political stance towards immigrant participation, their practices concerning local associations with immigrant constituencies, and detailing the URBAN project, the re-housing programme and its effects. The concluding section will show how these processes came together in reconfiguring the associations' roles and scope of participation in local politics, and discuss possible scenarios for the evolution of the emerging political opportunity structure.

The National Context and its Development

Statistics concerning foreigners provide for only an educated guess about the numbers of immigrants and ethnic minorities, because Portugal has no statistical sources adequately designed for these recent developments as yet. The numbers of foreigners holding residence permits up to 1998 is evidence of the fast pace of immigration during the last decade (SEF, 1998).

These figures also allow the identification of the major groups involved. In 1998 Africans, mostly from former Portuguese colonies, now Portuguese Speaking African Countries (PSAC), accounted for almost half the total foreign resident population; Europeans come in second place. The greatest increase, however, came from Asia.

The heterogeneity of motives and settlement patterns has been mentioned in earlier studies (e.g. Bastos and Bastos, 1999; Cordeiro, 1997; Fonseca, 1997; Machado, 1994, 1997; Pires, 1990). They suggest that a rough periodisation should distinguish a first period of immigration from the PSAC in the 1960s (following shortages in national labour force); a second period, following African de-colonisation (Pires et al., 1987); and a third one, still going on, beginning when Portugal joined the European Community in 1986. It was during the latter that the bulk of those usually lumped together under the term 'immigrants' came to Portugal.[2]

We can also identify three distinct occupational groups.[3] The first is composed of the more qualified segments of foreign labour force (Brazilians and Europeans). The second includes an amalgam of skilled or unqualified labour and business owners (Mozambicans).[4] Finally the third group combines all the other nationalities, heavily represented in manual labour, be it in public works and building, manufacture, or personal and domestic services (Capeverdians – by far the largest group –, Angolans, Guineans, and Santomese) (Cordeiro, 1997).

About 4 per cent of the population of the whole LMA[5] in 1997 did not hold Portuguese nationality,[6] double the national percentage (Cordeiro, 1997).[7] Although the settlement patterns of the different nationalities vary greatly, African concentration in the LMA makes this region the major concentration of economic immigrants in the country.[8]

National surveys of Portuguese public opinion consistently show that Gypsies are traditionally the minority group most discriminated against. Other communities, easier to identify as immigrants (for example Brazilians or Asian Indians), lag well behind in the polls. Blacks, however, ranked second in the public's feeling of 'excessive presence', two and a half points behind the Gypsies according to a 1995 poll. It placed public opposition to the presence of black people dangerously close to 50 per cent (*Público*, August 2, 1995).[9]

African immigrants are over-represented in slums and shanty towns, as well as in manual unskilled labour, constraining their ability to cope with their present situation (Baganha, 1998; Baganha et al., 2000; França, 1992; Silva et al., 1989). The high levels of school drop-outs and lower success rates among African youngsters are even more worrying, since they suggest problems stored up for the future (Justino et al., 1998; Machado, 1996). This situation is worsened by the fact that the lowest success rates occur where immigrant communities are largest, in the LMA (and especially in Oeiras municipality) (Cordeiro, 1997). And it is not very likely that the second generation, better educated than their parents, and more socialised into Portuguese society, will be willing to continue the same 'survival strategies' as their parents (Portes, 1994). Furthermore, their comparatively low school success and high drop out rates may prevent them from taking advantage of new mobility opportunities that rely heavily on educational qualifications.

These social disadvantages persist despite formal equality of access to most social rights. Access to health, education, job training, social welfare has no formal restriction – which in some cases even applies to undocumented immigrants.[10] Responsibility for implementing the right to education on behalf of immigrant children lies with the State, according to the Constitution (Article 74). Since the late 1980s, educational policies have aimed to incorporate cultural diversity in the school system, including the creation of a specific organisation attached to the Ministry of Education for that purpose in 1991. 'Cultural mediators' were created in 1998, aiming to facilitate ethnic minority youths' integration in school. Since 1996 impoverished immigrants have been a priority case for granting the minimum public wage. In sum, the granting of social rights shows a definite intention not to discriminate against foreigners and to prevent social exclusion.

The same holds for the access to two resources perceived as scarce, and therefore sensitive: housing and work. The Special Re-housing Programme launched in 1993 to replace shanty towns by social housing does not mention any nationality-based restrictions on eligibility. The 1998 law concerning foreigners' access to work did not abolish all restrictions, but major obstacles were tackled. Furthermore, special training programmes designed to help adaptation to changing labour market conditions include immigrants and ethnic minorities as specific cases. Trade unions have also been very active, participating in important activities concerning immigration and ethnic minorities, in spite of the delicate balance between protecting foreigners and avoiding nationals' disaffection. Two such activities are worth mentioning: (1) lobbying by the *ad hoc* Co-ordinating Secretariat for the Legalisation (SCAL) for the legalisation of undocumented immigrants; and (2) the making and implementation of the guidelines to fight racism and xenophobia in the work place and moonlighting, inscribed in the Strategic Agreement negotiated between the State and social partners in 1996. As well as extending social and economic rights of work and job security to foreign workers, these actions also aim at reducing unfair competition of foreign undocumented, underpaid and unregulated workers.

Political Developments at the National Level[11]

The Portuguese government only publicly accepted the label of 'country of immigration' in the 1990s. It then started to put in place an institutional and juridical framework specifically designed to cope with this emerging phenomenon (Guibentif, 1996).

The first 'extraordinary regularisation process' of illegal foreign residents (1992-1993), together with a 1993 Government Resolution targeted at immigrants' social exclusion, mark the official recognition of the problem (Machado, 1994; SOPEMI, 1995). After a long period of complacency towards the presence of illegal immigrants, its growing visibility and the problems it created in the context of EU pressure for enhanced border controls pressed for a solution. The 1981 nationality law, which enforced *jus sanguinis* over *jus soli* and withdrew the automatic right to Portuguese citizenship formerly granted to anyone born on Portuguese soil, also seems to have created a generation of unaware undocumented foreign residents whose legal status had to be dealt with. The first regularisation process was an attempt to clear the existing situation before tightening border controls. It gave one (supposedly last) chance for undocumented immigrants to get stay permits, under a specified set of conditions (e.g. minimum time of residence and proof of having a job and means of subsistence). The other side of the coin was the passing of specific legislation (on education, social security, job training, etc.) designed to reverse the social exclusion of documented immigrants.

This process led to an unprecedented mobilisation of immigrant associations, NGOs, and Catholic organisations, voicing strong criticism in the mass media about the way it was devised and conducted. A major criticism was that it was implemented through a border police department without direct or indirect collaboration from immigrants' associations, allegedly causing misinformation and distrust among the target populations. The stringency of eligibility conditions, with the burden of proof resting on the applicant, and the toughening of conditions for those who were not able to legalise were also denounced.

This dissatisfaction and its effects on public opinion were taken up by the Socialist Party (PS) then in the opposition. The PS rallied the political outcry against immigrant and ethnic minority exclusion and made pre-election commitments to address immigration issues with wider participation of civil society organisations, namely immigrants' associations. Since the 1991 elections, PS had had a formal agreement with some major national immigrants' associations (Cape Verde, Angola and Guinea-Bissau) to include one of its members on the list of eligible MPs (Machado, 1992). This political commitment was taken further during the regularisation process. But, though this Socialist MP was sometimes referred to by some interviewees as a 'representative' of the immigrant and ethnic minorities,[12] no single political party can claim to monopolise their representation. Conversely, no pressure group targeted at the immigrant and ethnic issues stands out in the political party system in Portugal. The importance assumed by Socialists – or people somehow connected to PS – in these issues is mainly the result of a decade rallying opposition to the PSD government (1985-1995) from within civil society.

In 1993, Lisbon's Socialist-led Town Hall furthered the process with the creation of a consultative council for immigrants and ethnic minorities affairs, thus strongly emphasising the party's commitment to the problem and to a solution based on political participation. Almost immediately after PS ended ten years of centre-right government in the 1995 national elections, the creation of a High Commissioner for Immigration and Ethnic Minorities (HCIEM), reporting directly to the Prime Minister, became the most visible part of the new framework. The appointed HCIEM, a former member of the Lisbon council for immigration and ethnic minorities, went on to create a national Consultative Council to advise him, with the participation of national immigrants' associations as representatives of these populations' interests. This Council came into effect in 1998. Another measure adopted immediately after the Socialist government was elected, and also one of its election promises, was to put in place a second 'extraordinary process of immigrants legalisation' in 1996. This relied on the involvement of the associations, NGOs and other civil society organistions (many of whom had in the meanwhile organised as a major lobbying group, the above-mentioned SCAL). This proved to be a major mobilisation event for national and local immigrants' associations, who provided a very active medium for the diffusion of information, reassurance and support to applicants and the general on-the-ground implementation of the regularisation campaign.

Another crucial change in the political opportunity structure was the granting of political participation rights to foreigners in local elections in 1996, subject to reciprocity from sending countries. At present this limits it to Capeverdians and Brazilians, among the larger foreign populations residing in Portugal. Besides its direct effects on political participation, the voter registration campaign and the electoral campaign that preceded the first local elections to take place under the new rule, held in 1997, were also an important experience of involvement by both national and local associations in the formal political process. Such data as are available, however, show that participation in the local elections involving non-EU citizens was low (see Table 8.1).

Table 8.1   Registered voters in 1997 local elections

	Capeverdians	Brazilians
Portugal	9,572	732
LMA*	9,038	289
Oeiras	1,378	23

* Lisbon and Setúbal districts

Source: STAPE (Technical Secretariat in Support of Electoral Processes).

But foreigners' political participation in Portugal shows differing behaviour by the two relevant national groups, in Portuguese local elections and their own homeland elections.[13] The number of Capeverdian electors registered for local elections was more than double that for elections in Cape Verde itself. The relative distribution of voters matches residential concentrations of Capeverdians legally residing in Portugal. By contrast, among Brazilians the number of registered electors in the 1997 local elections was five times less than registered to vote in Brazilian elections. This suggests a lower level investment in Portuguese polity, and conversely a still strong attachment to Brazilian political affairs, reflecting their recent settlement in Portuguese soil. Conversely, Capeverdians show a more tangible connection to the Portuguese polity. This is corroborated by the presence of politicians of Capeverdian descent in local political administration in the LMA.

Organisations Involved in Immigrant Issues

The developments sketched above obviously tended to give growing importance to the roles of immigrants' associations, and other civil society organisations involved with the issues of immigrants' and ethnic minorities' inclusion and participation. The associative landscape is heterogeneous, both at national and local levels, depending on the scope of intervention, members' skills and nationality, endorsement of a religious orientation or not, and relations with the sending country's government among other factors.

Over the last few years, the building of federations of associations at both national and European levels has been on the agenda of some associations.[14] The creation of the Consultative Council to the HCIEM, including representatives of all the Portuguese-speaking countries' associations, might well enhance and consolidate these changes. The increasing importance of the EU in defining guidelines and programmes targeting immigrants and ethnic minorities on a European scale also favours the development of such forms of organisations with greater scope.[15]

The Catholic Church and related organisations also play an important role beyond the limits of social solidarity and support, with far reaching consequences (including Caritas, Centro de Estudos Padre Alves Correia, and Obra Católica das Migrações, OCM). They made visible interventions during the legalisation process of immigrants and the public discussion of a new wage labour law. The stance it took during the latter enabled OCM to strengthen its position as a fundamental partner of national associations and as a mediating structure with the central government.

Non-religious and non-governmental organisations mainly initiated by Portuguese nationals (for instance SOS Racismo and Olho Vivo) have a more diffuse and encompassing intervention. They acquired high public visibility in 1996, when they organised the only major anti-racist demonstration in Lisbon after skinheads murdered a young black man. Otherwise, their action is more directed toward linking with other organisations to put more effective pressure on decision making.

The Case of Oeiras

Oeiras is one of the eighteen municipalities included in the LMA. It borders Lisbon municipality to the East, and has a lengthy waterfront along the Tagus estuary. Its mild natural climate and proximity to the capital helps explain why it was a holiday and weekend resort into the 1950s. As a result, the waterfront is more built-up than districts further inland. Population migration into the capital from the rest of Portugal and then the decentralisation from Lisbon caused a rapid increase in population density to over 3,300 inhabitants per km^2, four times that of the LMA as a whole, according to 1991 census data. Settlement patterns consistently converged on a dominantly suburban type.[16] The most recent figures for population growth, however, show a slowing down of this trend (Fernandes, 1997) (see Table 8.2).

Table 8.2   Change in area and population 1970-1991 (census dates)

	1970	*1981*	*1991*
Area (km²)	62.22	45.84	45.84
Population	68,265	149,328	151,342

Source: Fernandes, 1997, pp. 25-6, 93.

The suburbanisation process eventually created the need for new territorial and administrative arrangements. In 1979, part of Oeiras territory was turned into a new municipality; yet the population went on growing. Since the territorial reorganisation, the centre-right party PSD has always been in office in Oeiras Town Hall. In the 1997 local elections, their majority was even increased (Fernandes, 1997).

Immigrants' Residential Segregation: From Shanty Towns to Re-housing Projects

One of the main reasons why PSD is so popular is the Town Hall's implementation, since 1985, of a municipal housing programme, including re-housing of shanty town populations. This scheme was intensified after 1993 in line with the national Special Re-housing Programme (SRP). Survey data show the precarious housing situation of immigrants and ethnic minorities in Portugal. They are heavily concentrated in the LMA and over-represented in slum areas (França, 1992; Silva et al., 1989), mostly on the outskirts such as Oeiras. The large influx from Africa after de-colonisation contributed strongly to the growth of peripheral shanty towns. These were vast residential agglomerates of *ad hoc* built houses and sheds made of brickwork, wood, and foil[17] among other materials, with very poor collective infrastructure. Their elimination was the goal of the 1993 SRP. According to the SRP census conducted in 1993, Oeiras municipality had one of the largest shares of shanty dwellings in the LMA – over 10 per cent of the total – in spite of an existing municipal re-housing programme (Morais et al., 1997). This stood in sharp contrast with its high overall standards of living and the development of an important tertiary and hi-tech industry pole in the area. To a great extent, the growth and resilience of some of these shanty towns is the outcome of the influx of low-skilled economic immigrants.

There is spatial segregation of immigrants only in the sense of this pattern of over-representation. This is not to say that these shanty towns are in any way 'ghettos' exclusively built and dwelt in by Africans. Some older Oeiras inhabitants have lived in such precarious conditions for over thirty years: internal migrants from rural areas who first settled in Oeiras in the late 1960s, who never could afford moving into the formal housing market, and whose children and grandchildren were raised in an underclass environment. They mainly settled along the administrative borders between Oeiras and Lisbon and among scattered and disused farmland.

Later immigrants, mostly from the Cape Verde islands, were immediately channelled towards these slums, where they found accessible and affordable opportunities for settlement. Both the shanty towns and the re-housing quarters that are replacing them are inhabited by lower-class residents mixed by ethnicity. By 1993, one third of the 3,165 families dwelling in shanties recorded in Oeiras SRP census were headed by foreign citizens, three quarters concentrating in five *nuclei* lying in a narrow strip along the eastern border of the municipality.[18] The Town Hall has been re-housing both nationals and foreigners irrespective of their legal status. In local politics the housing problem is perceived to take priority over the issue of residential or legal status, which belongs to national government. Data available on municipal re-housing projects therefore reflect a very similar distribution by nationalities: nearly one third of their inhabitants are foreigners (not counting Portuguese nationals of foreign descent) (see Table 8.3). The lowest percentage of immigrants corresponds to the older quarters, dating from before the immigration wave.

Oeiras now ranks among the most successful municipalities in implementing the SRP. Taking advantage of the head start provided by the previous re-housing scheme, from 1993 on virtually all shanty towns are being razed, as municipal quarters are made available to relocate their households, mostly through subsidised leasing contracts.[19] The improvement in living conditions for these people thus comes at the cost of a higher claim on their incomes, a fact that has an important bearing on ensuing political processes, as we shall comment on below.

Table 8.3   **Municipal re-housing projects in Oeiras (rented houses only) (1998)**

	Number of housholds	Number of people living	Households of foreign origin[a] (%)
Outurela/Portela	128	397	38
Bugio	180	309	20
Medrosa	44	155	5
Moinho da Portela	90	354	35
Pombal	326	1,091	33
Laveiras/Caxias	400	296	33
Alto da Loba	440	220	34
Encosta da Portela	364	1,202	32
Quinta da Politeira	160	191	23
Ribeira da Lage	166	527	49
Bento Jesus Caraça II	74	240	3
Bento Jesus Caraça (PER)	40	251	48
Luta Pela Casa	100	[b]	0

[a] According to 'head of household' (i.e. the holder of the municipal rental contract) nationality
[b] Data not available

Source: CMO, 1997; Divisão de Habitação, CMO, 1998; Fernandes, 1997.

Although a substantial share of the SRP funding comes from the national budget, the specific implementation procedures and criteria are largely left to the Town Hall. One of the major features of the way Oeiras conducted the process was the option for dispersion. Shanty town dwellers were redistributed among a larger number of smaller re-housing neighbourhoods, which were also far more scattered throughout the municipal territory than the previous sites. At the same time, there was a deliberate policy not to make 'block relocations', that is, populations were spread around. Former neighbourhoods were consciously disregarded in house assignments. No re-housing neighbourhood was made up of households coming from one single shanty town, and all shanty town populations were divided among several re-housing quarters. This was a deliberate ploy to weaken slum solidarities and localisms, intended to foster internal differentiation and remove community obstacles to social mobility. As we shall see, this option had far-reaching consequences for the structure of the local associative field.

Even though the effects of re-housing on the social and urban landscape have generally been received positively, both among the concerned population and the surrounding residents, the new quarters retained some of the stigma of the old shanty towns. There are concerns voiced in interviews, survey data and often in the press about security, youth gang offences and drug dealing. Youth deviance prevention through sports and culture activities and even school coaching is therefore one of the main goals of local associations working with immigrants.

Immigrants' Associations and Their Relations with the Town Hall

Until recently the official position of Oeiras Town Hall has been not to recognise any form of collective body claiming to represent immigrants' and ethnic minorities' interests, be it immigrants' associations, NGOs, religious or anti-racist organisations. Abiding by liberal principles (Penninx, 2000), immigrants are seen as plain citizens like any others, and their claims addressed as individual claims to individual problems: local authorities' foremost task, it is said, is to integrate them into the mainstream, not to promote their separation. The key note has therefore been strong opposition to the setting up of a specific institutional frame for dealing with immigration and ethnic minorities issues. The main argument is that there are no specific group problems, at least inasmuch as the Town Hall is concerned, and that there are only individual problems – foremost among them the inability to access to the housing market. Thus, the idea of institutional representation of minorities co-operating with public officials to design and implement Town Hall decisions or guidelines is rejected. In contrast with current national government orientations and the institutions being created in some other municipalities of the LMA, Oeiras Town Hall has, up till now, consistently rejected the idea of an immigration council, as well as any kind of formal group interest representation.

Nonetheless, the actual experience of municipal officials led to the recognition of some specific minorities' situations. In turn, this is reinforced by the intermediate levels of local public administration in charge of co-ordinating specific departments, and therefore translating general policy guidelines into concrete municipal interventions, which often reflect a *de facto* recognition of cultural differentiation and specificity. In spite of the official rhetoric, local politicians do accept that the only way to counter the stigmatisation of immigrants and ethnic minorities is using (even manipulating) the cultural diversity of the municipality as one of its distinctive symbols.

Looking more closely at the substance of some of the requests and claims by local associations and actually satisfied by Oeiras Town Hall, one cannot therefore fail to notice some ambiguity. Funds and other forms of support are granted for special education and training in Portuguese language, funds are delivered for showing African cultures to youths of immigrant descent, financial aid is given to groups of youngsters to visit their parents' or grandparents' African countries, municipal facilities are made available to house foreigners' associations, and so on. Although the first kind of support is consistent with the aim of promoting assimilation into the mainstream, the others clearly facilitate specific ethnic group identities, in apparent contradiction with the affirmed principles. This is probably seen as a way of facilitating integration, smoothing their relations with the municipal government. Such targeted initiatives, however, are confined to strictly cultural domains.

Because there is no public support for overall group representation, but rather to specific activities, the non-recognition by Oeiras Town Hall of formal intermediary representative bodies encourages the burgeoning of small and diversified associations (Mouzelis, 1995; Schmitter, 1984; Soysal, 1994), mostly presenting themselves under the guise of neighbour-hood sports and culture associations[20] rather than by ethnic or national denominations. But the composition of their leadership and constituencies, the nature of their activities, and the goals they specify in interviews clearly identify them as immigrants' associations, adapted to the circumstances they were born in and to the structure of opportunities that local policies offer them (see Table 8.4). They generally benefit from several forms of support from the Town Hall (including municipal facilities), and their activities are funded as any other (Portuguese) local association, provided they can meet the necessary requirements of planning activities.

The three-way relationship between the Town Hall, immigrants' and ethnic minorities' associations, and political actors in the sending countries provides an important context for framing local authorities' activities. The establishment of privileged inter-city relations with municipalities in Portuguese-speaking countries (PSC) is part of the Town Hall's strategy. In this context, among the existing nine twin partners of Oeiras, seven belong to PSC (in Cape Verde, São Tomé, Angola, and Brazil), and co-operation is quite intense. Such links clearly privilege cities in Portuguese-speaking African countries, especially those led by political parties having similar liberal references. One of the associations found in Oeiras – Espaço da Comunidade Caboverdiana-Concelho de Oeiras (ECC-CO) – is directly supported by the Capeverdian government.

Table 8.4 **Associations in Oeiras: total and with immigrant and ethnic participation (1998)**

Places/parishes	Total	Having heavy immigrant and ethnic minorities participation
Outurela/Portela	8	5 (Outurela/Portela Residents' Association; Espaço da Communidade Caboverdiana – Concelho de Oeiras (ECC-CO); União dos Estudiantes Caboverdianos de Lisboa; União Desportiva de Barronhos (nearly inactive))
Carnaxide	7	0
Linda-a-Velha	16	6 (Associação Cultural e Desportiva da Pedreira dos Húngaros; Cabojovem; Associação Fúnebre da Pedreira dos Húngaros; Associação Juvenil Luso-Africana; Associação de Moradores Bento Gonçalves; Comissão para um Realojamento Condigno*)
Algés	13	3 (Associação dos Amigos da Mulher Angolana; Associação dos Naturais e Amigos do Bié e Anabié; Grupo Cultural Cristo Rei – Centro Social e Paoquial)
Linda-a-Pastora	3	0
Dafundo	3	0
Cruz Quebrada	3	1 (Associação de Solidariedade Social Assomada)
Oeiras	15	0
Paço de Arcos	11	0
Porto Salvo	13	0
Barcarena	8	0
Valejas	1	0
Talaíde	1	0
Oeiras	102	15

* Pressure group composed by local associations leaders (from a shanty town known as Pedreira dos Húngaros)

Source: Embassy of Cape Verde; High Commissioner for Immigration and Ethnic Minorities; Oeiras Town Hall.

The URBAN Programme

Along with the re-housing programme, since 1995 there has been an important ongoing initiative that targets the same populations in a specific area: the Oeiras URBAN programme, undertaken by the Town Hall as part of the European URBAN programme. Its aims are both physical rehabilitation of degraded urban areas and social inclusion of excluded populations, i.e. those placed in the public housing projects. Thus, while immigrant or ethnic minorities are not its main concern, their presence has to be acknowledged as one of the major social features of the populations being dealt with. This is clearly reflected in the guidelines for Oeiras's URBAN programme, which include such activities as creating and fostering local organisations that promote intercultural friendship, or support for multicultural approaches in schools. In fact, the programme's core philosophy is the idea of partnership between the public institutions and local actors representing communities' interests.

In order to characterise these partnerships, a distinction must be made between local and extra-local initiatives, and whether or not they have a link to the local community. Cross-tabulating these two attributes, we get three types (see Figure 8.1).

For example, when trying to obtain municipal local facilities for their head office, the Outurela-Portela Residents' Association argued that they were a local initiative, by people living in the neighbourhood, whereas other organisations had been granted such facilities although their members came from 'outside'. This was the case for ECC-CO, an association of Capeverdian nationals, which was granted municipal local facilities under the URBAN programme. Because it was organised by middle class professionals and other well-educated people, municipal officials expected it to promote initiatives maintaining and diffusing Capeverdian culture. This illustrates one of the possible top-down strategies for fostering local interlocutors that may function as channels into the larger immigrant community and a possible representative interlocutor. Most of the local interviewees who had heard of it, however, considered ECC-CO to be an outsider's association with few links to the community. Assuming the facilities were granted to all local Capeverdians, they complained that ECC-CO leaders acted as if it was their exclusive turf, paying no attention to local inhabitants. Town Hall officials echoed the locals' disillusion, acknowledging the inability so far evidenced to articulate with local community.

Figure 8.1   **Local associations in URBAN programme (1998)**

	Associations built up by local inhabitants	*Associations coming from 'outside'*
Embedded in local community activities	*Type 1* Outurela/Portela Residents' Association; 18th May Residents' Association; Aliança Operária Futebol Club da Outurela; Soc. Musical Simpatia e Gratidão	*Type 2* Associação Portuguesa para a Defesa dos Menores e da Família; Apoio; Ludoteca; Clube de Jovens (includes Associação Olho Vivo* and Marco Aurélio football school)
Having few or no links with local community		*Type 3* Cl. Desp. Veteranas de Angola; Espaço da Comunidade Caboverdiana (ECC-CO); União dos Estudantes Caboverdianos; Ajuda Internacional; UNIAP; Narcóticos Anónimos

* An antiracist organisation

In contrast, another initiative generated from above, but with a rather different scope, was remarkably successful. Marco Aurélio, a renowned Brazilian footballer who played in Portugal, was granted the use of local facilities to create a football school for youngsters. URBAN programme support of this activity is anchored in the same logic: creating opportunities for African-descent and Portuguese-majority youths to interact and to experience diversity in an integrative way. The Football School, contrary to the case of ECC-CO, is considered by the URBAN team as a success, and by local community as a type 2 institution. This kind of association, however, successful as it may be in promoting sociability among different parts of the community, can hardly be expected to lead to local representation, or to organised participation by migrant groups or ethnic-cultural minorities.

In fact, although a general philosophy of organised participation by local populations, including a multicultural dimension, may contrast the URBAN approach to that of the Town Hall, its implementation seems to be hindered by the population's lack of orientation to associative participation, as well as by the weakness of such direct participation traditions in Portugal's society and politics.

Furthermore, it may be noted that type 1 organisations do not have ethnic or cultural minority groups' participation and representation functions. Most of them were in fact generated by the local community long before immigrant presence began to be felt. The only exception is the Outurela-Portela Residents' Association, created as a direct outcome of the re-housing process, a topic we shall address below. Type 2 organisations, whose creation or local presence derives directly from URBAN activities, have an important local role. Their relation to multiculturalism, however, as defined by the URBAN sources, has more to do with social mixing and friendly relations between cultures than with a specific mode of civic incorporation. Furthermore, they are experiencing difficulties in establishing self-sustained leadership – people do take part in the activities, but hardly in their organisational and leadership tasks, the very ones that might be more conducive to sustained civic participation. All organisations with foreign national references that we find in the location fit into type 3, even those that benefited from URBAN support: not only were they 'imported', but they have few links with local immigrant or immigrant-descent populations and are in fact rather estranged by them.

Mobilisation Processes and Changes in the Political Opportunity Structure

The top-down partnership model informing the URBAN project thus has some part in activating local associations, but with little success in the realm of self-organisation and interest representation by local minority groups. In contrast, the re-housing process brought about consequences with possible far-reaching effects – especially as they combined with the local impact of processes induced by the national-level policies we have briefly outlined above.

Changes in the spatial pattern of settlement after re-housing had a major effect on the associations. Because of the policy adopted by the Town Hall, the local associations born in the shanty towns saw their former constituencies spread throughout the municipal territory. Together with the funding requirements, this introduced an organisational challenge that only a few were able to meet, outgrowing their local origins and their dependence on neighbourhood relations and moving up to a municipal level of action.

At present, there are two of the former shanty town neighbourhood immigrant and ethnic minority associations that remain particularly active in this expanded sphere of intervention: Assomada Solidarity Association and Pedreira dos Húngaros Culture and Sports Association. Both began as neighbourhood sports and culture groups in two different shanty towns (Alto de Sta. Catarina and Pedreira dos Húngaros). They catered mostly to Capeverdians, and are now being relocated in municipal facilities in the new re-housing neighbourhoods. Together with ECC-CO, (a national Cape-verdian association with headquarters in Oeiras granted under the URBAN programme, and with more explicit political concerns but enjoying far less support from the local community), they are the most prominent associations now competing for the 'pole position'. Competition to rally collective representation is growing, resorting to the capacity of influencing local authorities or even achieving the support of political actors in their countries of origin. Although some evidence points to incipient attempts of collaboration between some of them, the uneven capacity of securing and combining different kinds of resources (such as political support in their homeland and in Portugal, and local mobilisation of populations) makes it hard to anticipate the outcome.

The re-housing process proved effective in strengthening associative dynamics in yet another way. As a massive welfare investment with tangible results for people formerly excluded from formal housing, it was expected that it would enhance trust in political institutions, among immigrants as well as among the impoverished Portuguese covered by the programme. To a certain extent this happened, especially if the results were compared to situations in nearby municipalities where re-housing either lagged behind or had not even begun; but the effects were ambiguous and more complex than anticipated by the Town Hall. Survey data show that there is trust in the ability of public institutions to generate better life opportunities, and a fair degree of residential satisfaction among re-housed people with all but one of the dimensions we inquired about: the costs of new housing.[21] This dissatisfaction, however, is crucial, as it relates to the distrust about equity in the actions of the political institutions.[22] In fact, it triggered the most significant mobilisation process up to date, the 1995 protest against rent increases planned by the Town Hall. The old residents' associations, mainly of Portuguese working class and close to left-wing parties, and the new ones, established specifically to address this issue, were hand in hand opposing the City Hall.

One important aspect underlying this protest is that local government was not just a welfare provider, it also became a landlord towards whom dissatisfaction with neighbourhood life and housing conditions could be voiced. Political decisions had to be taken concerning social equity in renting arrangements in relation to household income and size. This meant that the beneficiaries were raised from being 'poor dependants' to being responsible contributors to housing costs, in line with their assessable income, and based on needs defined individually rather than collectively. There were immediate complaints about unfairness in income assessment and about what was perceived as 'taking back with one hand what was given with the other'. Furthermore, the later re-housing operations coincided with a decision to update older municipal leases, which had been kept at low values for a long time, and to make them dependent on household income at the same time. This caused a convergence of interests between the older working-class neighbourhoods, that were more organised and politically closer to left-wing opposition against the city government, and the more recent one who took advantage of the former's organisational experience. During 1995, rivalries between the more-established Portuguese working class and newly re-housed residents, including immigrants, were momentarily put aside and collective protest broke out. The new residents' association bring together a high proportion of immigrants and ethnic minorities, both in rank-and-file and in leadership positions. In this process, a new leadership emerged from immigrant grassroots, and a whole new experience in political mobilisation and negotiation through representatives left its mark. It should also be noted that this is a two-way process, as the Town Hall, despite its formal refusal to deal with group representatives, nonetheless uses these associations' leaders as intermediaries to reach the immigrants and ethnic minorities populations when needed.

The other significant instances of mobilisation to date are related to the policy developments at the national level mentioned in the first section. The most significant developments were the extraordinary regularisation processes for undocumented immigrants in 1992-1993 and 1996, and the registration campaign for immigrant voters for local elections, under the 1996 law. Unlike the other mobilisation efforts discussed so far, these were specifically addressed to immigrants. Although top-down initiatives were taken (by central and local level authorities, the embassies, national associations, and the Catholic Church), local co-ordination was secured by local groups. This gave the local government and the immigrants' associations a greater awareness of these associations' important role as campaigners and information brokers, and their possible importance as political partners. In the second regularisation process, local associations formally collaborated with state institutions in promoting legalisation, informing applicants and helping to file requests. The more explicitly political process of campaigning for enrolment and for voting in the 1997 elections brought some associations' leaders (both the older sports and culture clubs and the more recent residents' associations) into formal participation with local government officials and political parties' representatives.

The granting of electoral rights proved to have a very important effect in restructuring political opportunities for participation. All competing parties included people linked to local immigrants' associations, trying to capture a share of this new contingent of voters. One association leader of Capeverdian origin was elected to Municipal Assembly for the Socialist Party, and three others were elected as PSD candidates to the Parish Board (the president of a re-housing neighbourhood residents' association, the president of the Pedreira dos Húngaros Sports Association, and the vice-president of Assomada[23]). Thus, even though no formal minority representation bodies have been institutionalised, community leaders were elected into mainstream politics who are regarded as representatives of this segment of the municipal population and were co-opted in that capacity.

Further developments along these lines are hindered, however, by a weak overall level of formal participation by immigrants, either in the associations or in political actions. Besides the specific (albeit important) situations outlined above, bottom-up mobilisation is generally low. Although access to specific electoral data has not been authorised by the relevant institutions, voting turnout seems to have been low among immigrants. How does this relate to attitudes towards political participation? In the survey we mentioned above, involving both majority-descent underclass and lower classes and ethnic minorities, we tried to assess whether there are significant differences related to ethnic belonging or immigrant status, or whether the recorded differences could be explained by contextual and structural factors.

As Sayad (1999) suggests, one often expects immigrants to be some sort of 'model citizens'. Soysal (1994) shows that they tend to reproduce the dominant patterns of the host society. Political and civic participation is generally very modest in Portuguese society. This pervasive withdrawal from the public sphere ends up making public intervention 'almost always necessary for everything' (Lucena, 1982, p. 909; see also Cabral, 1995; Cruz, 1995; França, 1993; Santos, 1994). This is the matrix that moulds the opportunity structure for participation both for immigrants and nationals.

Following Hirschman's (1970) typology, we asked whether municipal authorities could be influenced (if not, *exit*), should be controlled (*voice*), or should be trusted and left alone to perform their tasks (*loyalty*). The research results show that ethnic minorities do indeed express more inclination to make claims and are more critical of municipal power (Marques et al., forth.). When asked whether the best way to solve problems was individually or collectively, minority ethnic belonging again makes a difference: ethnic minorities tend to prefer collective solutions, while ethnic majority respondents' answers reveal a much more balanced position between the two poles. Since ethnic minorities widely overlap with immigrant communities, the experience of poverty may be perceived as one momentary step in a ladder leading to upper layers of opportunity. The potential for collective participation seems therefore to exist among immigrants, and more so than among their Portuguese counterparts of comparable status (see also Justino et al., 1998).

This attitude is not, however, fully translated into effective civic mobilisation. According to the same survey, membership in voluntary associations can vary widely; however, non-participation is paramount. In the 'crumbled' framework of voluntary associations to which these people belonged, those promoting segmented local activities (humanitarian, sports, culture) override organisations aiming to mobilise and represent the communities at top levels of political decision (political parties, regional and national associations, residents committees). The results also suggest wider differences among municipal neighbourhoods, rather than a clear differentiation between the answers of ethnic minorities' and ethnic majority's respondents. So, contextual factors such as the neighbourhood, the degree of penetration of the associations in neighbourhood life, or the way residents' protest was conducted back in 1995 seem to be indeed powerful in explaining how the prevailing institutional matrix affects both national majority's and ethnic minorities' participation. On the other hand, interview data show that formal politics is not generally trusted. It is thought of as a non-issue or even a motive of estrangement by local communities' members. In contrast with the 'collective voice' outlook that still resonates with the echoes of the 1995 protest, this disaffection towards formal political institutions may prove to be the major obstacle to taking full advantage of the new set of political opportunities that has recently emerged.

Conclusion

We begin this conclusion by recalling Soysal's (1994) idea that immigrants tend to accommodate their citizenship practices to the institutional matrix offered to them by the host society. In this respect, what they find in Portugal, and Oeiras is no exception, is a weakly structured civil society with low levels of participation, without an organised tradition of formal group interest representation in the public and political sphere. On the other hand, they also find a weak welfare state, with comparatively few resources to redistribute and offering little incentive to make them feel they have a stake in the political process.[24] In the municipal arena, the position adopted by Oeiras local government not to acknowledge any intermediate form of collective interest representation, and the support policy targeted at specific initiatives of a mainly cultural nature, has encouraged a fragmented associative structure, working at neighbourhood level and based on very informal face-to-face dynamics.

These are perhaps the main reasons why the partnership-oriented assumptions of the EU URBAN programme, which included local civil society actors capable of collective interest representation, met with so little success in Oeiras – much as the programme has achieved in many other aspects of local development. Those assumptions tried to impose a framework based on a kind of participatory democracy where there was simply no ground for it to take root.

However, the interplay between local and national level developments has had more profound effects in reshaping opportunities for local political participation by immigrants.

On the one hand, major welfare policies addressing the re-housing of shanty town dwellers, (many of whom had immigrant origins), made clear that there was a stake for collective participation. Longstanding demands on housing have been satisfied in the process, but in keeping with Maslow's (1963) hierarchical scheme of need-satisfaction, their very satisfaction opened the way to frustration of emergent needs at higher levels. As the basic needs of housing conditions and residential security were partially met, new ones arose around concerns about fairness, equity, and self esteem, all aspects of quality of life. It is around these new needs that unprecedented protest mobilisation occurred in 1995, planting the seed for minorities' participation in organised action. It seems that a cumulative process is operating, where claiming social rights follows the enhanced civic awareness, which in turn results from the self-awareness as stakeholders of social and economic rights (Castles and Davidson, 2000; Marshall,

1992). The re-housing process had another indirect effect on the structure of the local associative field, because of the spatial redistribution of the pre-existing neighbourhood associations. The selection process has caused a hecatomb among small local associations, but has considerably strengthened the 'survivors', who are now facing an entirely new phase of striving to achieve interests monopolisation and therefore the recognition as legitimate interlocutors both by local authorities and the population (Schmitter, 1984).

Processes at higher scales intertwined with these local ones in shaping the new opportunity structures. The protests against the 1992-1993 regularisation process brought national immigrants' associations and related pressure groups into the arena of political struggle, along with the full emergence of an 'immigrant social problem' in collective awareness (Oliveira, 2000). The political realignment since the Socialist Party's election in 1995 also contributed to added weight of associations. The satisfaction of their claim for greater participation in the extraordinary regularisation process, via the collaboration of immigrants' associations, set the stage for the mobilisation and mediation capacities of the local associations and their leaders to become apparent both to themselves and to local government. The same may be said of the 1997 campaign for local electoral enrolment and voting.

In Oeiras, rather than formalised corporate bodies or partnerships, the institutional framework for the emerging forms of interest articulation was provided by the direct co-optation of associations' leaders into mainstream local politics, creating the opportunity for some of them to be elected locally. The fact that this move was performed by the political party in office as well as by its political opponents shows that, while collective intermediate bodies are still rejected in principle, collective immigrant references can carry weight in voting turnouts, and must therefore have some share of the political space. The 1996 law conferring voting rights on immigrants in local elections makes this possible. But its effects in local politics were decisively shaped by pre-existing local conditions and processes, both in the form and in the content of political participation. Local welfare policies and the social movements they generated, with their blend of trust in local government for the accomplishment of the re-housing process and distrust as to the equity of its conditions, seems to have been strategic in fuelling this embryonic political inclusion (Castles and Davidson, 2000; Marshall, 1992).

These gains, however, are as yet fragile. Elites of immigrant origin are becoming aware of the ways local (and national) politics work, and learning the ropes to achieve effective participation. But some degree of disillusion is unavoidable. Elected politicians complain of the minimal political weight their new positions carry in the complex world of local administration. And this participation still involves limited parts of the immigrant population. Formal associative affiliation is small-scale and fragmented, youths' disaffection is great and mistrust of politics and politicians widespread. Voting turnouts in 1997 were comparatively low among immigrants, and unless the new leaders can secure a stable constituency of immigrant vote, their newly-gained political participation may well erode in the near future.

Notes

1   The research on which this chapter is based was funded by PRAXIS XXI [projects CSH/840/95 and SOC/12104/98], and by Oeiras Town Hall [project *Renovação Urbana*]. We acknowledge Tiago Ralha, Ana Rita Cordeiro, António Sá and Alexandra Vasconcelos for their collaboration in data collection. A special note of appreciation is owed to David Justino, former Oeiras alderman for housing, who gave us full support for data gathering and all sorts of institutional contacts; his suggestions and comments during the frequent informal contacts we had with him were also much appreciated.

2   A national press content analysis showed the infrequent use, until very recently, of the term 'immigrant' (frequently confused with emigrant), and the common use of terms such as African and Capeverdian as synonyms (Guibentif, 1991).

3   According to the former CITP (Classification Internationale Type des Professions – 1968) classification scheme, used by SEF (Borders and Foreigners Service) until 1998.

4   Among whom are counted many Asian Indians, either self-employed in commerce or working as clerks (Ávila and Alves, 1993; Bastos, 1990; Malheiros, 1996).

5   Portuguese administrative territorial organisation defines three geographical unit levels: the *Freguesia* (parish), the smallest jurisdiction, with limited autonomy; the *Concelho*, corresponding to the municipal area; and the *Distrito*, under the rule of a central government representative. Only the governing bodies of the first two (*Junta de Freguesia* [Parish Board], *Assembleia de Freguesia* [Parish Assembly], *Câmara Municipal* [Town Hall] and *Assembleia Municipal* [Municipal Assembly]) are elected locally.
The percentage in the text is an underestimate. The administrative definition of the LMA (the whole *distritos* of Lisbon and Setúbal) is taken here in its broadest sense, for the source presents data at *distrito* level, thus encompassing municipalities that by the more precise definition should be excluded, and where immigrant presence is so far scarce. The population of immigrant origin is further underestimated because statistics only acknowledge the holders of residence permits and nationality, leaving out all those having acquired Portuguese citizenship, as well as many temporary visa holders.

6   83.2 per cent of whom are from Portuguese Speaking Countries (PSC).

7   Corresponding data for foreigners living in Oeiras are not available – census data will not be used because they are outdated and very unreliable (Cordeiro, 1997).

8   On PSAC immigrants, see Cachada et al., 1995; França, 1992; Honório, Evaristo et al., 1999; Machado, 1991, 1998; Pires, 1993; Saint-Maurice, 1997.

9   See further analysis of public opinion in Vala et al. (1999), about new forms of racism towards Blacks; and Marques (1999) relating it with distrust toward the opportunity structures. See also the press analyses by Cunha et al. (1996) and Guibentif (1991), and the thorough collection of national polls by Baganha (1996).

10   For example, an agreement on free healthcare for these foreigners was settled between a NGO (SANITAE), and Lisbon Regional Health Administration, in August 1998 (*Público*, August 27 1998).

11   We shall refer only to major developments before 2000, when an important change in the law regulating the presence of foreigners occurred.

12   To be sure, she is of Capeverdian origin, and a member of the Capeverdian Association. The MP she replaced is of Guinean origin, and a member of the Guinean Association.

13   Data on voting adapted from Marques et al. (1999).

14   For instance, the Forum of the Capeverdian Diaspora Associative Movement (March 1998, in Lisbon) devoted one of its panels to discuss this topic (Correia, 1998).

15   Correia, *ibidem*.

16   It should be kept in mind that the suburban growth pattern in Southern European countries differs from the Central and Northern European one.

17   Hence their current Portuguese designation, *bairros de lata*, literally 'tin foil quarters'.

18   Figures provided by Oeiras Town Hall. The number refers to households headed by a foreign citizen. This is a conservative estimate of ethnic minorities, since we found mixed households headed by Portuguese citizens, and immigrants or their descendants having acquired Portuguese nationality are not counted. A tentative census by a religious organisation (Centro de Estudos Padre Alves Correia) in 1994/1995 counted 11,124 individuals of African origin, irrespective of nationality, living in Oeiras shanty towns and public re-housing projects (Cachada et al., 1995).

19   Buying their new houses, however, is only an option for those few families with enough income to afford a bank loan. In some municipal neighbourhoods, a share of the new flats was reserved for sale to buyers not coming from shantytowns.

20   Which also occurs with Portuguese voluntary associations (Bacalhau, 1994; Cabral, 2000; França, 1993).

21   Surveys were performed in 1996, 1997 and 1998 in seven re-housing neighbourhoods with significant presence of immigrants, covering a total of 724 cases (Marques et al., forth.).

22   This aspect is more thoroughly discussed in Marques and Santos (forth.).

23   The latter, however, is not of immigrant origin, although he has a leading role in what might be locally considered as an immigrants' association.

24   As Castles puts it, social rights satisfaction may lead to political participation (Castles and Davidson, 2000, p. 105), thus reversing the steps in Marshall's model (1992).

References

Ávila, P. and Alves, M. (1993), 'Da Índia a Portugal: Trajectórias Sociais e Estratégias Colectivas dos Comerciantes Indianos', *Sociologia: Problemas e Práticas*, vol. 13, pp. 115-33.

Bacalhau, M. (1994), *Atitudes, Opiniões e Comportamentos Políticos dos Portugueses: 1973-1993*, Ed. Mário Bacalhau & T. Bruneau, Lisbon.

Baganha, M.I. (1996), *Immigrants Insertion in the Informal Market, Deviant Behaviour and the Insertion in the Receiving Country*, Centro de Estudos Sociais, mimeo report, Coimbra.

Baganha, M.I. (1998), 'Immigrant Involvement in the Informal Economy: The Portuguese Case', *Journal of Ethnic and Migration Studies*, vol. 24, pp. 367-85.

Baganha, M.I., Marques, J.C. and Fonseca, G. (2000), *Is an Ethclass Emerging in Europe? The Portuguese Case*, FLAD, Lisbon.

Baganha, M.I. and Peixoto, J. (1997), 'Trends in the 1990s: The Portuguese Migratory Experience', in M.I. Baganha (ed.), *Immigration in Southern Europe*, Celta, Oeiras, pp. 15-40.

Bastos, J.G. Pereira and Bastos, S.P. (1999), *Portugal Multicultural: Situação e Estratégias Identitárias das Minorias Étnicas*, Fim de Século, Lisbon.

Bastos, S. Pereira (1990), 'Espaço Doméstico, Espaço Simbólico e Identidade: Um Olhar Indiano Sobre o Viver Indiano na Cidade de Lisboa', in *Actas do Colóquio Viver (n)a Cidade*, GES-LNEC/CET-ISCTE, Lisboa.

Cabral, M. Villaverde (1995), 'Equidade, Estado Providência e Sistema Fiscal: Atitudes e Percepções da População Portuguesa', *Sociologia. Problemas e Práticas*, vol. 17, pp. 9-34.

Cabral, M. Villaverde (2000), 'Exercício da Cidadania Política em Portugal', in M.V. Cabral, J. Vala and J. Freire (eds), *Trabalho e Cidadania*, ICS-ISSP, Lisbon, pp. 123-63.

Cachada, F. et al. (1995), *Os Números da Imigração Africana*, Cadernos CEPAC (2), Lisbon.

Castles, S. and Davidson, A. (2000), *Citizenship and Migration: Globalization and the Politics of Belonging*, Macmillan, London.

CMO (1997), *Dez Anos de Habitação*, Town Hall, Oeiras.

Cordeiro, A.R. (1997), *Immigrants in Portuguese Society: Some Sociographic Figures*, SociNova Working Papers (4), FCSH-UNL, Lisbon.

Correia, C. (1998), 'A Orgânica das Instituições Associativas: Formas Superiores de Organização', Paper presented at the Forum do Movimento Associativo Caboverdiano na Diáspora, Lisbon, 11 pp.

Cruz, M. Braga da (1995), 'Processos Sociais e Políticos em Portugal', in *Instituições Políticas e Processos Sociais*, Bertrand, Lisbon, pp. 299-503.

Cunha, I.F., Queiroz, J., Ribeiro, P., Figueiras, R. and Policarpo, V. (1996), *Os Africanos na Imprensa Portuguesa: 1993-1995*, CIDAC, Lisbon.

Esping-Andersen, G. (1993), 'Orçamentos e Democracia: O Estado-providência em Espanha e Portugal, 1960-1986', *Análise Social*, vol. 28, pp. 589-606.

Fernandes, A. (1997), *A Geografia de Oeiras: Atlas Municipal*, Town Hall, Oeiras.

Fonseca, M.L. (1997), *The Geography of Recent Immigration to Portugal*, Centro de Estudos Geográficos, Universidade de Lisboa, Lisbon.

França, L. (ed.) (1992), *A Comunidade Caboverdeana em Portugal*, IED, Lisbon.

França, L. (ed.) (1993), *Portugal. Valores Europeus e Identidade Cultural*, IED, Lisbon.

Guibentif, P. (1991), 'A Opinião Pública Face aos Estrangeiros' in M.C. Esteves (ed.), *Portugal, País de Imigração*, IED, Lisbon, pp. 63-74.

Guibentif, P. (1996), 'Le Portugal Face à l'Immigration', *Revue Européenne des Migrations Internationales*, vol. 12, pp. 121-40.

Hirschman, A. (1970), *Exit, Voice and Loyalty*, Harvard University Press, Cambridge.

Honório, F. and Evaristo, T. (eds) (1999), *Estudo de Caracterização da Comunidade Caboverdiana residente em Portugal*, Cape Verde Embassy in Portugal, Lisbon.

Justino, D. et al. (1998), 'Children of Immigrants: A Situation in Flux Between Tension and Integration', in *Metropolis International Workshop. Proceedings*, FLAD, Lisbon, pp. 273-304.

Lucena, M. (1982), 'Transformação do Estado Português nas suas Relações com a Sociedade Civil', *Análise Social*, vol. 18/72-73-74, pp. 897-926.

Lucena, M. (1985), 'Neocorporativismo? Conceito, Interesses e Aplicação ao Caso Português', *Análise Social*, vol. 21/87-88-89, pp. 819-65.

Machado, F.L. (1991), *Etnicidade em Portugal: Aproximação ao Caso Guineense*, ISCTE, mimeo report, Lisbon.

Machado, F.L. (1992), 'Etnicidade em Portugal: Contrastes e Politização', *Sociologia: Problemas e Práticas*, vol. 12, pp. 123-36.

Machado, F.L. (1993), 'Etnicidade em Portugal: O Grau Zero da Politização', in M.B.N. Silva et al. (eds), *Emigração/Imigração em Portugal*, Fragmentos, Lisbon, pp. 407-14.

Machado, F.L. (1994), 'Luso-Africanos em Portugal: Nas Margens da Etnicidade', *Sociologia: Problemas e Práticas*, vol. 16, pp. 111-34.

Machado, F.L. (1996), 'Minorias e Literacia: Imigrantes Guineenses em Portugal', in A. Benavente (dir.), *A Literacia em Portugal*, Fundação Calouste Gulbenkian & Conselho Nacional de Educação, Lisbon.

Machado, F.L. (1997), 'Contornos e Especificidades da Imigração em Portugal', *Sociologia: Problemas e Práticas*, vol. 27, pp. 9-44.

Machado, F.L. (1998), 'Da Guiné-Bissau a Portugal: Luso-guineenses e Imigrantes', *Sociologia: Problemas e Práticas*, vol. 26, pp. 9-56.

Malheiros, J.M. (1996), *Imigrantes na Região de Lisboa: Os Anos da Mudança*, Colibri, Lisbon.

Marques, M.M. (1999), 'Attitudes and Threat Perception: Unemployment and Immigration in Portugal', *South European Society and Politics*, vol. 4, pp. 184-205.

Marques, M.M., Ralha, T., Oliveira, C. and Justino, D. (1999), 'Between the "Lusophone Community" and European Integration Where do Immigrants Fit In? Immigration and Citizenship in Portugal', unpublished paper presented at the Carnegie Endowment for International Peace conference on *Citizenship: Comparison and Perspectives*, FLAD, Lisbon.

Marques, M.M. and Santos, R. (forthcoming), 'Welfare and Immigrants' Inclusion in a Context of Weak Civil Society: Associations and local politics in Oeiras', submitted to *South European Society and Politics*.

Marques, M.M., Santos, R., Ralha, T. and Cordeiro, R. (1998), *Oeiras City Template*, Multicultural Policies and Modes of Citizenship < http://www.unesco.org/most/p97oeira.doc > .

Marques, M.M., Santos, R., Nóbrega, S. and Araújo, F. (forthcoming), *Renovação Urbana no Concelho de Oeiras: Uma Avaliação Sociológica*, (provisory title), Town Hall & Celta, Oeiras.

Marshall, T.H. (1992) [1950], 'Citizenship and Social Class', in T.H. Marshall and T. Bottomore, *Citizenship and Social Class*, part I, Pluto Press, London, pp. 3-51.

Maslow, A. (1963), *Motivación y Personalidad*, Sagitario, Barcelona.

Morais, I.A., Duarte, G., Vieira, B. and Madruga, M. (1997), *Caracterização do Programa Especial de Realojamento na Área Metropolitana de Lisboa*, AML, Lisbon.

Mouzelis, N. (1995): 'Modernity, Late Development And Civil Society' in J. Hall (ed.): *Civil society: Theory, history, comparison*, Polity Press, Cambridge, pp. 224-49.

Oliveira, N. (2000), *O discurso político sobre as minorias imigrantes: a construção de uma 'questão'*, SociNova Working Papers (16), FCSH-UNL, Lisbon.

Penninx, R. (2000), *Participation of Immigrants Through Their Organizations: Political Visions on Multiculturalisms and their Implications*, SociNova Working Papers (14), FCSH-UNL, Lisbon.

Pires, R. Pena (1990), 'Semi-Periferia versus Polarização? Os Equívocos do Modelo Trimodal', *Sociologia: Problemas e Práticas*, vol. 8, pp. 81-90.

Pires, R. Pena (1993), 'Immigration in Portugal: A Typology', in M.B. Rocha-Trindade (ed.), *Recent Migration Trends in Europe*, Universidade Aberta, Lisbon, pp. 179-94.

Pires, R. Pena et al. (1987), *Os Retornados: Um estudo Sociográfico*, IED, Lisbon.

Portes, A. (1994), 'The Informal Economy and its Paradoxes', in N. Smelser and R. Swedberg (eds), *The Handbook of Economic Sociology*, Princeton University Press, Princeton, pp. 426-49.

Santos, B. de Sousa (1994), *Pela Mão de Alice: O Social e o Político na Pós-Modernidade*, Afrontamento, Porto.

Saint-Maurice, A. de (1997), *Identidades Reconstruídas: Caboverdianos em Portugal*, Celta, Oeiras.

Sayad, A. (1999), *La double absence*, Ed. du Seuil. Col. Liber, Paris.

Schmitter, P.C. (1984), *Neo-Corporatism and the State*, EUI Working Paper (106), European University Institute, Florence.

SEF (1998), *Relatório Estatístico Anual*, < http://www.sef.pt./Relatorios/relat_estatistico_-anual_1998.htm >

Silva, M. et al. (1989), *Pobreza Urbana em Portugal*, Centro de reflexão Cristã, Lisbon.

SOPEMI (1995), *Trends in International Migration: Annual report 1994*, OECD, Paris.

SOPEMI (1998), *Trends in International Migration: Annual report*, OECD, Paris.

Soysal, Y. (1994), *Limits of Citizenship. Migrants and Postnational Membership in Europe*, University of Chicago Press, Chicago.

Vala, J., Brito, R. and Lopes, D. (1999), *Expressões dos Racismos em Portugal*, ICS, Lisboa.

9 Citizenship in a Local Key: A View from Paris

RIVA KASTORYANO AND JOHN CROWLEY

Introduction

The idea of citizenship in a local key is perfectly intelligible, as one of us argues in more depth in the Afterword. However, whether there actually is a local political space is an empirical issue. Nothing in the structure of 'community' issues necessarily relates them to territorially circumscribed politics. In the light of this theoretical framework, what is interesting about the French case is precisely the difficulty of pinning down locality or territoriality for political purposes. The reason is not primarily France's statist, centralist, Jacobean or *républicain* political culture or tradition. This undoubtedly exists and remains powerful (Crowley, 2000a). However, there have been major changes in the past fifteen years. Furthermore, a range of 'urban' issues has produced new forms of mobilisation and identity. What makes it unreasonable to talk of *local* citizenship, or even of citizenship in a distinctively local key, is therefore not the hegemony of the national level, but rather the complexity of the intertwined and cross-cutting territorialities and localities that characterise contemporary France. The local arena is simply one of those within which citizenship is played out.

We start here by describing the area – a small section of the northwest suburbs of Paris – chosen as an empirical reference. The second section will first summarise the legal and administrative context, with particular emphasis on developments since the major decentralisation reforms of 1982, then analyse briefly the political-ideological context of French debates over this period, which has been characterised by complex interactions between a primarily national discursive framework and strongly territorialised policy implementation and mobilisation. The third section will offer some evidence about the local politics of citizenship in the chosen suburbs and set it in the broader context. The empirical conclusion, which is in line with most other French studies, is that attempts to revitalise citizenship at the local level – or to promote specifically local citizenship, which may or may not be the same thing – have on the whole been

173

unsuccessful in their own terms. That is not the end of the story, however, because the terms themselves must be criticised. The fourth and final section takes a more general perspective on citizenship as it relates to the issues of multiculturalism and draws some conclusions from the development of the French multicultural agenda. In many ways, this is more apparent at the national level of ideological discourse than at the local level of political practice (in itself an interesting reversal) and, far from contradicting traditional French assimilationism, is in many ways an aspect of it. It is often assumed that more subtle and differentiated perspectives on citizenship are necessarily linked to group-based identity politics. France offers an important illustration of a rather different configuration.

The Changing 'Red Belt' of Paris

The Île-de-France Region is the richest and most populous part of France. It includes the city of Paris and the surrounding departments, extending considerably beyond the Greater Paris Area to rural municipalities in the Departments of Seine-et-Marne and Essonne in particular. Even within the long-urbanised core of the Region, social-economic circumstances are highly diverse. As in most French cities the centre is comparatively privileged, although even within the city of Paris sharp distinctions exist between the exclusive residential areas in the centre, south and southwest, and the more mixed areas in the east and north. The suburbs show similar diversity and a similar polarity. At a more detailed level, patterns of inequality are highly complex: rankings of municipalities on the basis of, say, income, housing quality and unemployment are by no means homogeneous. In no sense, therefore, are *les banlieues* a uniform social space.

Migration has long been a major factor in the Region, and its patterns reflect the general complexity. Successive waves and high intra-regional mobility have combined to erase many traces of historical patterns of settlement. Nonetheless, they remain perceptible, and in addition some recent migratory movements have not yet substantially dispersed. Thus, while residential clustering is on the whole limited, some local concentrations are visible to even the most casual observer: for instance, in Paris, the 'Chinatown' in the portion of the 13th *Arrondissement* around Place d'Italie, the smaller one in Belleville, or the strong West African presence in the portion of the 18th *Arrondissement* extending from Barbès-Rochechouart to the Porte de Clignancourt; or, in the suburbs, the Portuguese presence in the northern suburbs of Aubervilliers, La Courneuve and Stains, the

Sephardic Jewish community in Sarcelles, or the Italian community in Nogent-sur-Marne to the east.

It is equally difficult to give a uniform *political* picture of this socially heterogeneous region. While the regional level of government has, since the decentralisation reforms of 1982, acquired political significance, and has a range of potentially controversial competences including infrastructure, development, and higher education, it is by no means the main focus of political activity. The older and better-established municipality and department retain greater symbolic significance and, especially in the area of urban policy (within which much of the 'multicultural' agenda is in practice subsumed), have greater administrative competences. Furthermore, even an area the size of a municipality is politically and socially heterogeneous: the scale of 'the local' is a question that cannot be addressed without detailed empirical analysis. From the first direct regional elections in 1986 until 1998, the regional council of Île-de-France had a right-wing majority; since the elections of 1998, which saw countrywide losses for the mainstream right, the majority has shifted to the left.

In view of the general context, and in order to provide a better focus on local issues, the Paris study focuses on four contiguous munipalities in the northwestern part of the near suburban area – from east to west, Saint-Denis, Saint-Ouen and Épinay-sur-Seine (all in the Seine-Saint-Denis Department) and Clichy (in the Hauts-de Seine Department). Saint-Denis, Saint-Ouen and Clichy form a continuous block running from east to west along the boundary of the city of Paris. They are part of the traditional, but now fraying, *ceinture rouge* ('red belt') of Communist-run localities at the gates of the city.[1] Épinay is contiguous with Saint-Denis to the southeast, but does not touch Paris. In social-economic terms, the municipalities are comparatively poor in a comparatively rich region, as shown by a range of indicators such as taxable income per household, home ownership and composition of the labour force. In terms of housing quality and unemployment, the area is deprived compared not just to the Region, but to the country as a whole. In migratory terms, the municipalities all have a higher than average foreign population (around 25 per cent over the past two decades, compared to 13 per cent for the Region, and 6.5 per cent for France as a whole).[2] Because they were thoroughly urbanised well before the Second World War, they also show traces of a very diverse series of cycles, including in particular Spanish and Italian migration in the inter-war years and immediate post-war period, North African and Portuguese migration in the 1960s and 1970s, and migration from sub-Saharan Africa since the late 1970s.[3] Although the area is fairly homogeneous in broad outline, the municipalities also exhibit some interesting peculiarities and complexities. In order to illustrate them, Saint-Denis and Saint-Ouen will be profiled in rather more detail.

Saint-Denis (population 85,792 in 1999) is the second largest municipality in the Seine-Saint-Denis Department. While it remains a comparatively deprived urban area, it has been the beneficiary of substantial public investment in recent years. The most spectacular project was the new national stadium (Stade de France), built on a typical brownfield site (a former gasworks) and bringing with it substantial upgrading of transport infrastructure. The soccer World Cup of 1998, for which the Stade de France was specifically built, also caused an influx of investment in tourist-related activities. This built on and extended a phase of city-centre regeneration begun in the late 1970s. As a result, distinctions between neighbourhoods (*quartiers*) within the municipality have sharpened and, while the city continues to have a 'bad reputation', there are signs of 'yuppie' movement into some of the more desirable areas. Current property prices in Saint-Denis are roughly 40 per cent lower than in the contiguous district of Paris (the 18th *Arrondissement*) despite easy access both by public transport and by car. However, regeneration, while it has had a significant impact on the urban landscape, remains incomplete in social-economic terms. Unemployment remains significantly higher than the regional average, and skilled jobs created in Saint-Denis tend to be filled by commuters from outside. It will be of considerable interest to follow the impact on local employment of the major new office developments around the Stade de France: as is frequently the case in well-situated comparatively deprived areas, job creation may not produce jobs for local people.

What is most distinctive about Saint-Denis is the existence of a strong and deeply rooted political culture or tradition. Saint-Denis is not strictly a 'suburb' of Paris, but a separate and ancient city connected historically with the royal house of France, members of which were traditionally buried in the medieval basilica. Only at end of the nineteenth century did urbanisation of the northern parts of Paris and the industrial development of Saint-Denis itself make the two cities contiguous. Empirical studies suggest that historical depth is still a perceptible feature of *dionysien* identity, and the municipality has indeed invested significantly in the cultivation of local memory.

Furthermore, Saint-Denis has a strong and justifiable self-perception as the paradigmatically industrial city. Because of the logistical advantages of its geographical position, the city was structured, as early as the third quarter of the nineteenth century, around heavy industry. As a result it attracted considerable immigration, from other parts of the Greater Paris Area as well as from the provinces or abroad, producing a politically powerful residential and occupational working-class clustering. Powerful Socialist and, from the mid-1920s, Communist movements flourished in this social context. Especially in the post-war period, Saint-Denis developed as, in some respects, a Communist society – one, that is, structured around the Party. Recruitment of members was organised through a variety of satellite organisations, such as welcoming structures for the workers and youth groups, as well as through an active social policy directed at the population generally. As in other long-standing Communist municipalities, significant traces of these structures survive to this day. Saint-Denis is thus, in French political mythology, the archetypal 'red suburb' (Bacqué and Fol, 1997).

Over the past twenty years, however, Saint-Denis has been strongly affected by major structural changes. Social deprivation rather than industrial employment has come to summarise both the city and the Seine-Saint-Denis Department as a whole. During the 1960s, industrial plants relocated away from Paris and its suburbs. The metallurgical and chemical sectors, historically dominant in Saint-Denis, were among the sectors most prominent in this respect, and the new wave of tertiary employment only partly compensated for the job losses. In addition, shifting patterns of employment broke the strong local link between residence and work, and tended to harden redundancy into long-term unemployment. As a consequence, while manual workers still represent a large proportion of the labour force, Saint-Denis is no longer defined or structured by them.

For reasons that are linked in complex ways to these social shifts, municipal Communism is also in decline, not just electorally but also as a mechanism of social integration. In the late 1970s, the Communist Party was still by far the largest in the Department, where it held all nine parliamentary seats. But by 1981 it had lost 25 per cent of its votes, and by 1988 a further 50 per cent of its reduced total. The trend has stabilised over the past decade, but with no evidence of improvement. Even in the Seine-Saint-Denis – where, thanks to active social policies and a high degree of patronage, the Party has maintained a strong electoral base –, its position in terms of council and parliamentary seats depends crucially on Socialist support. This is the case in the city of Saint-Denis, where the Communist Party had enjoyed a hegemonic position from 1945 to 1978. Even the united left, however, which won 64.7 per cent of the vote in 1983, achieved only 54.5 per cent in 1989 and 46.2 per cent in 1995. In that year, for the first time since 1945, a second round of voting was necessary.

The votes lost by the Communists seem to have gone mainly to the Front National (FN), which, as early as 1983, won 9.3 per cent of the vote in municipal elections (well above its national average of 7.5 per cent at that time). Since 1992, the FN has won an average of 20 per cent to 25 per cent of the votes in Saint-Denis.

Saint-Ouen (population 39,646 in 1999) provides a contrast with its much larger neighbour in terms of a number of features that are of possible interest for the analysis of local political processes. It is, first of all, a comparatively wealthy municipality, not because its population is richer than in Saint-Denis but because of the unusually high business tax base. On the one hand, much more of Saint-Ouen's industry has survived than in Saint-Denis. Alongside historically important industries such as the automobile sector, there are, among other major sites, a large oil depot, an electricity-generating plant, and one of the largest waste incinerators in the north of Paris. On the other hand, 'brownfield' redevelopment started earlier than in Saint-Denis and has been successful in attracting tertiary employment. The prime area for such development, in the southwest, is indeed shared with neighbouring Clichy, which has benefited equally. Finally, and most unusually, Saint-Ouen benefits from the *puces* or flea market, a historic and listed area, in the south-west, that covers nearly 20 per cent of the municipality. Covering everything from junk to exclusive antiques, the market is a major tourist attraction, and a substantial source of income for the municipality. Property taxes in Saint-Ouen are approximately half the level in Saint-Denis.

Secondly, the town has been little affected by the housing developments of the past 30 years. Social housing has mainly taken the form of compulsory purchase of existing buildings, and there are only three high-rise developments, of limited extent. Residential infrastructure is therefore poor, but the physical structures of social inequality are rather different from most other areas of northern Paris. Saint-Ouen also has an unusually high level of individual houses and owner occupation – combined with low property prices (roughly the same as in Saint-Denis), this leads to substantial 'yuppification' pressure, which the municipality has sought to regulate using its compulsory-purchase powers. As a result, the town exhibits a fairly high level of social mixing on a micro-geographical level, more similar to the 18th *arrondissement* of Paris than to the northern suburbs generally (Clichy shares this feature), but also, like Saint-Denis, a sharp disjuncture between residence and employment. High unemployment co-exists with high levels of job availability and creation within the town.

Thirdly, because of the size of the town and the comparative wealth of the municipality, the web of Communist control, which has eroded in Saint-Denis, remains dense and powerful. Although the Communists are required to govern in coalition, the Party is still the channel for political and social expression: most voluntary-sector activity is closely co-ordinated by the authorities, and the level of patronage (particularly as far as municipal employment is concerned) is high. As a result, the authorities are very active in pre-empting local political initiatives. Neighbourhood committees, youth organisations, planning initiatives and so on are usually created, and on the whole successfully controlled, by the council. While there is, in one sense, a considerable degree of grass-roots democratic activity, Saint-Ouen has not, to date, exhibited the kind of genuinely autonomous mobilisation seen in Saint-Denis in the context of the Gérard Philippe Theatre or of the illegal residents collectives. The contrasting study of Saint-Ouen and Saint-Denis is therefore of particular interest in evaluating the significance of municipal initiatives (compared to 'bottom-up' mobilisation) for local politics.

The Institutional and Ideological Context: Jacobinism, Decentralisation, and the 'French Model'

The idea that there is a distinctive 'French model' of statehood and nationhood pervades French academic and political debate and is widely echoed in comparative analysis. This model – often labelled 'Jacobin' – supposedly defines both politics and nationhood exclusively by reference to the state, and therefore leaves space neither for multiculturalism nor for local forms of democracy. There is some historical truth in this picture, and it retains powerful ideological significance (Crowley, 2000a). As a current description, however, and particularly as a framework for explaining differences between France and her European neighbours with respect to multicultural policies and modes of citizenship, the 'French model' is woefully inadequate.

France, first of all, is not now a noticeably more centralised state than many of its European neighbours. Of course, even the Jacobin model leaves space for local politics. Any system with competitive local elections – which France has had continuously from the 1870s – could hardly do otherwise. Nonetheless, it was true that elected authorities at the communal (*conseil municipal*) and departmental (*conseil général*) level were administrative sub-divisions of the state rather than autonomous modes of political organisation, and their competence remained strictly circumscribed by the prerogatives of the *Préfet*, the territorial representative of the state. From the 1960s, however, the subordinate status of the local came to be regarded as both technically inefficient and ideologically questionable. As state activity expands, and as planning assumes precedence over legislation, centralisation tends to suffer from information bottlenecks and unpredictable compliance. For instance, the active management of urban space became, in France as in other countries, a policy priority in the years after the Second World War. But such management depends crucially on the ability to predict responses to decisions made in respect of housing development, the siting of institutional, commercial and industrial facilities, transport investment and so on. And prediction requires, at the very least, extensive knowledge about the opinions, preferences and projects of local residents, and is arguably all the more reliable that the population is committed to, and not simply affected by, the policies. Participatory planning thus has, at least to some extent, an internal technocratic logic. Its significance is however powerfully reinforced by the critique of technocracy, which combines rejection in principle of Jacobin centralisation, as riding rough-shod over local specificities, and rejection of the tendency of planning to be, in practice, insensitive to both local feelings and to environmental considerations.

Responding to the build-up of these pressures, a law of 1982 fundamentally reshaped local government, replacing the hierarchical relationship between the *Préfet* and the local authorities by partnership. The spirit of the reform was not simply to give greater autonomy to local authorities, but to change their very character. Changes in voting rules were introduced to revitalise party politics and an increased emphasis was put on civil society as a locus of citizenship and democracy. In the debates of the period, a 'new citizenship', based on the concrete activities of the voluntary or 'third' sector (*secteur associatif*), was contrasted favourably with the abstract 'statist' citizenship of Jacobinism (Bouamama et al., 1992). The 'new' citizenship was judged to be of particular significance for immigrants, excluded from mainstream politics by alien status and by racism; and for young people, alienated from traditional politics, and furthermore excluded when also the victims of racism. As we shall see, enhanced opportunities for migrant participation in local politics were a key feature of decentralisation. Similarly, urban policy (*politique de la ville*), as it emerged in the 1980s in the context of rising crime and unemployment and occasionally violent 'youth'[4] mobilisation, was predicated on incorporating disaffected sections of the population in the local political system through the promotion of voluntary activity and mainstream party affiliation. While the link between decentralisation and democratisation was largely implicit in the reforms of the 1980s, it has become increasingly significant in the past decade. A series of laws have imposed on local authorities new responsibilities to promote participation, particularly in planning processes, and the notion of 'local democracy' has now a fairly precise legal, and not simply ideological, meaning (Baguenard and Becet, 1995; Blondiaux et al., 1999; Crozel, 1998; Delemotte and Chevallier, 1996; Neveu, 1999).

The interpretation of French 'local democracy' remains controversial both politically and analytically. Firstly, its territorial inscription is obscure. Legal requirements to enhance information, consultation, and to a certain extent participation, apply to municipalities, departments and regions. They are, therefore, agnostic as to scale and institutionally awkward in light of the complex relations between these three levels, and between the *collectivités territoriales* and local governance generally. A feature of the French system is overlapping competence: while the responsibilities of the three levels are distinct, the distinction is not functional. For example, all levels are involved in education. As a result, demarcations are politically arbitrary, and overlapping competence leads to the creation of a vast range of *ad hoc* bodies to handle multilevel partnerships. Such bodies are not subject to the legal requirements of 'local democracy'; and in practice their accountability is elusive. Similar problems arise even when responsibility is not functionally divided. A range of issues that cannot, for technical reasons, be managed at communal level are shifted upwards to intercommunal bodies representing metropolitan areas with no specific democratic structures and which, unsurprisingly, prove prone to corruption. Plans to amalgamate municipalities into coherent citywide authorities tend to encounter insuperable resistance.

A symmetrical difficulty arises at the sub-communal level. French municipalities are quite small units of urban governance: in the Île-de-France Region – with the exception of the city of Paris itself –, populations of around 50,000 are typical. However, even at this level, the scale of democracy is at issue. On the one hand, mechanisms for direct participation risk overload or irrelevance. As discussed in the following section, 300 to 400 people represent an excellent turnout for a consultative meeting with a broad agenda – and of those, only 20 or fewer are likely to speak. More focused events are usually far less well attended. On the other hand, except at election time or in the context of major infrastructural decisions, even the communal political agenda is fragmented and heterogeneous. The broad characterisation in the previous section fails to do justice to the complexity of local politics, of which voting patterns are a crude but convenient illustration. Polling stations in this area represent geographical groupings of between 1,000 and 3,000 voters. In Saint-Denis and Saint-Ouen, there has in recent years been a ratio of roughly 2 to 1 between the Communist votes in the highest and lowest polling stations; Clichy shows similar variability, although the absence of a dominant party makes the pattern more difficult to read. The neighbourhood (*quartier*) is, to this extent, a more relevant 'local' scale for many purposes, bringing together territorially defined identities and issues. Indeed, service delivery is often organised at the neighbourhood level, and the *quartier* serves as a normative reference for much of the literature on 'local democracy'; as a consequence it is a focus for official processes of consultation and participation. But neighbourhoods are at best administrative units. They have no true democratic dimension and, in particular, due to the blocked-list system of proportional representation, no dynamic of election and accountability. The research summarised here, which is consistent with other studies (Blondiaux et al., 1999; Neveu, 1999), suggests that consultative processes entirely disconnected from decisions tend to become depoliticised and to discourage participation (see the next section). This does not mean, of course, that the neighbourhood is the correct scale for local democracy – simply that the municipality demonstrably is not.

If France is not, as one would sometimes think, entirely run from Paris, neither is multiculturalism simply an import that ideological protectionism has kept off the market. Of all western European countries, France is the one where immigration has the oldest and deepest significance. Indeed, in the desire to formulate a new model of local democracy, specific forms of exclusion related to immigration were a major consideration. France, in other words, has been structurally unable to avoid multicultural questions, and has provided answers that, while distinctive in many ways, nonetheless fall within the general rubric of multiculturalism.

The issues raised by immigration over the past thirty years have often been framed in a local context, and indeed largely addressed by policies implemented, and often even conceived, locally. Their formulation, on the other hand, has been determined by ideological debate at the national level centring on competing interpretations of the 'French model'. However, such debate did not take place in a vacuum. It represented a response to a series of very practical policy challenges arising from territorial fragmentation and multiculturalism. The highly abstract 'model' therefore serves primarily as a language of political debate. It undoubtedly imposes constraints, but also leaves scope for differentiated local responses and for considerable pragmatic flexibility even at the national level. The position of Islam in France is a helpful illustration.

The politicisation of Islam reflects, in complex ways, a perceived crisis of the French model of state-centred nationhood. Since the early 1980s, the political landscape has been reshaped by the mobilisation of young people of North African origin (called in French *Maghrébins*) against exclusion from mainstream French society, and by the hostility to such mobilisation that has fuelled the political success of the anti-immigrant Front National. The intersection of religion and social exclusion thus marks the limits of abstract universalism – although whether this requires abstract universalism to be reaffirmed against religion, jettisoned, or reconfigured, is an open question.

The French multicultural movement, which became influential in the 1970s, defined itself by the critique of abstract universalism. It rejected both 'integration' as a constraint applying peculiarly to immigrants and the exclusive link between nationality and citizenship, framing its rejection by the appeal to the 'new' conception of citizenship. Among the (limited) practical expressions of multiculturalism in the 1970s were schemes for the teaching of 'langues et cultures d'origine', and in many localities greater interaction with voluntary organisations and some degree of special provision (including religious facilities for Muslims). After the election to the Presidency in 1981 of François Mitterrand – whose Socialist Party was the main proponent of multiculturalism –, a number of new measures were introduced. Perhaps the most important was the removal of restrictions on the creation of voluntary organisations (*associations*) by foreign residents. In combination with the decentralisation reforms of 1982, this transformed the local opportunity structure for migrant activity. However the new policy was not simply permissive. Using finance as leverage, both the central state and local authorities were instrumental in promoting migrant organisation, and thereby forms of 'community' solidarity within French society that the ideological model defines as unacceptable. But a key objective – and one explicitly consonant with the ideological model – was to deny space to Islamic mobilisation in neighbourhoods with large Muslim populations (Kastoryano, 1996).

An unintended but predictable effect of this complex strategy has been to increase the salience of Islam. The inevitable competition between social, cultural and religious organisations and the informal division of labour among them has actually encouraged demands for the 'recognition' of Islam,[5] and thereby stimulated fear of it as a threat to nationhood (Cesari, 1997). This is encapsulated by the well-known *affaire des foulards* in 1989.

The suspension from school of three young girls who refused to remove their *foulards* (headscarves) in class prompted a furious national debate. It showed the persistence of Jacobinism in French politics (Kastoryano, 1996), but also that Jacobinism is a political cleavage, not a uniform 'model'. The divisive issue in this case was the interpretation of the key concept of *laïcité* (roughly but inadequately translated as 'secularism'), which is both a controversial ideological touchstone of Jacobinism and a consensual positive constitutional principle. Interestingly, the outcome was a compromise. The current situation is that Islamic dress is discouraged, but tolerated when a pupil really insists on condition that no religious militancy is involved. Considerable discretion is granted to head-teachers in implementing the guidelines, and where necessary the courts have been the final arbiters.

What this means in practice is the establishment of a bargaining relation between the secular state and the putative representatives of a community organised around religion. While it has no place in the ideological 'French model', this pluralistic framework – which is of course unremarkable in comparative terms – can be shown to apply quite generally to the dynamics of cultural issues in French politics (Kastoryano, 1996). As an unintended consequence, voluntary organisations have, in turn, been restructured in federation around Islam in order to negotiate its recognition by the state. At the same time, however, in a superficially contradictory way, the state's refusal to acknowledge religious associations has made Islam a focus of identity, since it is a source of pride for some groups to act independently of the agencies that subsidise supposedly secular cultural associations. A space is thus also created for an oppositional Muslim identity. In a second stage, the unintended promotion of competing forms of 'Islam in France' has pushed the state to seek clarification, which means in practice the promotion, so far with limited success, of a distinctively 'French' form of Islam. Such an unremarkably pragmatic political framework suffices to show that France cannot be adequately described solely by reference to its dominant ideological model of statehood and nationhood.

The Local Politics of Citizenship

The 'local', as we have seen, occupies an ambiguous position within the French model of nationhood. Depending on whether one adopts a pro-Jacobin or anti-Jacobin stance, the enhancement of local citizenship can be seen as part either of the problem or of the solution to the crisis of French national identity. As the previous section shows, however, this contrast is overdrawn: the 'local' does not conflict with the overall model, but fits into it. Thus, the local and national politics of multiculturalism exhibit the same characteristics: practical flexibility in negotiation with societal interests on the basis of their ability to mobilise, but framed and limited by an ideological suspicion of such flexibility, which is therefore disguised and denied. A further twist in the local context is that the flexibility is to a significant extent endogenous – all the more so that decentralisation offers a greatly expanded opportunity structure – whereas the ideological frame is an exogenous national constraint. It remains to be seen how this two-level structure plays out in practice.

The local politics of citizenship reflects the emergence of new kinds of claims that fit poorly within established structures. These claims are a consequence both of the opportunity structure created by decentralisation and of the new salience of 'urban' issues. Their 'newness' is a three-fold challenge to the 'openness' of the public sphere in that they bring forward new *actors*, new *issues* and new *discourses*. They also challenge the technical efficiency of policy, especially in view of the indeterminacy of an 'urban' agenda of inclusion that can be interpreted as easily in terms of justice as of social control. As far as the area studied here is concerned, the dominant national context is the expression of (shifting) perceptions of the problem of the *banlieues*. However, partly because of the instability of the national context, partly because, as we saw in the first section, our area differs in social and geographical characteristics from more peripheral northern and northwestern suburbs, there are significant local peculiarities.

In broad outline, two major shifts are perceptible in the policy context directed at the *banlieues* between the early 1980s and the late 1990s. On the one hand, citizenship, interpreted in moral as much as political terms, has become the normatively dominant mode of inclusion. As nationality has dropped down the political agenda, citizenship has referred increasingly to a mode of participation in society rather than a binary legal status (Kastoryano, 1996). On the other hand, multiculturalism – which was initially either celebrated or rejected out of hand – has gradually been reframed as an issue of justice.

Conversely, what is constant – and in many ways distinctively French – in the policy context is the refusal to define the 'problem of the *banlieues*' as ethnic, 'racial', cultural or even political. The social housing of the 1970s was part of slum-clearance programmes designed to remove the *bidonvilles*, or shanty towns, on the margins of many cities, and in some cases, of which Saint-Denis was typical, decaying city-centre buildings.

Because of the social geography of migration in the post-war period, many of the beneficiaries of the re-housing programmes were immigrants, and the '*banlieue* problem' could therefore be defined plausibly in 'post-migratory' terms (themselves ambivalent, of course, since they can be given either a racist or an anti-racist spin). In fact, however, exclusion is defined as a *social* phenomenon, for which the remedy must also be social: a *politique de la ville* directed at the city *per se* and designed to benefit its inhabitants as such, and not as members of 'ethnic groups' or 'minorities'. Positive action has thus always been thought of in territorial terms – even when it was clear that urban space was in fact 'ethnically' coded. Similarly, grass-roots mobilisation – even when visibly and self-consciously led by people with what would be called in other countries an ethnic background – has generally adopted the territorial policy framework. Whether this reflects sincere subscription to the 'Republican' model or simply recognition of the need to pay lip service to it is unclear – but in terms of political sociology it makes little difference. After all, to say that exclusion is *social* is simply a truism. Racism and *anomie* are nothing if not social phenomena (Crowley, 2000b).

Certainly, it is striking how pervasive is the *language* of citizenship in the municipalities studied at the end of the 1990s. One finds it, as one would expect, to define processes of participation and consultation, but also, more interestingly, to frame normative expectations of behaviour. Thus, in the Charter for community policing (*police de proximité*),[6] displayed as a poster in every police station, officers are called on to behave as 'model citizens'. Similarly, the promotion of citizenship is an explicit objective of youth policy in all the municipalities studied. Expectations, however, are not simply institutional. Citizenship also serves to summarise 'good behaviour'. For example, in the Hauts-de-Seine, including Clichy, a 1999 campaign against litter and dog dirt was entitled *Ville Propre, Ville Citoyenne*. Again, in Saint-Ouen's 2000 consultation exercise (*Rencontre pour la Ville*), citizenship turned up as a *leitmotiv* in discussions not just about participation (one of six tabled themes) but also about 'living together', 'sharing the city' and the environment (*cadre de vie*). Not only was the discourse of the local authority framed in such terms, but the participants in the public meeting and the people interviewed in the filmed survey prepared for the event reproduced it, apparently quite spontaneously. Of particular significance in this respect is crime, which is increasingly presented rhetorically as the ultimate negation of citizenship in the dual sense that the denial of citizenship might be regarded as one of its causes and that good citizens do not commit it. It would be an exaggeration to say that France has adopted the 'Third Way' slogan 'tough on crime, tough on the causes of crime'. However, from being non-existent even 15 years ago, thinking about crime in terms of a balance of rights and responsibilities expressed in the language of citizenship has become a significant strand of public debate. The growing implication of local authorities in crime prevention, expressed institutionally by the *Contrats Locaux de Sécurité* that the state has been promoting since 1998, has undoubtedly facilitated this shift.

A consequence of the new language of citizenship has been to erode the rigid distinction, stressed by 1980s versions of the 'Republican model', between the citizen, who supposedly has no social 'determinations', and the ordinary 'encumbered' member of society. In current debate, on the contrary, the idea that racism is a denial of citizenship has become commonplace. As a result, practical measures to combat routine discrimination have, for the first time, become a significant plank of integration policy. Multicultural concerns are thus expressed in the language of citizenship. The shift is very clear at the national level, but how it plays out locally depends strongly on specific ideological contexts. In right-wing authorities, such as Clichy until 1995, suspicion dressed as colour-blindness is the dominant attitude towards political activity defined in cultural or 'ethnic' terms – and the successor Socialist administration follows a similar line. The orthodox Communist line of a municipality such as Saint-Ouen is also deeply suspicious about the political language of multiculturalism, and refuses to use it to describe any aspect of municipal policy. Colour-blind class-based mobilisation remains the normative political template. However, when one looks at what is actually done, a more complex picture emerges. On the one hand, cultural diversity is explicitly recognised as legitimate: the denial of diversity is therefore a denial of citizenship. This theme was both deliberately introduced into the *Rencontre pour la Ville* and embraced when expressed by participants in the admittedly uncontroversial form of the rejection of assimilationism. Furthermore, the local authority is actively involved in the celebration of diversity through annual festivals and its financial support for a range of cultural groups in the municipality. On the other hand, and probably more importantly, multiculturalism is a technique, applicable in particular to youth policies that is designed to enhance their efficiency. In line with the findings of other French research, targeted recruitment, tacit proportionality, negotiation with powerful grassroots organisations and content sensitivity are widely applied, even when they are ostensibly rejected as inappropriate. The objective remains strictly defined as mainstream participation, but its very compatibility with multicultural techniques is a significant shift. Finally, Saint-Denis, while not radically different from Saint-Ouen, is more open to multicultural concerns, partly because the marginal position of the leading local-council faction within the Communist Party gives it greater room for manoeuvre. The city has, in particular, become the focus of post-national mobilisation by, and in support of, illegal aliens claiming legalisation. In Saint-Ouen, on the other hand, while the Communist Party is in principle committed to 'papers for all', the local authority has refused to get involved in the movement, and has taken a hard line against forms of direct action such as occupations of vacant buildings.

As we consider the place of culturally defined actors within the local political system, questions of rhetoric shade into questions of participation. In this respect, two kinds of participation are at stake: specific modes not based on legal citizenship, to take account of the high proportion of foreign residents; and forums separate from the mainstream representative system, in order to correct its rigidity and often inappropriate scale. Furthermore, especially in comparative perspective, it is important to examine the place of cultural diversity within the mainstream representative system.

The last point is the easiest to analyse. Members of what would be called in other countries 'ethnic minorities' have gradually achieved a significant – although still far less than proportionate – place in local politics. National representation, on the other hand, is still minute. However, their presence does not reflect the development of 'ethnic politics'. The initial opportunities for incorporation were often provided, at the end of the 1980s, by local bosses looking for 'ethnic brokers' (Geisser, 1997). In practice, however, such a role offered benefits neither to ethnic social movements, which were strongly opposed to attempts at co-optation, nor to aspiring politicians, for whom ethnicity would have been a career dead-end. The failure and rapid disappearance of such strategies suggests very strongly that the current French opportunity structure is inimical to ethnic politics, quite apart from the ideological constraints of the Republican model. Ethnic politics exists, if at all, outside the representative system in some voluntary organisations, particularly those with a strongly religious orientation. They are excluded, on the whole, from formal participation, and in any case tend to reject it on principle. Active political involvement on the part of members of 'ethnic minorities' tends therefore to follow traditional paths of patronage, often based on tokenism, and apprenticeship within mainstream political institutions. The municipalities studied here, where there are hardly any elected representatives from recently constituted minorities, are entirely typical.

Specific representation has been on the agenda since the 1970s, when the exclusion from participation of aliens came to be formulated as a limit to democracy.[7] However, it has been defended, if at all, only as a transitory measure or as a kind of halfway house. The two dominant positions have consistently been that political rights at the local level should either be extended to aliens within mainstream institutions, or restricted to nationals on principle. A few cities have, at various times, experimented with consultative foreigners' councils, but none of the experiments had major significance, and no national framework has ever been adopted. None of the municipalities studied here have used such mechanisms. In practice, therefore, the French debate is a national one about the extension of municipal voting rights to non-EU aliens. The Socialist Party committed itself in the 1970s to such a reform, but the proposal was never put into effect: at the time of writing (October 2000) it is again on the political agenda.

The meaning of local citizenship, especially from the multicultural perspective, is therefore primarily determined by the range of participatory processes that have developed since 1982 alongside the mainstream representative system. As discussed in the preceding section, these processes aim generically at solving the problem of democratic *scale*. A full survey is not possible here, but some useful pointers can be gained by distinguishing between rather different kinds of processes.

A first category includes consultation exercises in the context of planning procedures. Since 1994, these have been obligatory for a wide range of decisions. On the other hand, they have a very weak legal standing. Not only do they not have a clearly defined format, but also the local authority is actually forbidden from soliciting any kind of binding decision from a consultative forum. In particular, the courts have struck down local referenda framed as decision-making polls. In the area covered by our research, the process is usually that a well defined project, drawing on wide-ranging prior consultation with institutional (e.g. the department or the region) or other (e.g. business) interests, is publicised through a range of media including periodical newsletters, the local press, and *ad hoc* packages. Once some degree of familiarity has been achieved, a meeting or a series of meetings is called. In addition to general announcements – which people tend notoriously not to notice – invitations are also delivered directly to letterboxes. The opportunity to participate is thus fairly genuine, and makes no distinction in terms of legal status. Furthermore, meetings are scheduled at times that are convenient for many people (early evening on weekdays or Saturday morning), and a free buffet and drinks afterwards offer a further incentive to come along. However, attendance is typically small (30 to 50) and heavily skewed towards men in the 35 to 65 age bracket. Self-selection, in other words, operates to exclude precisely those local residents who are least effectively represented by the mainstream political system. In view of the context of the meetings, such exclusion is arguably not very serious. The format is exclusively *informative*: elected officials explain to the population the reasons for and features of the proposed project, and those who speak do so to request clarification (in practice more such requests tend to be expressed informally after the meeting than during it). Political discourse is minimal both from the platform and from the floor: at this stage, what is at stake is purely technical. This does not mean, of course, that infrastructure projects are never controversial: on the contrary, they invariably are. However, compromises are reached through closed bargaining between constituted interests, and by the time the issue is opened to citizen involvement, everything is already cut and dried. As one would expect on theoretical grounds, politicisation, when it does occur, tends therefore to take the form of demands for, or attempts to create, a genuinely public space in which the agenda itself is up for discussion. Far from using established consultative procedures, it presumes their rejection. The construction in Saint-Denis of the Stade de France is an example of the limits of tightly managed consultation, but while the controversy about the interests of local residents who claim to have been ignored at the planning stage drags on, it has so far failed to develop a truly political dimension.

A rather different kind of process is broad-based consultation with a fairly open agenda aimed at shaping priorities for future municipal action. The *Rencontre pour la Ville* exercise in Saint-Ouen in June 2000 was a typical example, and can be described briefly for illustrative purposes. It was organised in exactly the same way as the planning meetings, but such processes differ in that no immediate decision is at stake, and therefore no prior official project restricts the options. Conversely, the absence of any clear agenda leads to a loss of focus. The Council had sought to address this by arranging a prior consultation exercise (a 'survey' – *enquête* – conducted by a team of journalists from the local newspaper)[8] and drawing from it the six very broad themes mentioned earlier, around which the public meeting was structured. The main features of the meeting correspond to results from research in other French cities, with some interesting peculiarities. Attendance was some 250, and unlike the planning meetings was a fairly representative sample of the population, including in particular a significant number of people in the 18-25 and over-65 age brackets.

Contrary to some findings (Neveu, 1999), therefore, attendance did not seem to be strongly correlated with political resources or capital.[9] Active participation was inevitably more skewed (only about 15 members of the public spoke), but not in any obvious age, gender or class pattern. Nor was the cultural (or 'ethnic') diversity of the audience manifestly distorted. In terms of discourse, on the other hand, previous findings were strongly confirmed (Blondiaux et al., 1999; Neveu, 1999). First of all, the degree of spontaneity was very low. While there was no platform, and while television screens were arranged to offer all participants a uniform view of the speakers as they spoke,[10] the meeting was chaired and in effect managed by the journalist who had been responsible for the prior survey. The chairing was flexible and sensitive, and imposed few constraints on the speakers (the meeting overran its time by nearly three hours), but was nonetheless highly normalising: there were no outbursts, incidents, interruptions or controversies; and in fact no debate at all. Secondly, the meeting was highly depoliticised. Although the Mayor was present, sitting next to the chairman, along with a number of councillors and officials, many of whom spoke, politics almost never emerged. From the tone of the meeting, local government might be judged a purely technical matter of management. In her opening statement, the Mayor even strenuously, and improbably, denied that the meeting had anything to do with the 2001 municipal elections. With regard to party-political discourse, self-censorship was complete. Although a couple of speakers did claim Communist Party membership as a preface to their statement, there was nothing approximating to a Party speech. On the other hand, membership of voluntary organisations was put strongly forward. Nearly all speakers took the floor as officials of *associations* and justified their special knowledge and interests in those terms. The implications – which clearly point to the limited descriptive content of the 'new citizenship' model – are that most *associations* are, and are perceived to be, non-political; and that truly political voluntary-sector activity tends to be set within interest-group pluralism rather than participatory politics.[11] Thirdly, in the absence of any agenda for political decisions, the meeting became a rather empty 'listening' exercise, and was indeed summed up as such by the Mayor. On the whole, no one with a real political agenda would bother turning up.

If we generalise from this case, building in a range of other findings, it seems fairly clear that consultative processes, even when they have a participatory format, do little to correct differential patterns of participation in, and influence over, local politics – in a word, patterns of *power*. They may indeed be an amplifier of as much as a corrective to mainstream institutions. Saint-Denis' experience of a third kind of local democratic processes – institutionalised consultation on a participatory basis – points in the same direction. There is little doubt about the sincerity of the local council's efforts to promote neighbourhood democracy through its neighbourhood initiatives (*démarches quartiers*). The fact that the local Communist Party has an interest in renewing its declining electoral support, especially in light of its awkward relations with the national Party, does not qualify this sincerity, but merely explains it. Meetings are held regularly – usually about every two months – in each of the city's neighbourhoods. Anyone may attend. They are supported by direct contacts between the Council and neighbourhood organisations, which aim at setting the agenda and exploring options. A major drawback of the processes discussed previously – the lack of any interface between interest group bargaining and participatory deliberation – is thereby at least partly addressed. In addition, the neighbourhood forums send delegates to an annual citywide meeting. However, the Council's own assessment of the process is at best mixed. While attendance is typically good, and while the meetings are useful as sounding-boards, they tend to exclude precisely those groups – the young, migrant women, and to a lesser extent the old – whose voices are already inadequately heard – or, in the case of the first group, are heard stridently, but outside and against the political mainstream.

Multiculturalism 'à la Française'?

Anyone looking for multiculturalism 'on the ground' in France as a counterweight to ideological Republicanism at national level will understandably be disappointed by the evidence offered here. To the extent local politics offers scope for multicultural concerns to be expressed, it is not in terms of citizenship – and certainly not of a 'new' model of citizenship – but rather in the familiar terms of a balance of political power. And since minorities with multicultural concerns tend to lack power, they tend to be overlooked. The general tendency, however, should not hide some important complicating factors. Minorities may have more resources than sometimes realised – which means that the weakness of local multiculturalism may be less of a problem than often thought. Some of these resources are highly conventional: numbers for instance. The political consequences of the social geography of migration are familiar from many countries, and France is no exception.

In this field of politics as in others, organisation may compensate for lack of numbers. However, for fairly obvious reasons, organisational capital is often more productively invested at the national level. The development of the *beur* movement of the 1980s is a good example. It emerged primarily in the context of localised mobilisations. Community structures often referred specifically to urban territories – as in the best known example, the pioneer movement of the Jeunes Arabes de Lyon et banlieue –, and local authorities were leading actors in the promotion of pragmatic multicultural policies (Geisser, 1997). That these were aimed, often quite explicitly, at the development of new modes of social control only reinforces the point. However, the local focus was rapidly eroded. The organisation that emerged as the public face of the multicultural agenda – SOS Racisme – was, from the outset, national, although it did function to some extent as an umbrella for a range of local bodies. And its specific resources were equally national: its close links with the Socialist Party and, partly as a direct result, its capacity for effective media management. Both the hegemonic claims and the 'style' of SOS Racisme caused considerable resentment among local activists who perceived themselves as more 'rooted' and more authentic. After the influence of SOS Racisme began to wane in the early 1990s, mobilisation again became more local – but precisely for that reason also became less visible and influential. A constant theme that comes up in discussions with activists is the existence of a kind of 'double bind': to exist means to go political and to go national; but to do so is to lose any reason for existing.

If the voluntary sector was the sole promoter of multicultural concerns in France, the story of the 1990s would be one of decline. In fact the opposite is demonstrably the case. In the 1980s, it was judged necessary to mobilise around the slogan '*la France, c'est comme une mobylette – ça marche au mélange*',[12] precisely because denial that post-migratory social diversity had anything to do with 'France' was at the heart of the Front National discourse in its first phase. At the end of the 1990s, nearly everyone celebrates the 'multicoloured' soccer team that won the 1998 World Cup and the 2000 European Championships. In the 2000 edition of an annual poll conducted by a magazine to rank the 50 most-admired French people, the socially committed priest Abbé Pierre, who had topped the poll for as long as anyone could remember, came second to the soccer star Zinedine Zidane. Such things are trivial in one sense, but they do seem indicative of a transformed climate. Strong measures against routine racial discrimination were judged so unlikely in the 1980s that they were hardly argued for; at the end of the 1990s, they are a policy priority for the national government: every police station now has a poster encouraging people to know their rights and to press charges if they regard themselves as having been the victims of discrimination. The official Haut Conseil à l'Intégration, which in the late 1980s was a promoter of ideological Republicanism, now calls for the creation of a body analogous to the British Commission for Racial Equality in order to reinforce the application of anti-discrimination laws. Mainstreaming, in other words, is a crucial ideological resource, but it is one that, by its very nature, is national rather than local – grassroots mobilisation can deploy it, but not directly produce it.

To offer a full analysis of the new French political context, within which multicultural concerns have moved from the margins to mainstream, would be beyond the scope of this chapter. All we can offer are some indications about the apparent connections between the move to the mainstream and the *nationalisation* and *politicisation* of the issues. In two respects, the connection is a contingent one. It is a fact about France that, despite decentralisation, there is no sub-national locus of legislative authority. Therefore, any mobilisation aimed at changing the law is necessarily national on purely strategic grounds, however rooted it may be in local issues and forms of mobilisation. In other political systems, the situation may well be different. It is similarly a fact about France that its 'political field' is entirely polarised by Paris. To some extent this is a reflection of the history of nation and state building and of the power of the dominant normative model of statehood. However, in more mundane ways, it is also linked to the institutions of the Fifth Republic and the structures of the media. Any rational political strategy is therefore necessarily Paris-centred.

Nonetheless, the *way* in which issues that emerge locally are nationalised is not reducible to a tactical choice of terrain. The issues themselves are transformed by the change of scale. As discussed in the introduction to this volume, the language in which specific claims can be generalised is one that must be detached from immediacy and rephrased in more abstract terms of justification – and the constraint is all the more powerful that the power resources backing the claim are weaker. The changing multicultural agenda fits, therefore, into a broader framework that includes a range of 'diversity' issues that bring into play common abstract principles of justice. The period during which the French multicultural and anti-racist movements have declined while multicultural concerns have moved into the mainstream is also a period during which gender, sexuality, regionalism and human rights have been at the top of the political agenda. On our analysis, this is not a coincidence. Each of these areas points to a common internal difficulty within the dominant French conceptions of statehood and nationhood, and therefore promote – in ways that are sometimes indirect and obscure – a shared alternative political language. The difficulty is that the requirement of abstraction expressed by Republican citizenship falls unequally even as it claims to embody equality. The implications are different depending on whether the category under discussion is women (the Constitution has been revised to embody the principle of *parité*, or numerical equality of political representation), same-sex couples (who can now enter into a 'civil solidarity pact' giving them most of the legal, social and tax rights of married couples), regional minorities (who have so far been only partly successful in their demands for recognition), illegal aliens (some of whom established rights that had previously been denied in the legalisation process of 1997-1998) or 'ethnic minorities' (claiming equal citizenship in a context of widespread racism). Nonetheless there is a common agenda here – and indeed a broadly overlapping set of political mobilisations, which suggests that the phenomena cannot be analysed solely in terms of 'identity politics'. Furthermore, it is undoubtedly an agenda of citizenship. It is pointless, however, to think of it as belonging to a single, uniform political scale. What is empirically inadequate about the idea of local citizenship in a country like France is that it neglects the extent to which, for very good reasons, what emerges locally is played out nationally – and *vice versa*. Conversely, what is normatively inadequate about the critique of national citizenship is that it tends to presume that there is a 'real' or 'natural' scale, compared to which the nation is somehow artificial. In fact, the evidence suggests that, by their very nature, political issues cut across geographical scaling. Any attempt to tie the public 'sphere' to a determinate spatial or institutional location is therefore self-defeating. The modes of citizenship – thankfully, from a normative democratic perspective – defy exhaustive definition.

Notes

1   The Communist Party, with Socialist support, does however retain control of the *conseil général* of Seine-Saint-Denis.
2   Figures by nationality are the only ones systematically available in France. In view of French nationality law, which makes naturalisation easy and imposes French nationality on many French-born foreigners, there is no straightforward way of deriving 'ethnic' data from nationality data. For the purposes of this paper, it is unnecessary to go into to the complex issues raised by the production of 'ethnic' data.

3   Based on figures from the 1990 census (the last systematically available at the time of writing), there were 1,377,416 foreigners resident in the Île-de-France Region, of whom 238,955 were Algerian, 155,674 Moroccan, 75,965 Tunisian, 59,572 Spanish, and 51,001 Italian. There were 154,877 foreigners from sub-Saharan Africa. The Algerian, Italian and Spanish populations declined by 19, 22 and 30 per cent, respectively, between 1982 and 1990, which gives some indication of the impact of migratory cycles on the statistics. Over the same period, the Moroccan population increased by 26 per cent, the sub-Saharan African by 50 per cent, and the Turkish by 117 per cent (40,795 in 1990).

4   While the issue cannot be discussed in detail here, the quotation marks serve to underline that shifting meanings of the word 'youth' (*la jeunesse*, itself gradually replaced by *les jeunes*) were at the heart of the political and policy processes of the 1980s. In current usage, 'youth' has almost entirely parted company with age and come to designate a social-behavioural type, with derogatory and often implicitly racist connotations. The parallels with the social-political construction of 'black youth' in the UK are fairly obvious (Gilroy, 1987; Solomos, 1988).

5   There are some 4 million nominal Muslims in France, about half of whom (including the *Harki* community) are of Algerian origin. Quotation marks are required around 'recognition' because it is precisely as an undefined and arguably empty concept that the word has attained universal currency in debates about religion in general and Islam in particular.

6   The development of the *police de proximité* (which is substantively very similar to what is called in the UK community policing) is the outcome of a long-running process, but has been particularly promoted by Jean-Pierre Chevènement, as Interior Minister in the Jospin government from 1997 to 2000. It is relevant that Chevènement represents in ideological terms the most dogmatically Republican fraction of the current coalition (to the point of resigning in September 2000 over opposition to devolution for Corsica) and was, as a superficially paradoxical consequence, the promoter of a range of initiatives – including the new forms of anti-discrimination policy mentioned below – that represent a French form of pragmatic multiculturalism.

7   Naturalisation in France is fairly liberal, but a combination of identity considerations and restrictions in the state of origin on dual nationality discourage many resident aliens, even of very long standing, from requesting it.

8   How this was done and why it was done in this way was not explained to participants. As is usual in such cases, 'public opinion' was simply taken for granted as an objective datum. The empirical details require further research.

9   Quite apart from other published findings, there are reasons from our research, as noted in the first section, to think that Saint-Ouen is unusual, perhaps because of the survival of a Party-structured civil society. Certainly evidence from Épinay and Saint-Denis suggests the familiar conclusion that participation in 'open' consultative processes is lowest for groups that are the least mobilised with respect to the mainstream representative system.

10   Such staging is interesting, as it might almost have been designed to pre-empt the usual objections against such meetings. We are unable at this stage to say if this was self-consciously the case.

11 In particular, despite the diversity of the audience, and despite the reference to multicultural issues in the opening film, nothing of multicultural significance with any political edge came up in the meeting.
12 The slogan turns on an untranslatable pun. *Mélange* means 'mixture' (here in the sense of 'diversity') but also the peculiar fuel that mopeds run on, which is a mixture of petrol and lubricant oil.

References

Bacqué, M.-H. and Fol, S. (1997), *Le Devenir des Banlieues Rouges*, L'Harmattan, Paris.
Baguenard, J. and Becet, J.-M. (1995), *Démocratie Locale*, PUF, Paris.
Blondiaux, L., Marcou, G. and Rangeon, F. (1999), *La Démocratie Locale: Représentation, Participation et Espace Public*, PUF, Paris.
Bouamama, S., Cordeiro, A. and Roux, M. (1992), *La Citoyenneté dans Tous Ses États: De l'Immigration à la Nouvelle Citoyenneté*, CIEMI/L'Harmattan, Paris.
Brunet, J.-P. (1980), *Saint-Denis, la Ville Rouge, 1890-1939*, Hachette, Paris.
Butzbach, E. (ed.) (1989), *Les Immigrés et la Participation à la Vie Politique Locale*, Syros, Paris.
Cesari, J. (1997), *Faut-il Avoir Peur de l'Islam?*, Presses de Sciences-Po, Paris.
Crowley, J. (2000a), 'France: The Archetype of a Nation-state', in L. Haagendoorn, G. Csepeli, H. Dekker and R. Farnen (eds), *European Nations and Nationalism: Theoretical and Historical Perspectives*, Ashgate, Aldershot, pp. 67-106.
Crowley, J. (2000b), 'L'identité Collective Comme Configuration Politique: L'exemple du Racisme', *Cahiers politiques*, no. 5, pp. 9-30.
Crozel, B. (1998), *Urbanité et Citoyenneté: Attention, Démocratie Urbaine*, L'Harmattan, Paris.
Delemotte, B. and Chevallier, J. (1996), *Étranger et Citoyen: Les Immigrés et la Démocratie Locale*, L'Harmattan, Paris.
Geisser, V. (1997), *Ethnicité Républicaine: Les Élites d'Origine Maghrébine dans le Système Politique Français*, Presses de Sciences Po, Paris.
Gilroy, P. (1987), *'There Ain't No Black in the Union Jack': The Cultural Politics of Race and Nation*, Unwin Hyman, London.
Kastoryano, R. (1996) *La France, l'Allemagne et Leurs Immigrés: Négocier l'Identité*, Armand Colin, Paris.
Neveu, C. (ed.) (1999), *Espace Public et Engagement Politique: Enjeux et Logiques de la Citoyenneté Locale*, L'Harmattan, Paris.
Solomos, J. (1988), *Black Youth, Racism, and the State: The Politics of Ideology and Policy*, Cambridge University Press, Cambridge.

Copes with a Different
Type of Migrant

MICHAEL ALEXANDER

Introduction

Tel Aviv is a relatively young city. Since its founding in 1909, the city has grown rapidly through the absorption of successive waves of Jewish immigrants coming from a widely varied Diaspora. Most of today's Tel Avivis, their parents or grandparents emigrated from the cities of Europe, from towns in Russia, from villages in the Maghreb and the Middle East. But since the mid-1990s this city of immigrants has had to cope with a different type of immigrant – non-Jewish 'foreign workers'. The influx of overseas labourers has occurred at an astonishing rate within the space of a single decade. From a few thousands at the beginning of the 1990s, labour migrants in Tel Aviv are now estimated at between 20,000-60,000, or anywhere between 5-15 per cent of the city population (the official municipal population, not including the migrants, is 350,000).[1] Migrants in Tel Aviv account for between tenth to a third of the country's total population of foreign workers.[2]

The rapid growth of overseas migrants in Israel is due to their role as replacement labour for Palestinian workers. However, unlike the Palestinians, who commuted daily into the region from the nearby Gaza Strip and West Bank, the overseas labour migrants remain in Tel Aviv. New 'foreign worker communities' composed of mostly illegal residents from Africa, Latin America, the Philippines and elsewhere, have formed. This is a previously unknown phenomenon in Tel Aviv. Israeli society, increasingly fragmented by political and ethnic divides, does not know how to cope with the new challenge of the settlement of non-Jewish labour migrants. Government policies reflect this indecision.

The Municipality of Tel Aviv, tired of waiting for national-level decisions, has initiated its own policies toward the labour migrants. In 1998 a new Mayor was elected who promised to 'stop ignoring the foreign workers in Tel Aviv'. In 1999 the Municipality opened MESILA, the first Aid and Information Centre for the Foreign Community in Tel Aviv. MESILA in effect challenges the national government policy, which regards all non-Jewish migrants as temporary. Meanwhile, the migrants themselves are making their first claims toward basic rights. Paradoxically, the best organised are the illegal migrants. Of these, only the African community has mobilised politically, in the form of the African Workers Union.

This chapter will focus on the interaction between the 'first Hebrew City' and its first wave of non-Jewish immigrants, whose settlement is challenging the basic tenets of Israeli society. The first part sketches out the particular context of non-Jewish migrants in Israeli society, describing the historical context of migration to Tel Aviv, including the latest 'migrant wave' – overseas labour migrants. Next we describe the institutional context, particularly the difference between national and municipal policies toward migrants. We shall claim that Tel Aviv's policies are challenging and even pre-empting national policies. In part three we describe the self-organisation of the migrant communities in Tel Aviv. We focus on the 'illegal' African community and how it has successfully mobilised. We conclude that the particular migration regime in Israel has resulted in a paradoxical situation whereby the undocumented migrants are freer to organise and mobilise, in contrast to their legal counterparts. We shall claim that currently the illegal labour migrants in Tel Aviv and the Municipality have a common goal at the national level – to change government policies. At the local level, however, the municipal policy and migrant needs may differ, and this could lead to less favourable relations between the host city and its labour migrant communities in the future.

The Israeli Context: Can Tel Aviv be Compared to European Cities?

When referring to migrants and ethnic minorities in Tel Aviv, it is important to understand the special context of Israel as an ethnically-based immigration society.[3] From pre-statehood and until the 1990s, immigrants to Israel were overwhelmingly Jewish, and until recently Jewish Israelis (accounting for 82 per cent of the population) were mostly immigrants. In 1995, 39 per cent of the Jewish population had immigrated to Israel, and an additional 40 per cent were children of immigrants (Shuval and Leshem, 1998). Israel's *raison d'être*, ideology and institutions are still largely based on the 'ingathering of the Diaspora', i.e. on Jewish immigration which the state actively encourages and assists. According to the Law of Return (1950) based on *ius sanguinis*, Jewish immigrants are automatically granted

Israeli citizenship upon their arrival, including immediate voting rights and generous government subsidies.

In regard to non-Jews, however, Israel clearly defines itself as a non-immigration country. It is almost impossible for a non-Jewish migrant to obtain Israeli citizenship or even permanent resident status, unless (s)he marries an Israeli and/or converts to Judaism (neither is easy). Israeli terminology reflects this well: Jewish immigrants are termed *olim* (from the Biblical Hebrew 'to arise' to the Land of Israel), while labour migrants are termed *ovdim zarim* (foreign workers), a term connoting alien-ness and transience. The neutral term *mehager* (immigrant) is rarely used in Israel, outside academia.

Until the 1990s there was virtually no non-Jewish immigration to Israel (although the last wave of *olim* following the breakdown of the Soviet Union contained a large proportion of non-Jews, see below). However, the massive recruitment of overseas foreign workers, beginning in 1993, created the first real non-Jewish migration in the country's history, concentrating on Tel Aviv. Until recently, 'minority' in Israel has meant first of all the indigenous Arabs within the state. The 'Israeli Arab minority' (mostly Palestinians and Beduin) accounts for 18 per cent of the national population. Here we do not deal with the Palestinian ethnic minority in Tel Aviv, or with the Jewish migrants to the city, beyond the brief summary below.

This chapter focuses on the labour migrants in Tel Aviv, who have arrived in the 1990s. Their settlement is reminiscent of the processes familiar in Western European cities since the 1970s. Nevertheless, including Tel Aviv in a survey of multicultural policies and modes of citizenship in European cities is problematic. Israel is not in Europe, although it often pretends to be. Tel Aviv, the most westernised city in Israel, may be called a hybrid – partly European, partly Middle Eastern. Furthermore, the ideology of Israel as a 'Jewish state' makes Tel Aviv a special case in terms of migration and ethnicity. Thirdly, the Israeli migration regime, which binds foreign workers to specific employers and leads to systematic exploitation (see below), has created a paradoxical situation where illegal workers live under threat of deportation, but often have better living and working conditions than legal workers. This situation shapes the character of migrant organisation and mobilisation, as we shall see.

Finally, the political context of the Israeli-Palestinian conflict directly affects the character of labour migration in Tel Aviv. The rapid growth of foreign workers – from some 15,000 in 1990 to an estimated 200,000 today – is largely due to their role as substitutes for Palestinian labour in the country's dual labour market. This substitutive role also explains Israeli attitudes toward the overseas migrants. On the positive side, they are welcomed as a non-threatening substitute for the Palestinian workers, who were seen as a potential danger. On the other hand, the Palestinians commuted back to their homes every night, while the overseas labour migrants remain in what have become 'foreigners' neighbourhoods'. All of these contexts have profound consequences for the interaction between migrants and the city of Tel Aviv.

So, can Tel Aviv be compared to European cities, with regard to the interaction between cities and migrants? I believe it can. Firstly, in terms of urban development patterns and economic and political structure, the Tel Aviv Metropolitan Area (1997 population: 2,539,100) is similar to European cities. The similarity between Tel Aviv and European cities is also clear in the local reaction to labour migrants. As far as the illegal immigrant is concerned, 'Fortress Europe' is not so different from 'Fortress Israel', and the composition of labour migrants in Tel Aviv is strikingly similar to that of European cities. Indeed, it appears impossible to isolate any variable in the 'migrant-city equation' that is common to all the European cities in this book, and is not also true for Tel Aviv. Tel Aviv may be unique, but so is every city in this survey.

Nevertheless, two points are crucial to understanding the special case of migrants and ethnic minorities in Tel Aviv. One is the polarised difference in Israel's attitude toward migration, between Jewish and non-Jewish migrants, both in civil society and institutionally. The other point is the ethnically-based labour market dualism that evolved since at least the 1960s, based on cheap Palestinian labour. The rapidity and magnitude of the overseas worker phenomenon in Tel Aviv, as well as the migration regime, is largely due to their replacement role instead of Palestinian workers.

The Historical Context of Immigration to Tel Aviv

The city of Tel-Aviv-Yafo[4] is located on the eastern shore of the Mediterranean Sea, and is surrounded by the Tel Aviv Metropolitan Area (TAMA) which contains 42 per cent of Israel's population. The TAMA incorporates nearly 70 local authorities including 22 municipalities, and is likened to the Randstad in Holland, in terms of urban density, interdependence of functions and national dominance.[5] Thus, although Jerusalem is the political capital, Tel Aviv is the demographic and economic centre of Israel.

Tel Aviv has been undergoing economic restructuring since the beginning of the 1980s. While the manufacturing sector has been shrinking, there has been a boom in the service sector. Forty per cent of the Israeli workforce in the financial and business services now work in Tel Aviv. Altogether, over 300,000 people are employed in the city, of which 37 per cent reside in Tel Aviv and the rest commute.[6]

Economic growth has been offset by steady residential population decline. In the early 1990s population loss to the suburbs was offset by a certain amount of central city residential growth, and temporarily by the Russian migration wave. However, the most significant demographic change since the mid-1990s has been the settlement of foreign workers – although this does not yet appear in the municipal statistics.

Jewish immigration and the Arab minority: 1909-1989   Tel Aviv was founded in 1909 as a suburb of Yafo (Jaffa) by 60 Jewish families who wanted to escape the overcrowding of the ancient port town, and to establish the 'first Hebrew City'. Its spectacular growth was thereafter based on Jewish refugees coming from Europe, North Africa and the Middle East. Immigration from Europe raised the population to 34,000 by 1925, turning the Yafo suburb into a real town, with a business area, the first hospital, theatre and philharmonic. Another wave of immigrants mostly from Germany tripled the population to 100,000 by 1935. Further immigration doubled the population to 200,000 by 1947, creating the need for massive public housing projects.

Israel's War of Independence (1947-1949), involving battles with local Palestinians and the neighbouring Arab states, resulted in massive population movements on both sides. An estimated 70,000 Palestinians from Yafo fled almost overnight in 1948, and became refugees. In 1950 the nearly deserted city of Yafo was annexed to the Municipality of Tel Aviv, the remaining 4,000 Palestinians becoming Israeli citizens and residents of 'Tel Aviv-Yafo'. Today the Arab population of Tel-Aviv-Yafo (roughly 60 per cent Muslim and 40 per cent Christian) has grown to some 16,000. Most of the Arabs live in Ajami neighbourhood in Yafo, altogether comprising 25 per cent of Yafo's residents and about 4 per cent of Tel-Aviv-Yafo's population.[7] In the last municipal elections (1999) two Yafo Arabs were elected to the City Council, one on an Arab list and another on a leftist list, meaning they are slightly over-represented in the City Council.

While Yafo's Palestinian population fled, Tel Aviv-Yafo's numbers swelled to 345,000 by 1951. Jewish refugees from the Arab countries and from the European Holocaust were housed in deserted Yafo and in hastily built residential areas. Tel Aviv's population peaked in 1963 at 394,000. From the mid-1960s until 1988 the city's population slowly decreased as a result of suburbanisation. Between 1989-1994 another migration wave arrived, following the disintegration of the Soviet Union. Nearly 26,000 Russian immigrants settled in Tel Aviv, constituting 7.4 per cent of the city population by the end of 1995.

Between 1989-1994, the disintegration of the Soviet Union resulted in nearly 26,000 Russian immigrants settling in Tel Aviv, constituting 7.4 per cent of the city population by the end of 1995. The Russian immigrants first settled in Yafo and in the poorer neighbourhoods in the southern part of Tel Aviv, due to lower rental prices and the presence of relatives from the previous Russian immigration wave in the 1970s. Within a few years many improved their economic position (Menahem, 1993). The poorer neighbourhoods abandoned by the upwardly mobile Russian immigrants in the mid-1990s were soon filled in by the foreign workers. The wave of Russian *olim* (approximately 700,000 arrived in Israel between 1990-1993) was the first in Israel's history to include a high proportion of non-Jews, coming as family dependants and under false papers. Current estimates are that a third or more of the Russian immigrants to Israel are not Jewish. This may mean that this population will find it more difficult than Jewish *olim* to integrate into Israeli society, and may even constitute a new 'ethnic minority'. In the last decade the Russians have quickly and successfully entered the Israeli political game at the national level (two Russian immigrant parties in the Knesset). In the last municipal elections, however, the Russian parties did not run local lists in Tel Aviv.

Labour immigration: 1993-2000   Understanding the massive influx of migrant workers to Tel Aviv requires a knowledge of the foreign worker phenomenon at the national level. From 1956 to 1987 the Israeli economy became dependent on Arab workers, developing an ethnically based dual labour market. After 1967, Palestinians from the occupied West Bank and Gaza Strip began to commute daily to work in Israeli cities and towns. By the late 1980s some 120,000 workers, or 9 per cent of the labour force in Israel, was Palestinian – less than half of them legal workers. The construction and agricultural sectors became especially dependent on Palestinian labour, which constituted 45 per cent and 25 per cent of their workforce, respectively. In 1987 the Palestinian uprising (*intifada*) broke out. A series of terror attacks in Israeli cities in the early 1990s led to frequent closures of the Territories and government bans on employment of Palestinians. This led to increasing pressure from the construction and agricultural lobbies on the government to allow recruitment of foreign workers. In mid-1993 the government decided to allow large-scale recruitment of workers from overseas as a 'temporary' solution to the shortage of Palestinian workers (Bartram, 1998; Fischer, 1999; Schnell, 1999a).

The entry of overseas labour migrants into Israel, both legal and illegal, was massive. Until 1993, overseas migrant workers were a marginal factor in Israel. The change in government policy in 1993 led to a drastic increase in the number of permits for foreign workers – from some 10,000 permits in 1993, to almost 70,000 in 1995, and peaking at about 100,000 in 1996. Since 1997 government policy has been reducing the number of permits. Estimates of the number of foreign workers with permits in 1999 are around 80,000-90,000. Seventy-five per cent are employed in construction (mainly Romanians), 15 per cent in agriculture (mainly Thais) and 10 per cent in domestic services (mainly Filipinos).[8]

Parallel to the increase in legal labour migrants there was an increase in illegal immigrants (without a stay and work permit).[9] There is general agreement that for every documented foreign worker in Israel there is at least one undocumented migrant. Current estimates of the number of undocumented foreign workers in Israel vary widely, and most probably the number is around 100,000. In effect, overseas workers, estimated at around 200,000 legal and illegal migrants, have replaced the Palestinians who now account for only 4 per cent of the local workforce.

In Tel Aviv there is no official census of foreigners by the local authority, but there are several estimates, ranging from 25,000 to over 60,000.[10] The percentage of 'illegal' foreigners in Tel Aviv is high, estimated at 70-80 per cent of the local migrant worker population (Schnell, 1999b; Tel-Aviv-Yafo Municipality, 1999b). This is due to dominance of the service sector in Tel Aviv, which employs mostly illegal workers, rather than construction and agriculture sectors. Undocumented labour migrants in Tel Aviv come from over thirty countries, mostly from Africa, East Asia, Latin America, East Europe and the former Soviet Union.[11]

The diversity of the labour migrant population in Tel Aviv may derive from the fact that Israel did not have colonial relationships that could account for the origin of its foreign workers. Another reason may be that Israel is a target country with an 'added spiritual value' for immigrants of Christian background from around the world. Many labour migrants come as tourists or pilgrims and stay on to work. The aura of living in the Holy Land also strengthens the motivation for chain migration and family reunification. For Israel, it is politically difficult to curtail the flow of pilgrimage tourists in an attempt to limit illegal immigration.

Africans comprise the largest and possibly most veteran group of foreign workers, arriving first in the late 1980s. Between 5,000 to 10,000 are estimated to be living in Tel Aviv, nearly all of them illegal.[12] The African migrants come mostly from Ghana and Nigeria, but also from Democratic Republic of Congo (formerly Zaire), the Republic of Congo, Central African Republic, Ethiopia, Ivory Coast, Sierra Leone, Mauritius and South Africa. The South American migrant community comes mainly from Colombia, Ecuador, Bolivia, Chile and Venezuela. Both these groups enter the country under tourist visas and then remain to work illegally. Kemp et al. (2000) note the characteristics common to the African and Latino migrant communities: a great majority are illegal; a high percentage of families with children; a relatively educated population; well-developed communitarian patterns of organisation.

The East Asians, mostly single Filipino women and a smaller number of single Thai men and women, are employed legally as caregivers and live at their employer's residence, or illegally as domestic help and in restaurants. Workers from Eastern Europe are imported by the construction industry primarily from Romania, in organised groups of single men. As with the East Asians, an unknown amount of foreign workers who arrived with permits have left their legal employers and continue to work illegally. Workers from the former Soviet Union are estimated to have become in recent years the largest group of undocumented workers (Fishbain, 2000). Other nationality groups in Tel Aviv include Poles, Turks, Indians and Chinese, mostly men working in the construction sector. An unknown number of labour migrants originate from Arab countries (mostly Jordanians, but also from Egypt and Maghreb countries). Most reside in Yafo, after having crossed the border into the Palestinian Authority and then continued into Israel (Schnell, 1999b).

The foreign worker population in Tel Aviv resides mostly in the poorer, southern neighbourhoods, with a significant concentration in the 'core neighbourhood' of Neve Sha'anan, between the old and new Central Bus Stations. A 1997 survey of this area showed that 70 per cent of the local population were labour migrants (Schnell, 1999a).[13] The core area, with its foreign workers' cafes and meeting places, also serves a broader population of labour migrants living and working outside of Tel Aviv, who converge on Neve Sha'anan on the weekends and holidays. Some even hire apartments together in southern Tel Aviv to serve as their weekend homes. For the migrants, this concentration clearly provides them with a feeling of community and security – although making them easier targets for police deportations as well. For the Israelis, the foreign workers' geographical concentration has intensified their presence in Tel Aviv in the eyes of the local population, media and politicians.

Tel Aviv's Challenge to the National Migration Regime

Israel is a highly centralised country with most authority resting in the hands of governmental ministries.[14] The rules regarding the employment of overseas labour in Israel are extremely restrictive. 'Legal' foreign workers are those with a valid stay and work permit issued by the Ministry of Interior, which is limited to a specific employer. This permit is issued via the employer for one or two years, renewable for several years, depending on the employment sector. The employer is responsible for 'his' foreign workers' housing, work conditions and health insurance. In effect, man-power agencies are largely in charge of this process. These responsibilities are routinely violated by the agencies and employers, and routinely un-enforced by the government, due to lack of manpower and governmental indecision. Since the stay and work permit of a migrant worker is linked to a specific employer, moving to another employer makes one 'illegal'. This bonding of foreign workers to a specific employer who can make them illegal simply by dismissing them, encourages massive exploitation by em-ployers. Thus, the Israeli migration regime makes the situation of legal workers often more difficult than that of illegal workers. Although the latter face the threat of deportation, they are free to choose their workplace, housing, etc. In fact, many migrant workers abandon their legal employer in order to earn better wages and improve their living conditions, thus entering the illegal migrant population (Bar-Zuri, 1999; Drori and Kunda, 1999; Rosenhek, 1999).

Between 1993-1996 government policy was to effectively ignore illegal workers. Quotas for legal foreign labourers in each sector were set from time to time, with the construction and agricultural lobbies pressing to increase, and the Ministry of Interior pressing to limit, the number of permits. In late 1996 the government decided to reduce the number of work permits for migrants and set a target of 1,000 deportations per month of illegal workers. The number of deportations did grow, but remained a fraction of the level intended.

The new Labour-led government which came to power in June 1999, while not outlining a clear policy concerning the foreign workers, in prac-tice decreased dramatically the deportations of illegal migrants. In addition, different ministries have raised the need to reform the current situation, which is considered unsatisfactory by all sides (except the employers and manpower agencies), including the possibility of formulating a limited, temporary legalisation for certain groups of migrant workers. A committee in the Ministry of Health has recommended the inclusion of children of foreign workers (regardless of legal status) in the national health insurance plan, on a limited basis. In January 2000 an amendment was passed to the 1991 Law on migrant labour, tightening the employers' responsibilities toward their legal foreign workers. However, without proper enforcement, exploitation of the legal workers is expected to continue. Meanwhile, Prime Minister Barak ordered (in August 2000) the authorities to increase the deportation rate of illegal migrants, and to further decrease the number of permits issued to migrant workers.[15]

Municipal Policies toward Labour Migrants

Although local authorities in Israel are weak vis-à-vis the national government, Tel Aviv is relatively autonomous due to its economic centrality, which translates into a high municipal income from local taxes.[16] This independence was expressed in the opening in 1999 of a municipal service centre for the migrant workers in Tel Aviv (MESILA), the only one in the country. Since the majority of immigrants in Tel Aviv are illegal, this municipally-funded service openly defies the government policy of ignoring or deporting illegal migrants. Since then, Tel Aviv's policy has clearly aimed to push the government into assuming more responsibility for the migrant workers and their families, regardless of their legal status.

Tel Aviv's policy toward its foreign worker population developed informally within the municipal bureaucracy during the mid-1990s. It became official at the beginning of 1999, when the newly elected Mayor, Ron Huldai, stated that 'the Municipality of Tel-Aviv-Yafo must assume responsibility for the estimated 60,000 foreign workers in the city'. The Mayor and municipal Council, elected for five-year terms, govern Tel Aviv-Yafo. Since January 1999 Mayor Huldai (Labour) rules with an overwhelming majority coalition in the Council, leaving elected councillors with little influence. It is the Mayor and his administration that effectively make and run migrant policy in Tel Aviv.

The previous Mayor (1993-1998) deliberately steered away from official recognition of the 'foreign worker problem'. His stand was that the city would adopt no policy regarding the local migrant population as long as government policy was undecided. However, a *de facto* shift in local policy toward the migrants began within the professional municipal bureaucracy around 1996. Until then, municipal officials had regarded the migrant population at best as a temporary phenomenon, at worst as an 'urban threat' to the city's southern neighbourhoods. In 1996, for the first time, reports on the migrant population were written from within the Planning and Welfare Divisions, suggesting that migrant needs must be addressed. Neither paper mentioned migrant representation, and both papers were ignored at the mayoral level.

Meanwhile, the municipal departments, which had to deal with the migrants on a day-to-day basis, developed selective treatment policies, emphasising treatment of migrant children. Thus, municipal schools accepted migrant children, nearly all of them undocumented. In 1988, 1,674 migrant children were enrolled in local schools, out of an estimated (1999) 1,700 foreign workers' children residing in Tel Aviv, mostly under six years of age. The Municipality covers the full costs, which are normally subsidised by the Ministry of Education for Israeli children. Municipal social workers treated migrants regardless of their legal status, in cases of clear danger and provided emergency treatment especially to children. The Municipality's neighbourhood Mother-Infant Health Stations treated all migrant applicants – foreigners accounted for over 60 per cent of all cases at the Neve Sha'anan Station by 1998 – but other municipal health services were closed to the undocumented migrants (Tel-Aviv-Yafo Municipality, 1999b). The municipal Welfare Division pioneered the way in the *de facto* recognition of the migrant presence. In 1997 the Director of the Welfare Division assigned a municipal community worker to deal specifically with the migrant population. Her contacts with the labour migrant communities laid the basis for the foundation of MESILA two years later.

Between 1996 and the elections in late 1998 the realisation of a significant (and possibly permanent) labour migrant presence in Tel Aviv arose in the public consciousness, due in large to the local press. It did not develop into an election issue, however. After Mayor Huldai entered office he set up a Forum on Foreign Workers, an advisory body reporting to him made up of relevant municipal officials (for instance directors of relevant departments and MESILA) plus academic advisors. Intended to formulate new policy for the Mayor and co-ordinate actions toward the migrant population, the Forum meets irregularly and has no public representation. Neither migrants nor Israelis (e.g. local NGOs dealing with migrants) have representatives in the Forum, a step that would have alleviated its top-down character.

The most concrete expression of Tel Aviv's migrant policy was the establishment (July 1999) of MESILA, the Aid and Information Center for the Foreign Community in Tel-Aviv-Yafo. Located in the core migrant neighbourhood of Neve Sha'anan, the centre serves migrants (regardless of legal status) at three basic levels. Firstly, its volunteers and small staff of social workers provide individual assistance to migrants through information and counselling, in issues as varied as health, bureaucratic and legal problems, housing, and family violence. Often, MESILA serves as a mediator between migrants and Israeli institutions: ministries, employers, police, landlords, etc. Secondly, group activities such as courses on childcare, Hebrew language, etc. are intended to provide migrants with tools for dealing with life in Israel. Thirdly, MESILA aims to empower migrant communities by encouraging the organisation of local migrant leadership. The centre has initiated a series of meetings with migrant community representatives, such as leaders of the African Workers Union, pastors in the Latino and Filipino communities, etc.

Through MESILA (and its informal predecessor in the Welfare Department), the Municipality of Tel Aviv appears to have broken the suspicion with which the migrant community in Tel Aviv, most of them undocumented and fearful of deportation, had regarded any contact with the authorities. Previously, migrants turned only to NGOs such as Workers Hotline and the Association for Civil Rights in Israel for help. Now, a clear majority of the migrants coming to MESILA are 'illegals', mostly from Latin America and Africa. The government's first reaction to MESILA was mixed. Warnings from Jerusalem, recommending that the centre serve only documented workers, were followed by informal expressions of support for the new service, and finally by visits of government representatives, including several ministers, who praised the city's initiative.

Tel Aviv's current policy toward the labour migrants is primarily of a service nature. As a tool of empowerment for the migrant communities MESILA's influence is still unclear. Beyond MESILA, however, the city's migrant policy is still undecided, indeed, it is not at all clear whether a comprehensive policy toward the migrant community will develop in Tel Aviv. The issue of migrant representation is still taboo, and there are no formal participatory frameworks for the migrant communities in Tel Aviv. Presumably, the needs of the migrant communities are to be voiced through MESILA's director to the Forum on Foreign Workers. The possibility of including migrant representatives in the Forum is dependent on the decision of the Mayor. Although considered a liberal, Huldai is an ex-Air Force officer with a centralised style of governance (similar to Prime Minister Barak). It appears unlikely that he will agree to any formal participation of the migrant population, beyond a purely consultative arrangement.

Surviving in the 'Hebrew City': Organisation and Mobilisation

The Israeli migrant regime, as described above, discourages political mobilisation of labour migrants. The legal workers live in fear of their employer's wrath should they openly organise, while the undocumented workers live in fear of deportation. This same regime, however, has led to a paradoxical situation, where the undocumented migrants have greater freedom to organise, even to mobilise politically, than their legal counterparts. Thus, the Africans and South Americans, most of whom are illegal, have developed a wide variety of self-help and social organisations, while the Romanians (most of whom are legal) have not developed any social organisation. However, only the African community has succeeded in political mobilisation, through the supra-national African Workers Union. Interestingly, the AWU has succeeded in bringing the plight of the illegal African labour migrants to public attention, by raising 'two major themes explicitly aimed at mobilising Israeli public opinion and support' (Kemp et al., 2000). The first theme relates to the 'valorisation of personhood' (Soysal, 1994) that is, claiming rights divorced from national membership. The more prominent theme recurring in the African migrants' claims is to depict themselves as a 'community of suffering'. This theme deliberately speaks to Israelis' 'Jewish conscience', drawing parallels between the current hardships of the African migrant community in Israel, and those of the Jewish Diaspora in the past (Kemp et al., 2000). The AWU's strategy is described in the next section.

The African community is the most highly organised, having developed a large number of self-help communitarian associations which can be categorised as:

- social-cultural organisations such as churches, sports and music clubs;
- national and regional origin-based associations;
- rotating credit associations.

African associations in Tel Aviv are organised on national and regional lines, the oldest being of the Ghanaians, the most veteran migrant workers' community in Tel Aviv. Other associations include those of migrants from Mauritius Island, Central African Republic, Republic of Congo, Nigeria, and Democratic Republic of Congo. There is also a regional-tribal association of the Manding people. The supra-national African Workers Union, established in 1997, is the only pan-African, political association.

Fear of arrest and deportation remains the underlying reason for the underground nature of the African organisations. Dozens of 'underground' churches of various denominations operate in former stores and warehouses in southern Tel Aviv, in addition to at least two dozen 'underground' kindergartens, usually operating in private apartments, and one African community 'school' with 26 children between ages 3-12. African self-help organisations are patterned after the village associations. Rotating credit associations, based on non-formal arrangements of mutual aid and trust, provide money and loans to members in times of need. Social life focuses around churches, and pastors play an important role in community life.

Following the Africans, the Latino migrant communities in Tel Aviv have made several attempts to create a supra-national Latino association. These have failed due to personal rivalries, intrigues and power struggles. A Latin Workers Union (OTL) was established in 1998, modelled on the African Workers Union, with the active support of Israeli social activists and academics. It was a fragile and short-lived attempt that was abandoned after a series of police raids. Indeed, the Latino community blamed this mobilisation attempt as responsible for an escalation in arrests and deportations.

Although not mobilised politically, Latino migrant organisations flourish as religious, sport, and cultural associations. The South American migrant community has developed independent religious organisations, mostly Evangelist, supplementing the established Catholic churches in Yafo. Some of the Latino religious organisations have established connections with the Arab Protestant churches in Israel. Football teams and leagues also play a significant role. The weekly football games, accompanied by Latino food stalls and music, serve as the central supra-national event of the Latino community, in which information is exchanged, funds are raised, etc. The Latino migrant community also has a variety of self-help, cultural and recreational organisations, such as folklore ensembles and *tertulias*, informal discussion gatherings on social and political issues relevant to the Latino community.

The East Asian migrants, mostly Filipino women whose employment as caregivers restricts them to their employer's house during the week, have developed associations centred around the organisation of social activities on weekends and holidays. Filipino organisations include mutual help functions, such as raising money for emergency flights home. Some of the organisations take annual dues and issue membership cards. Catholic churches also provide a framework for mutual activities of the Filipino community, e.g. trips to holy sites in Israel (Von Breitenstein, 1999).

The Romanians (employed in the construction sector) are in Israel on a rotating basis, usually one or two years, and regard their stay as temporary. They are all single men and have no formal social organisation, beyond drinking together at established places. This appears to be the rule for labour migrants employed in construction from other countries as well (e.g. China). The only type of 'mobilisation' is ad hoc, when groups of workers raise grievances toward their employer about work and living conditions. These grievances are either settled within the workplace (sometimes by the employer dismissing the troublemakers and having them deported), or brought to the attention of Workers Hotline, the NGO dealing with these issues.

Migrant Mobilisation: The African Workers Union

The African Workers Union (AWU) was founded in July 1997 in reaction to the deportation policy implemented in the spring of 1997. Leaders in the African community at first tried, unsuccessfully, to petition the Supreme Court claiming violation of human rights. A series of informal meetings with Israeli parliament (Knesset) members, mediated by a journalist from the local Tel Aviv newspaper, led to a formal invitation to visit the parliament. Knesset members encouraged the AWU leaders (themselves illegal migrants) to create

> an official body of the African Community to work together with the Law Makers to come up with an honourable solution to government policy regarding migrant workers in Israel (AWU, 1999).

Following this meeting, the migrants submitted a policy proposal on the status of the African migrant community in Israel, and decided on the creation of the African Workers Union as the body that would represent the entire African community. Aided legally by a Knesset member, the AWU was officially registered in Israel as a non-profit organisation, although its membership is overwhelmingly made of illegal migrants! At a gathering in October 1997 religious and lay community leaders of the African community gave their support to the AWU (Kemp et al., 2000).

The AWU is characterised by a formal, bureaucratic structure, which typifies many of the African migrant community organisations. The self-appointed leadership includes a chairman, vice-chairman, general secretary, spokesman, etc. Although there is no formal mechanism of national representation, the positions are held by men from different countries in Africa.

According to the AWU *Newsletter* (AWU, 1999), the current leadership 'plans to establish definitive structures of the organisation' through general elections in the future. The AWU requires members to register and pay dues, and issues union ID cards – interesting for an organisation of illegal migrants who live under threat of arrest and deportation. The AWU's three main goals are:

- in the short term, to limit systematic deportation;
- in the medium term, 'to solicit the help of Israelis of good will in political activism, in order to find an honourable solution to the presence of Africans in Israel';
- in the long term, to achieve 'limited legal status for all migrant Africans' in Israel (AWU, 1999).

Beyond the stated political goals, the organisation's aim is to provide a 'common umbrella which will provide assistance and services' to all African workers. In its first two years of existence, the organisation has become an accepted lobbyist at the national level. AWU leaders have met with over thirty Knesset members and arranged visits to the Neve Sha'anan neighbourhood in an effort to secure support for favourable legislation regarding illegal migrants. At the local level, the AWU arranged visits for municipal officials and helped to organise a symposium in Tel Aviv on the deportation policy. If a foreign worker is invited to speak at a public forum on migrants in the city, it is invariably an AWU spokesman. AWU spokesmen have appeared at the four main universities in Israel to solicit support of the academic community, and met with the Secretary General of Amnesty International during his visit in Israel (AWU, 1999).

Aided by local media, local NGOs and several Knesset members, the AWU has succeeded in raising the plight of the African migrants before the Israeli public.[17] Israeli public opinion on the foreign communities is most favourable toward the Africans. However, AWU's primary goal – obtaining some kind of legalisation for the African migrant community – has not been obtained. Indeed, the first and only proposal for legalisation of the undocumented migrants in Israel, raised by then Interior Minister Scharansky, has been a blow to the Africans' hopes. It was based on granting yearlong work permits to illegal workers who have been in Israel for less than five years. This would exclude most of the African migrants, and include the newer groups of illegal labour migrants, mostly from the former Soviet Union. AWU leaders accused Scharansky, head of the Russian migrants' party, of wanting to enlarge his constituency (Fishbain, 2000).[18]

Mobilisation and Municipal Policies: Complementary or Contradictory?

Barely a decade has passed since labour migrants began settling in Tel Aviv. The Municipality only recently began to experiment with policies toward the local migrant population, and migrant mobilisation is still in its infancy. Yet several points can already be noted from the Tel Avivian experience, regarding migrant mobilisation, municipal policies, and the interaction between them.

First, the migration regime of the host country has had a profound influence on the character of labour migrant organisation and mobilisation. In the Israeli case, this regime has led to a paradoxical situation where the illegal migrant communities have formed well-developed networks of self-organisation, while the legal migrants have not. Until now, the labour migrant communities in Tel Aviv have not translated their well-developed social organisation into political mobilisation, with the one exception of the African community. The AWU has concentrated its efforts at the national political level, on improving the legal status of the African community, rather than on local, material improvements. It is unclear to what extent this juridical focus reflects the needs of the African community as a whole, the focus of the self-appointed leadership of the AWU, or the focus of Israeli human rights activists who have been instrumental in aiding the formation of the AWU.

Secondly, the national migration regime has influenced the municipal reaction to the labour migrants. The restrictive immigration regime and the exploitation of legal workers resulting from it encourages labour migrants to seek work in the illegal labour market. Tel Aviv has become the centre of the undocumented migrants in Israel, providing them with more job opportunities and the shelter of the big city. As migrant enclaves emerge in its poorer neighbourhoods, the city has had to deal with the urban conse-quences, as well as the needs of thousands of people that the government effectively ignores. In reaction, municipal service departments developed informal policies toward the migrants. These were formalised by the new mayor through the founding MESILA, whose goals and practice contradict national migrant policies. The gauntlet thrown at the government by the Municipality of Tel Aviv appears to be affecting national policies, as reflected in the reforms being considered at the ministerial level regarding the situation of undocumented migrants in Israel. To some extent the reform attempts may also be a result of the strategy of the AWU, which has raised public sympathy to the plight of the illegal migrants, without raising claims for permanent citizenship status that could be perceived by the public as threatening the Jewish character of the state.

Thirdly, the interaction between migrant mobilisation and municipal policies, although at first glance complementary, may in the long run be contradictory. At the national level the Municipality of Tel Aviv and the migrant organisations are co-operating (or using each other) to advance mutual claims on the new government. The Municipality is increasingly making its voice heard at the national level, demanding a fundamental change in government policy regarding the labour migrants residing in Israel. The migrants too, in the case of the AWU, have focused their attention on changes at the national level, primarily in the Knesset.

However, the Municipality appears to be interested firstly and primarily in improving migrants' living conditions at the local level, primarily through MESILA. The Municipality says that it cannot change the migration regime, but it can help improve daily life 'in the small but important things'. MESILA is thus encouraging the migrants to articulate their needs regarding education of the children, health care, housing problems, etc. in an organised fashion. The migrants, on the other hand, at least in the case of the Africans, are most disturbed by their illegal status and the threat of deportation. They feel that legalisation is the only solution, and appear less concerned about their living conditions.

There is still no talk of formal representation of the migrants at the local level, neither by the migrants nor by the Municipality. As long as the threat of deportation hangs over the undocumented migrants who make up the majority of the foreign worker population in Tel Aviv, it is difficult to imagine anything more than a consultative type of participation. Possibly MESILA may act as intermediary between migrant representatives and municipal policy-makers. Should the undocumented migrants attain some kind of legal status in the future, the possibility that they will raise political demands at the local level is very real, as we know from the European experience. That would probably signal the end of the current honeymoon between the Municipality of Tel Aviv and its labour migrant population.

Notes

1   In 1997 the official population of Tel Aviv was 348,600, not including the labour migrants. If we include the foreign worker population, the total city population may reach up to 400,000 residents.

2   The total number of foreign workers in Israel, according to official estimates for 1998, is about 170,000 (about half of them legal). Other estimates place the number as

200,000 or more, i.e. approximately 3 per cent of the national population (Ministry of Labour and Welfare, 1998). Some consider the government estimates to be low. The Israeli NGO Workers Hotline estimates there are between 200,000-250,000 foreign workers in Israel, of which 100,000 have legal permits.

3   See, e.g. Smooha (1990) on Israel as an 'ethnic democracy' and Yiftachel (1993) on Israel as an 'ethnocracy'.

4   Tel-Aviv-Yafo is the official name of the city, since the annexation of the Arab city of Yafo (Jaffa) to Tel Aviv in 1950 (see below). We shall use the term Tel Aviv to designate the entire city, noting Yafo separately when necessary.

5   The Tel Aviv Metropolitan Area was officially redefined in 1995 to include the Tel Aviv District (including Tel Aviv and three neighbouring cities) and Central District, plus the city of Ashdod in the Southern District. The TAMA thus covers most of central Israel. In 1995 the TAMA supplied 46 per cent of the work places in Israel and produced 50 per cent of Israel's GNP (Lerman and Shahar, 1996).

6   Based on employment figures, the main economic sectors of Tel Aviv are finance and business services (24 per cent); public services (21 per cent); commerce, restaurants and hotels (19 per cent); and industry (16 per cent) (Tel-Aviv-Yafo Municipality, 1996a).

7   Since the population census is based on respondents' self-definition of their religious identity, the exact number of Arab residents after 1990 is hard to ascertain. Until 1990 'non-Jewish' in Tel-Aviv-Yafo meant Muslim or Christian Arab. From 1990, however, with the new wave of immigrants from the Soviet Union, 'non-Jewish' no longer assumes Arab. In the 1996 census, 35 per cent of the respondents identifying themselves as non-Jews were Russian immigrants. According to the 1997 census, the total non-Jewish population in Tel-Aviv-Yafo (not including foreign workers) is 19,300, or 5.5 per cent of the city population (Tel-Aviv-Yafo Municipality, 1998a).

8   The legal foreign workers are employed in the construction industry (75 per cent), agriculture (15 per cent) and domestic and geriatric services (10 per cent) (Fischer, 1999; Schnell, 1999b).

9   The main 'entry routes' to Israel for illegals are: (a) entering on tourist visas (2-3 months) and remaining to work; (b) entering as legal workers and then leaving the legal employer; (c) increasing numbers of workers from Arab countries enter through neighbouring Egypt and Jordan and then 'disappear' within the Palestinian or Israeli Arab communities, thus entering the Israeli labour market (Schnell, 1999a).

10   The Municipality estimated in 1997 that there were some 60,000 foreigners in the city. The latest estimates (1999) by the Municipality are much lower, below 25,000. Among researchers, however, the estimates vary between 25,000-40,000 and some believe the numbers may be even higher than 60,000.

11   Undocumented labour migrants in Israel are estimated to be: 33 per cent Eastern Europeans, 17 per cent Asians, 15 per cent Africans, and 14 per cent Latin Americans (Ministry of Labour and Welfare, 1998).

12   According to the Ministry of Labour, Africans account for some 15 per cent of the illegal migrant workers in Israel, i.e. between ten to twenty thousand, of which the majority resides in Tel Aviv. Other estimates are lower, between 5,000-10,000 of whom the majority is in Tel Aviv.

13 According to an unpublished 1999 municipal estimate, between 8,500-10,000 foreign workers reside in the core area neighbourhoods, comprising between 50 to 60 per cent of their population.

14 Two government ministries are primarily responsible for policy concerning non-Jewish migrants: the Ministry of Labour and Welfare, and the Ministry of Interior. Conspicuously absent is the Ministry of Immigrant Absorption, which deals only with Jewish immigration. Before the last elections in May 1999, both these ministries were in the hands of the Orthodox Shas party, which is clearly antagonistic to non-Jewish migrants. In the first year of the new Labour-led government, the Ministry of Labour and Welfare was still controlled by Shas, but the Russian immigrants' party Israel Ba'Aliya controlled the Interior Ministry. Following the secession of these two parties from the coalition government, the two above ministries are currently headed by ministers from the ruling Labour Party.

15 The government has approved a draft law, to be submitted to parliament in October 2000, to regulate the detention and deportation of illegal foreign workers, introducing judicial review in the process.

16 Government payments accounted for only some 12 per cent of the 1997 municipal budget. However, in Welfare, Education and Health, the government's role in the municipal budget accounted for 45 per cent, 31 per cent and 22 per cent, respectively (Tel-Aviv-Yafo Municipality, 1998a). This limits the city's autonomy in these areas, which are important in local policy toward migrant residents.

17 The AWU is actively aided by the four main NGOs dealing with the foreign worker phenomenon, all operating from Tel Aviv: Workers Hotline (which provides office space for the AWU's administration); the Association for Civil Rights in Israel; Physicians for Human Rights; and the Hotline for Migrant Workers in Prison. The role of Israeli human rights activists, including the Tel Aviv journalist Einat Fishbain, in encouraging and facilitating the political activity of the African migrants was significant.

18 After being implemented on a limited and experimental basis in Eilat, Scharansky's proposal seems to have been shelved for the time being, due to widespread opposition from the Ministry of Labour on one hand, and human rights organisations on the other hand, and following his party's secession from the coalition and resignation from the Ministry of Interior.

References

AWU (African Workers Union) (1999), *Newsletter*, August 1999, Tel Aviv.

Bartram, D. (1998), 'Foreign Workers in Israel: History and Theory', *International Migration Review*, vol. 32, pp. 303-25.

Bar-Zuri, R. (1999), *Foreign Workers without Permit in Israel, 1998* (in Hebrew), Ministry of Labour and Welfare, Manpower Planning Authority, Jerusalem.

Breitenstein, T. von (1999), 'The Philippino Workers in Israel', in R. Nathanson and L. Achdut (eds), *The New Workers: Wage Earners from Foreign Countries in Israel* (in Hebrew), Hakibbutz Hameuchad, Tel Aviv.

Drori, I. and Kunda, G. (1999), *The Work Experience of Foreign Workers in Israel* (in Hebrew), Institute for Social and Labour Research, Tel Aviv University, Tel Aviv.

Fischer, H. (1999) 'Foreign Workers: Current Situation, Formal Framework and Government Policy', in R. Nathanson and L. Achdut (eds), *The New Workers: Wage Earners from Foreign Countries in Israel* (in Hebrew), Hakibbutz Hameuchad, Tel Aviv.

Fishbain, E. (2000), 'Foreigners Forever', *Ha'aretz*, Daily newspaper, English edition, February 25, 2000, p. B4.

Fishbain, E. (2000), 'The New Tel Avivians', Series of articles in *Ha'ir*, Tel Aviv weekly newspaper (in Hebrew), July 1997-July 1998.

Kemp, A., Raijman, R., Resnik, J. and Schammah Gesser, S. (2000), 'Contesting the Limits of Political Participation: Latinos and Black African Migrant Workers in Israel', *Ethnic and Racial Studies*, vol. 23, pp. 94-115.

Lerman, R. and Shahar, A. (1996), *Development Policy Principles for Tel Aviv Metropolitan Area*, Volume 1, Intermediate Report no. 2 (in Hebrew), The Institute for Urban and Regional Studies, Hebrew University of Jerusalem, Jerusalem.

Menahem, G. (1993), *Urban Economic and Spatial Restructuring and Absorption of Immigrants*, Paper presented at the International Workshop on Immigrant absorption, Technion, Israel Institute of Technology, May 1993.

Ministry of Labour and Welfare, *Foreign Workers in Israel: Statistical Report for 1997*, Presentation transparencies (in Hebrew) for Caesaria Conference, Manpower Planning Authority, June 1998.

Rosenhek, Z. (1999), 'The Politics of Claims-making by Labour Migrants in Israel', *Journal of Ethnic and Migration Studies*, vol. 25, pp. 575-95.

Schnell, I. (1999a), *Foreign Workers in Southern Tel Aviv-Yafo* (in Hebrew), The Florsheimer Institute for Policy Studies, Jerusalem.

Schnell, I. (1999b), *Incorporation of the Foreign Workers in Israel* (in Hebrew), Unpublished report for the Center for Social Policy Research in Israel, Jerusalem.

Shuval, J. and Leshem, E. (1998), 'The Sociology of Migration in Israel: A Critical View', in E. Leshem and J. Shuval (eds), *Studies of Israeli Society*, Volume 8, Transaction Publishers, London.

Smooha, S. (1990), 'Minority Status in an Ethnic Democracy: The Status of the Arab Minority in Israel', *Ethnic and Racial Studies*, vol. 13, pp. 389-413.

Soysal, Y. (1994), *The Limits of Citizenship*, University of Chicago Press, Chicago.

State Comptroller (1996), *1995 Annual Report*, No. 46 (in Hebrew), State Comptroller, Jerusalem.

Tel-Aviv-Yafo Municipality (1995), *Historical Survey of Master Plans*, Tel-Aviv-Yafo Master Plan Report no. 2 (in Hebrew), Planning Division, Long-Term Planning Department, Tel Aviv.

Tel-Aviv-Yafo Municipality (1996a), *Tel Aviv: Mediterranean Metropolis*, Planning Division, Long-Term Planning Department, Tel Aviv.

Tel-Aviv-Yafo Municipality (1996b), *Foreign Citizen Workers in T.A.-Yafo*, Draught report (in Hebrew), Welfare Division, Tel Aviv.

Tel-Aviv-Yafo Municipality (1998a), *Statistical Yearbook 1997* (in Hebrew), Center for Economic and Social Research, Tel Aviv.

Tel-Aviv-Yafo Municipality (1998b), *Districts in Tel-Aviv-Yafo*, Planning data (in Hebrew), Planning Division, Long-Term Planning Department, Tel Aviv.

Tel-Aviv-Yafo Municipality (1999a), 'The Foreign Worker Phenomenon and Urban Implications: Municipal Policy Background Paper', Draught paper (in Hebrew), Planning Division, Long-Term Planning Department, Tel Aviv.

Tel-Aviv-Yafo Municipality (1999b), 'Foreign Workers in Tel-Aviv-Yafo', Presentation trans-parencies (in Hebrew), Welfare Division, Tel Aviv.

Yiftachel, O. (1993), 'The "Ethnic Democracy" Model and Jewish-Arab Relations in Israel: Geographical, Historical and Political Angles', *Ofakim Geografia* (Geographical Horizons) (in Hebrew), vol. 37-38, pp. 51-9.

11 Contradictions of Inclusion in a Direct Democracy: The Struggle for Political Rights of Migrants in Zurich

HANS MAHNIG AND ANDREAS WIMMER

Introduction

Switzerland has become one of the most important immigration countries in Europe. If one looks at the percentage of people born abroad – an indicator commonly used in traditional immigration countries – the proportion of foreign born in Switzerland is about one fifth of the overall resident population (Haug, 1995, p. 28), a figure twice as high as the USA, and considerably higher than Canada. In Zurich, the economic centre and the largest city of Switzerland, immigration is even more important than on the national level, a phenomenon which mirrors the fact that migrants 'tend to concentrate heavily in larger urban areas', becoming 'the directly visible face of globalisation' (Penninx, 1998, p. 3).

How did the local authorities react to this process? Did they implement specific policies in order to respond to the presence of the large migrant population in Zurich? And the migrants, did they organise and make specific claims to local authorities? In the following pages we will try to give an answer to these questions. However, at the same time our aim is to look closer at the existing hypotheses concerning the inclusion of migrants in Western societies. Zurich may be regarded as a particular interesting case for studying the question of the local inclusion of migrants, because it has been described as one of the European cities with the most democratic institutional framework for policy-making (Neidhart, 1998). Furthermore, because the Swiss federal system gives municipalities substantial autonomy in several policy fields, they have a wider margin to implement immigrant policies than local authorities in other countries. These two institutional features seem to provide a political opportunity structure (see MPMC, 1997) particularly appropriate for the inclusion of migrant communities on

221

the city level. Several important studies of immigration and immigrant policy support this view: they are based on the implicit assumption that the more democratically organised a polity is the better are the chances for the inclusion of migrants. James F. Holliefield (1992, p. 232), for example, shows that the contradiction between economic interests and individual rights led in liberal societies to a converging 'expansion of civil rights for aliens and other minorities'. Gary Freeman, observing a general tendency for the fuller inclusion of migrants in the Western world during the last decades (1995a) goes even a step further claiming that this process has to be explained by the gradual 'unfolding of the internal logic of the core values of liberal democracy' (Freeman, 1995b, p. 912). Given the fact that the Swiss system of direct democracy, at the local as well as the national level, provides social groups through the popular initiative[1] and the referendum[2] with more opportunities to participate in the political process than political systems of the representative type (Linder, 1999, p. 236), one might reasonably imagine that Zurich is a city open to claims of migrants.

The following analysis, though, will show that this is not the case. Although over the last three decades there has been an increasing adaptation of Zurich's municipal institutions to the specific problems of ethnic minorities, there is still a reluctance to grant them full inclusion into society. This can neither be explained by the lack of mobilisation of the migrants, nor by the unwillingness or resistance of local policy-makers, but has primarily to be imputed to the opposition of important parts of the Swiss population who can articulate their hostility towards migrants through the instruments of direct democracy. We agree therefore with Patrick Ireland (1994) who thinks that Swiss political institutions have been detrimental to the inclusion of migrants.

This result leads us to a more general observation: our central hypothesis is that a fuller understanding of the dynamics of immigrant politics is only possible if we do not consider liberal democratic regimes in a holistic way. Literature on migration is full of examples that treat 'liberal democracies' as homogeneous entities. However, modern democratic regimes consist of two basic principles, according to the French theorist Jean Leca (1996, p. 231): 'the reign of the number' and 'the reign of the law'. In other words, in liberal democracies, the democratic element, the right to participate in political decisions, is counter-balanced by the constitutional element, the guarantee of human rights. As recent literature on European immigrant policy shows, migrants have often gained new rights because the corresponding decisions have not been made democratically, but 'behind closed doors' by the political elite (Guiraudon, 1998, p. 293) – the most prominent example being probably the granting of local voting rights to migrants in the Netherlands (Rath, 1988, p. 29). In other words, the inclusion of migrants is due to the liberal element in Western societies and not to the democratic one.

This hypothesis will be illustrated by the study of Italian immigrants and their struggle for political rights in the City of Zurich. The reason for choosing Italians is twofold. First they have been one of the most important migrant groups in Zurich since the end of the last century and have become the most important one after 1945. Second, since the 1960s, they have engaged in a widespread mobilisation, first for their civil then for their political rights, and gave birth to the most important migrant associations in Switzerland. Therefore after having presented some basic data on the city and its migrants and their children, we will first sketch the municipal immigrant policy during the last three decades, then present the mobilisation of Italian migrants and, finally, analyse the interaction between the two.

Zurich: An Immigration City

The City of Zurich is the largest of the 261 municipalities of the Canton of Zurich.[3] It is divided in 12 *Kreise* (boroughs) and 34 *Quartiere* (neighbourhoods); in 1997, 335,943 persons lived in the city. However, the metropolitan area of Zurich is far larger than the municipality alone and stretches over the limits of the Canton. In 1996 the agglomeration – officially defined as an area consisting of 100 municipalities – consisted of 948,537 persons (Statistisches Amt, 1997, p. 349), although certain authors suggest that the whole metropolitan area includes about 1.5 million inhabitants (Hitz et al., 1995, p. 225).

Zurich is the economically most important city of Switzerland: once the seat of machine and textile industry, its economy is today largely dominated by tertiary sector activities.[4] From 1965 to 1991 the share of the workforce in the secondary sector felt from 43.0 per cent to 18.5 per cent, whereas in the financial sector it increased from 9.6 per cent to 26.1 per cent. In 1990 about one third of the 500 biggest Swiss companies had their head office in Zurich, as well as three of the four largest Swiss banks and four of the six largest insurance firms. Of all foreign banks 59 per cent were located in Zurich. That is why certain authors consider that Zurich has the characteristics of a 'global city' (Hitz et al., 1995, pp. 219-20).

Immigration to Zurich

Immigration to Zurich has a long history and roughly corresponds to the migration patterns on the national level. After having been an emigration country for a long time, Switzerland became an immigration country in the last decades of the nineteenth century. In 1848 the new Constitution, and the victory of the liberal movement over the Conservatives made Switzerland a liberal 'island' on the European continent which attracted a significant number of political refugees (Vuilleumier, 1992, pp. 24-38). But it was the industrial take-off during the second part of the nineteenth century which led to immigration: the proportion of foreigners in the total population increased from 3 per cent in 1850 to 14.7 per cent in 1910. On the eve of World War I about 600,000 foreigners were living in the country, which was 15.4 per cent of the total population. Most of them came from Switzerland's neighbouring countries: Germany, Italy, France and Austria (Schlaepfer, 1969, pp. 13, 17, 82).

Migration to Zurich was even stronger: because of the booming construction industry foreigners made up 33.4 per cent of the total population in 1910 (see Table 11.1). Germans and Italians were the most important groups, the latter living concentrated in Aussersihl, a neighbourhood which became in 1896 the place of the so-called Italian riots (*Italienerkrawalle*), a violent outburst of anger and xenophobic resentments against Italians (Looser, 1986). During World Wars I and II the foreign population decreased significantly at both national and the city levels, falling in Zurich to 24,306 (6.8 per cent) in 1945.

Shortly after the Second World War, a new immigration cycle began. There was a steady and massive flow of foreign workers to Switzerland: on the national level their number increased from 285,000 in 1950 (6.1 per cent) to 983,000 (17.2 per cent) in 1970. For Zurich the corresponding figures were 32,000 (8.1 per cent) in 1950 and 70,000 (16.7 per cent) in 1970 (see Table 11.1). Most of them came from Italy and Spain and responded to the demand for unqualified workers in construction and in restaurants and hotels. Contrary to other European countries, the international economic crisis of 1973-1974 led to a massive return migration of foreign workers to their countries of origin. Between 1974 and 1977 the Swiss economy lost a tenth of its jobs: two thirds of those dismissed were foreigners and it is estimated that a large number of the unemployed left the country between 1974 and 1976 (Haug, 1980, pp. 7-8). Thus, Switzerland succeeded through its regulation system in making foreign labour an 'economic buffer' (Schmidt, 1982, p. 255). The share of foreigners in the total population fell to 14.8 per cent in 1980.

Table 11.1   Stock of foreign residents in Zurich (1900-1995)

Year	Foreigners	Swiss population	Total population	Foreign population (%)
1900	43,457	107,090	150,547	28.87
1905	51,700	116,800	168,500	30.68
1910	63,622	126,470	190,092	33.47
1915	58,569	141,662	200,231	28.25
1920	44,996	161,303	206,299	21.28
1925	37,882	172,892	210,774	17.97
1930	43,809	211,185	254,994	17.18
1935	35,310	281,847	317,157	11.13
1940	28,609	305,417	334,026	8.56
1945	24,309	333,075	357,381	6.80
1950	31,699	357,874	389,573	8.14
1955	36,659	380,692	417,351	8.78
1960	52,791	384,482	437,273	12.07
1965	67,242	366,623	433,865	15.50
1970	69,944	348,028	417,972	16.73
1975	70,542	319,071	389,613	18.11
1980	66,956	303,662	370,618	18.07
1985	72,712	286,372	359,084	20.25
1990	84,773	271,579	356,352	23.79
1995	101,465	259,361	360,826	28.12

Source: Leitbild 1998b, p. 57.

Although the number of foreigners in Zurich also decreased during the 1970s the logic of migration to the city began to follow a different path from the country as a whole. Their numbers rose from 67,000 in 1980 to 101,000 (28.1 per cent) in 1995, whereas on the national level their part in the total population only increased to 19 per cent in 1997. This divergent evolution can only partly be explained by the fact that migrants are increasingly moving to Zurich. Another important reason is the out-migration of the Swiss population from the city to the suburbs – a development also observed in other Swiss cities – which leads to a social polarisation between the big urban centres and the rest of the country (Leitbild, 1998b, pp. 51, 65).

The Main Characteristics of the Migrant Population

Swiss statistics only distinguish between foreigners and nationals. There is no registration of ethnic origin, as for example in the Netherlands and in the UK, which would permit the measurement of the numbers of ethnic minorities.[5]

Table 11.2   Composition of foreign residents in Zurich, by country of origin and percentage of the total foreign population (1996)

Country of origin	Number	Percentage of total foreign population
Italy	19,413	19.0
Republic of Yugoslavia*	16,172	15.8
Germany	9,806	9.6
Spain	8,026	7.9
Portugal	6,048	5.9
Turkey	5,825	5.7
Sri Lanka	3,905	3.8
Croatia	3,528	3.5
Austria	2,883	2.8
Macedonia	2,702	2.6
Bosnia	2,148	2.1
Greece	1,844	1.8
UK	1,222	1.2
USA	1,117	1.1
Other countries	17,409	17.2
Total of foreigners	102,048	100.0

* Serbia and Montenegro

Source: Statistisches Amt, 1997, p. 70.

In 1996, 85,767 persons (84 per cent) from the 102,048 foreigners living in Zurich were European in origin. Smaller numbers came from Asia (9,493), the Americas (3,977), Africa (2,579) and Australia (162). As Table 11.2 illustrates, the most important groups were the Italians (19 per cent of all foreigners), people from the Republic of Yugoslavia, the Germans, Spaniards, and Portuguese. The foreign population differs from the Swiss in Zurich along lines of religion. According to the census of 1990, 50 per cent of the Swiss were Protestant, 33 per cent were Catholic and a further 15 per cent had another or no religious affiliation.[6] Among foreigners however the proportions were quite different: only 8 per cent were Protestant and 55 per cent were Catholic, with 36 per cent recorded as having another religious affiliation or none (Statistisches Amt, 1997, p. 28). To this last group belong the Muslims, increasing from around 1,000 in 1970 to 8,700 in 1990 (just under 10 per cent of all foreigners) and the members of the Greek Orthodox Church. Recent estimates suggest that they are about 15,000 Muslims living in the city (Wittwer, 1996). The Greek Orthodox Church had 2,778 members in 1970 and 7,028 in 1990 (7.9 per cent of the total foreign population) (Statistisches Amt, 1996, p. 12).

Until the beginning of the 1980s the level of residential segregation in Zurich was relatively low and never became an issue of politics (Arend, 1991). But if one looks at the economic concentration of foreigners in Zurich's labour market one can distinguish two groups: on the one hand people from the German-speaking neighbouring countries (Germany and Austria), from Northwest Europe and from other OECD countries, who are mostly well-qualified and working in good positions. On the other hand immigrants from the traditional recruitment-countries – Spain, Portugal, former Yugoslavia, Greece, Turkey and other non-European-countries – who are concentrated at more than 90 per cent in branches which require only low qualifications (Bartal et al., 1998, pp. 43-4). The different groups have nevertheless diverse occupation-profiles (see Table 11.3): a fifth of the Italians work in sales and office jobs which require only low qualifications and about a quarter are occupied in metal-working, machine-building as well as construction and painting. Almost a fifth of the Spaniards and a quarter of the people from former Yugoslavia are working in the hotel and restaurant industry and higher proportions in construction/painting and cleaning. The Portuguese are concentrated in the same three sectors but even more strongly. Turks and Greeks are only concentrated in the service and not in the industrial sector: the three main occupation branches of the Turks are hotel and restaurant industry (21 per cent), sales and office jobs (15 per cent) and other occupations (19 per cent) whereas Greeks are distributed more evenly across the different branches (Ochsner, 1998, pp. 308-9). Women coming from the same countries of origin are highly concentrated (up to 90 per cent) in the hotel and restaurant industry, in sale and office jobs requiring low qualifications (for example cashiers), as nurses or hairdresser, and in the cleaning sector (Bartal et al., 1998, p. 44).

Table 11.3   **Distribution of employed foreigners according to nationality and branches in Zurich (in percentages) (1995)**

Branches	I [a]	S [b]	P [c]	E-Y [d]	T [e]	G [f]
Low-qualification jobs						
in the industrial sector						
Construction/painting	11	13	20	16	3	2
Metal-working/machine building	13	7	3	8	8	11
Textile	2	1	-	-	2	1
Low-qualification jobs						
in the service sector						
Hotel and restaurant industry	8	19	33	25	21	11
Sales/office jobs	20	10	4	9	15	18
Other occupations[g]	11	10	7	12	19	15
Cleaning	10	16	17	10	9	17
Hospital care	1	1	1	4	2	3
Public transports	6	11	5	6	8	5
Total low-qualification jobs	82	88	90	90	87	83
Other jobs	18	12	10	10	13	17
Total employment	100	100	100	100	100	100

[a] Italians; [b] Spaniards; [c] Portuguese; [d] Ex-Yugoslavian; [e] Turks; [f] Greeks;
[g] Unskilled workers and workers without indications on their profession

Source: Ochsner, 1998, pp. 303-9.

The Municipality's Policy on Migrants

As already stated, Zurich has been described as one of the European cities with the most democratic institutional frameworks for policy-making (Neidhart, 1998) because the so-called system of *direct democracy* gives social groups substantial opportunities to participate in the political process. The gathering of 4,000 signatures, for example, is sufficient to launch a popular initiative on the city level that has to be followed by a voting. If 4,000 signatures are collected against a decision taken in the Communal Council during the twenty following days, a referendum must be held.

Another peculiarity of the city's political system is linked to citizenship. In Switzerland the naturalisation procedure consists of three stages. The federal Constitution stipulates that, in order to get the Swiss nationality, one first has to become the citizen of a municipality and then of a canton. Therefore the candidates for naturalisation have to ask for the right of citizenship (*droit de cité*) from a municipality first (Centlivres, 1990). The federal Constitution prescribes that a foreigner, in order to apply for citizenship, has to prove that (s)he has lived legally in Switzerland for 12 years,[7] but the municipalities have the right to establish additional criteria, which are often grounded in an ethno-cultural logic: candidates for naturalisation have to prove that they are assimilated to the values and traditions of the local community. In addition, the naturalisation procedure is often very costly. Municipalities implement these principles in different ways: in large municipalities a special commission is responsible for treating the naturalisation demands of foreigners, whereas in small municipalities *all* the citizens decide on the requests (EKA, 1998). In Zurich, the Civil Section (Bürgerliche Abteilung), composed of municipal counsellors, is responsible for handling requests.

A further point has to be mentioned in order to understand immigrant policy in Zurich: contrary to other European cities, Zurich – and more generally Switzerland – was not confronted with such problems as migrant unemployment, social and ethnic segregation and urban violence until the 1990s. The federal admissions policy – which succeeded much better than other European countries' policy of using foreign workers during the international economic crisis of 1974 as an 'economic buffer' – guaranteed the country a very low unemployment rate for Swiss and foreigners alike. In the middle of the 1980s scholars could therefore affirm that in Switzerland 'the foreigner residing and being unemployed is rare, its social identity non-existent' (Bolzmann et al., 1987, p. 62).

Nevertheless, immigration became one of the central issues of Swiss politics during the 1960s and the first half of the 1970s, but in a different way than in other European countries: during this period a large campaign for a general reduction of the number of foreign workers took place. A couple of small political parties, rooted in the Canton of Zurich, achieved large public support for their claim that Switzerland was 'over-foreignised' (*überfremdet*) by the high number of immigrants. Using one of the instruments of direct democracy, these xenophobic movements succeeded in putting the government under pressure. They launched several popular initiatives demanding a radical cut in the number of foreigners living in Switzerland. Although these initiatives were rejected in popular votes, they nevertheless pushed the Swiss government to adopt a 'stabilisation policy' (*Stabilisierungspolitik*) – i.e. a more restrictive admission policy – in 1970 (Mahnig, 1998, pp. 178-9). However, because the so-called foreign-worker problem (*Fremdarbeiterproblem*) was defined as a question of reducing the number of migrants at the federal level, it has always been on the *national* and not on the *local* agenda.

Immigrants in Zurich from 1945 to 1990: A Marginal Issue

In the City of Zurich immigrant politics took a different form than at the national level. On the one hand, initiatives for a more open policy towards migrants were made by individual politicians sensitive to the problems of migrants, persons working in institutions in contact with migrants, citizens committed to the question for humanitarian or political reasons and the migrants themselves. These initiatives, which aimed for the fuller participation of migrants in the city's affairs, never found real support in mainstream political parties. However they were often accepted by the City Council (*Stadtrat*), which is the executive of the city, or the Communal Council (*Gemeinderat*), its legislative body, and led to the setting up of some immigrant-related institutions and policies. On the other hand, the xenophobic party National Action (Nationale Aktion, NA) tried to exclude migrants from a fuller participation in various fields. The Party never succeeded with its initiatives, but several times it was able to block decisions favourable to migrants made by the Communal Council by using the provision for a referendum.

In reaction to a demand from a centrist councillor, in 1968 the City Council set up the Municipal Commission for Assimilation Questions (Städtische Kommission für Assimilierungsfragen), later called Municipal Commission for Foreigners' Questions (Städtische Kommission für Ausländerfragen).[8] Composed of a number of 'experts', it was charged with making recommendations to the City Council and the Communal Council. A year later, the Co-ordination Office for the Questions of Foreigners (Koordinationsstelle für Ausländerfragen, KSA) was established in order to serve as a secretariat for the Commission and to co-ordinate the activities of different administrative services concerning migrants. The central task of these two institutions was therefore to provide mediation and information for immigrants as well as for Swiss.

However, the most important adaptations to the effects of migration were made within the education system – which is not organised at the municipal, but at the cantonal level. Because at the beginning of the 1980s the proportion of migrant children increased to up to 90 per cent of all pupils in some schools, the authorities feared an increase of school segregation (Schulsynode, 1983). In 1980 they set up a special service called Pedagogy for Foreigners (Ausländerpädagogik), later called Intercultural Pedagogy. In 1987 a comprehensive approach for intercultural education was adopted by the cantonal authorities (Truniger, 1995). The idea of this Service is to integrate intercultural learning in the common curriculum of the 'popular school' (*Volksschule*), which is regarded as a school for all pupils regardless of social or ethnic origin. At the same time courses in mother tongue and culture of origin for the children of a number of migrant groups were also set up, the *Kurse in heimatlicher Sprache und Kultur* (*HSK-Kurse*).

The activities of the Municipal Commission for Foreigners' Questions and the KSA did not produce such innovative results and the two institutions became increasingly criticised. In 1979 a report considered them to be inefficient and asked for a reform of their structure. The City Council therefore decided to set up a Foreigners' Parliament (*Ausländerparlament*): together with 15 Swiss members, 38 migrants would represent the most important migrant groups living in Zurich, in proportion to each nationality's numerical importance in the city. In order to emphasise its restriction to a consultative role, the Foreigners' Parliament was finally called Foreigners' Forum (*Ausländerforum*). In June 1984 the Communal Council approved the project by 67 against 11 votes. However, the National Action (NA) as well as the Swiss Popular Party (Schweizerische Volkspartei, SVP) launched a referendum against the Forum: the NA for xenophobic reasons, the SVP because it considered the new body as a 'waste of money'. The vote took place in a highly politicised atmosphere and in December 1984 64 per cent of the voters expressed themselves against the project.

Faced with this defeat, the City Council tried to keep decisions concerning migration within the limits of its own competence. In July 1985 it decided to include more migrant representatives in a new Foreigners' Commission: eight of the twenty members were immigrants. The decision was strongly criticised by the NA because, according to the party, it was against the will of Zurich's population. The City Council also transformed the KSA: in 1987 a new President was appointed and in 1988 the number of the office's employees was considerably increased because of the setting up of a new information service for migrants. In addition, the head of the Department for Social Affairs established a special information service for migrant women, called Infodona, in 1989.

The failure of the Foreigners' Forum was not the only political success of the xenophobic party however. The central focus of its activity was the question of naturalisation. The representatives of the NA in the Communal Council permanently claimed a restrictive reform of the access to citizenship, most often grounded in ethnic criteria (longer waiting periods for non-European candidates, ability to speak the local dialect etc.). Their claims were always rejected by a large majority of the local councillors. However, they sometimes succeeded in promoting their aims using a referendum. When in 1970 the Naturalisation Commission decided to ease the criteria of access to citizenship, the NA launched a referendum and in 1971 a majority of 61 per cent of voters decided against the reform. In 1978 the Party tried once more to fight a reform with a referendum. However, this time it failed: 54 per cent were in favour of the change. Almost twenty years later, in 1996, the successors of the NA, the Swiss Democrats (Schweizer Demokraten) succeeded once more in blocking a reform of the naturalisation procedure.

The Politicisation of Immigration during the 1990s

At the end of the 1980s the dynamics of immigrant politics in Zurich changed radically. Five developments are responsible for this change. First, unemployment increased sharply from the beginning of the 1990s, and this strongly affected migrants because of their high representation in the lowest segments of the labour market. If this problem concerned the whole of Switzerland, a second issue was more specific to Zurich: increasing spatial segregation. Compared to other European cities, segregation on the neighbourhood level cannot objectively be considered as a serious problem, even if the concentration of poverty in some high-rise buildings on the urban periphery has become a concern for the city. Segregation is, however, a problem at a wider territorial level: the migration of the middle classes from the city to its suburbs led to a loss of taxes and to an increased proportion of poor people living in the city (Meyrat-Schlee and Gafner, 1998).

A third important development was the expansion of the drug market in the beginning of the 1990s, which attracted a lot of foreign drug dealers and had therefore a negative impact on the perception of immigrants in general. Migrants from former Yugoslavia were particularly considered to be heavily involved in drug dealing in public opinion (Boskovska, 1999). A fourth problem was linked to the war in Kosovo: many Albanian workers, already staying for a long time in Zurich, had their families join them. The large-scale arrival of Albanian children and youngsters, struggling at school and completely excluded from participation in the labour market, confronted the city with the formation of ethnic street gangs (Hagmann, 1995). Once more it had a generally negative impact on public perception of migrants. Finally, there was the rise of a political actor, who tried to enlarge its constituency through the politicisation of these social problems: the SVP. In the 1960s the SVP was still a party representing the farmers and conservative rural middle classes, but during the 1970s and 1980s it developed into a modern neo-conservative party (Hartmann and Horvath, 1995). From the middle of the 1990s the SVP increasingly raised the issues of law and order and immigration as topics for electoral politics.

Facing this situation, the Mayor, the Social Democrat Josef Estermann, tried to follow a strategy of de-politicisation, favouring a policy of information and mediation. In 1993, for example, the KSA, which was charged with organising activities for the better mutual understanding of migrants and Swiss, launched the project *z'Züri dehei?* ('at home in Zurich?'). This tried to support social-cultural activities for migrants as well as Swiss. Furthermore, the Mayor presented himself as a supporter of a double-sided integration policy: he was in favour of fuller participation opportunities for migrants, but at the same time he wanted them to adapt to Swiss society and to respect their duties (NZZ, 1996). The central piece of the Mayor's strategy to de-politicise the immigrant issue was a White Paper on Integration (*Integrationsleitbild* or *Leitbild*), published in May 1998, which aimed at a new comprehensive approach for an integration policy in Zurich. The *Leitbild* considered the exclusion of an increasing number of migrants from the labour market as the central problem of the city and demanded improvements in education and vocational training for migrants. It also claimed that housing segregation and the concentration of migrants in certain neighbourhoods would become a more serious topic and asked for the implementation of a dispersal policy (Leitbild, 1998a, pp. 28-36).

However, the Mayor's strategy to calm down the immigrant issue could not prevent a number of political defeats. In January 1996 the Communal Council decided to ease some of the criteria for the naturalisation of foreigners. The changes adopted were modest, and because of the still restrictive rules, the Green Party and the Alternative Party voted against the changes, which were supported by all the other parties, except the xenophobic Swiss Democrats (SD). Arguing that the changes adopted would lead to a 'squandering of Swiss nationality', the SD launched a referendum. The vote took place in June 1996: 62 per cent of the voters rejected the changes. Two years later, in spring 1998, the Communal Council decided to subsidise a 'contact network' for migrants from Kosovo with 50,000 SFr. This time, the SVP launched the referendum against this decision, which was considered by the other parties as a reasonable project concerning an excluded group. In a popular vote on June 1998, 56 per cent of the voters agreed with the SVP and rejected the project.

Furthermore, the *Leitbild* did not have the effect its authors hoped: during the summer of 1998 it led to a considerable and very controversial debate. The SVP, on one side, claimed that there was no 'integration problem' in Zurich, but instead a 'foreigner problem' and therefore asked for a policy which would stop further migration to the city. The left, on the other side, represented by the Social Democrats, the Green Party and solidarity organisations, criticised the *Leitbild* because it demanded the 'assimilation' of migrants in central aspects of Swiss society and concentrated, according to them, only on their 'social deficits' but not on their social-economic contribution to Swiss society. Migrant organisations made similar claims and criticised the fact that they had not been associated to the setting up of the *Leitbild*. Faced with these critical reactions, the Mayor decided in November 1998 to rewrite the *Leitbild*. The new text was presented in September 1999. It tried to integrate many of the criticisms the first *Leitbild* received. In May 2000 the SVP refused to support to the new text however. It proposed a number of restrictive projects concerning immigration in the meantime. Parties on the left did likewise, however with an opposite content. These developments are a clear indicator that immigration will continue to occupy the political agenda as a controversial issue in the near future.

The Mobilisation of Migrants and Migrant Associations

Unlike in other countries (for example France), Swiss legislation does not require the registration of associations. Anyone, Swiss citizens as well as foreigners, can found an association. Therefore there is a large number of migrant associations in Zurich: in 1997 the KSA published a brochure enumerating 350 immigrant associations (Koordinationsstelle, 1997). According to nationality the Italians have by far the most associations (63); they are followed by Spaniards (25), Turks (23), Greeks (14), Tamils (9), Croats

(8), Albanians (7), Portuguese (6), people from the Republic of Yugoslavia (6) and Bosnians (4).

However, only scarce information is publicly available on the precise aims and actions of these organisations. A recent study suggests that the principal reason why migrants set up an association in Zurich is their wish to have their own place to meet and to foster their own culture. A second reason is the desire to establish networks of solidarity. In fact, there seem to be many links between the different associations (Mostert, 1999). Only a small number of migrant organisations have an explicit political or religious commitment. The organisations are often based on the same national or regional origin, but in case of Asians, Africans or Latin Americans the organisations transcend ethnic or national boundaries. The resources of the associations come mainly from within: about 60 per cent rely solely on the fees of their members for finance, 16 per cent receive financial support from the countries of origin and 22 per cent from the Swiss administration (Von Ah and Dobler, 1998, pp. 224-8). It seems that the majority of associations address themselves to first-generation migrants and has some difficulty in attracting the second generation.

Even if few migrant associations are politically active, some of them, mostly Italian organisations, have mobilised for their civil and political rights. If at the beginning their mobilisation took place along ethnic lines, in a second stage they allied with other migrant organisations, solidarity movements and labour unions. Because Italians' mobilisation has been up to now the most important, we will focus on Italian organisations, and especially on one, the Federazione delle Colonie Libere Italiane (FCLI), which also played a central role in the interactions with the municipality.

Italian Associations and the Role of the Federazione delle Colonie Libere Italiane

During the 1960s Italians made almost up to 60 per cent of all migrants living in Switzerland and they were still the most important group in 1998 with 334,594 persons (24.8 per cent of all migrants) (BFA, 1998). In Zurich they represented almost half of the migrant population at the end of the 1960s. Since then, however, their part decreased steadily: to 24,046 (32.8 per cent) in 1985 and to 20,290 (20 per cent) in 1995. In the same year they were nevertheless still the second most important migrant community in Zurich.

As some scholars have observed, the '*associazionismo italiano*' is particularly well developed in Switzerland. Although only a tenth of all the

Italian emigrants in the world lived in Switzerland in the 1970s, about a third of all their associations were established there (Leuenberger, 1984, p. 5). One of the reasons for this surprising phenomenon is the fact that Italian immigration to Zurich dates back to the nineteenth century. First numerically behind German and French immigrants, the Italians became the most important group before World War I (BFS, 1997, p. 33). When Italian workers arrived in Zurich after 1945 they found already a large array of well-established Italian institutions, associations and political organisations (see Morach, 1979). The most important institutions for the support of migrants is probably the Missione Cattolica Italiana di Zurigo which was founded in 1898, but various political organisations and labour unions played also a crucial role. The most important of them became the Colonie Libere Italiane in Svizzera.

The origin of this association goes back to the 1930s when the fascist government of Italy tried to control its migrants through the consulates. Italian anti-fascists of different political orientations set up the Scuola Libera Italiana di Emancipazione Proletaria in Zurich in order to escape this ideological control and to give their children an education free from fascist ideology. They also founded the first Colonia Libera Italiana (CLI) in Zurich, which together with twelve other *Colonie* became in 1943 the Federazione delle Colonie Libere Italiane in Svizzera (FCLIS). The aim of the Federation was to pursue the anti-fascist struggle for a new democratic Italy, on the one hand, and to defend the interests of Italian migrants, on the other (Leuenberger, 1984, pp. 136-7). With the end of the war many of the leaders of the FCLIS – who were often intellectuals – returned to Italy and the organisation fell into a crisis; from this moment on, however, the FCLIS became a real migrant workers' organisation (De Marchi, 1972, p. 49). To begin with, the FCLIS addressed its claims almost entirely to the Italian government: in 1954, for example, it launched a petition under the title *l'Emigrazione Più Povera d'Europa Paga il Passaporto Più Caro d'Europa*, asking the Italian government to abolish the high fees to obtain a passport. In the same year the FCLIS launched another petition for the right of social and medical assistance for the family members of migrants remaining in Italy. It also asked the Italian government to include migrant representatives in the commission for bilateral negotiations on immigration regulation between Switzerland and Italy (De Marchi, 1972, pp. 63-75; Grossi, 1985).

Though the FCLIS did not address claims to the Swiss government at that time, it increasingly became the object of official control because the Swiss authorities considered the association to be infiltrated by the Italian

Communist Party. During the Cold War FCLIS members were expelled for political reasons on several occasions and the organisation was under close police surveillance. In 1956 the response of the FCLIS was to calm down the issue by including an article in its statutes that the organisation would keep aloof from political action. But by 1963 it had organised a conference on *The Democratic Rights of Emigrants Workers*, launching a campaign for more freedom of political speech for migrants, which was restricted in Switzerland (Bresadola, 1974; De Marchi, 1972, pp. 60-2).

With the massive influx of Italian migrants during the 1960s the FCLIS grew and enlarged its activities: in 1964 it had about 14,000 individual members and counted 100 federated associations. Alphabetisation courses and evening schools for adults were developed (Grossi, 1985, p. 206). It was also during the 1960s that the FCLIS' defence of migrants' interests turned increasingly towards Swiss society. It tried to integrate the large number of Italian regional and cultural organisations and in 1970 the *Convegno Nazionale delle Organizzazioni degli Emigrati Italiani in Svizzera* was organised, with a participation of 427 organisations (De Marchi, 1972, p. 99).

The *Colonia* of the City of Zurich played a leading role for the co-ordination of the FCLIS' action, because it was the central body of the federation. However, because many of its members were active at the federal level, local activities got less attention than in other cities. As a result the number of its members – growing from 110 persons in 1945 to 320 in 1971 – was, compared to the 60,000 Italians living in Zurich in 1971, not very high (De Marchi, 1972, p. 167). One of the reasons for this was certainly the large variety of other Italian associations existing in the city. But political reasons also played a role: many of the members of the organisation were also members of the Italian Communist Party (PCI). At the end of the 1960s a permanent conflict between a group which wanted to bring the FCLIS closer to the PCI and a second group which wanted to keep the association autonomous broke out (De Marchi, 1972, pp. 165-6, 231-3). Nevertheless, in 1969 a cinema was opened, and it became an important centre of cultural and political debate.

The economic crises of 1974 and the subsequent policy of the Swiss government led to a decrease of membership in all the *Colonie*. But with about 10,000 members in the middle of the 1980s the FCLIS was still the largest migrant organisation in Switzerland and probably also in the world (Leuenberger, 1984, pp. 7-8).

The Interactions Between the Municipality and the Migrants

The real struggle by the FCLIS for civil and political rights in Switzerland began in the 1970s and took first place on the federal level. When at the beginning of the 1970s representatives of labour unions, Christian groups and left-wing organisations founded the committee Mitenand (Together) in order to launch a popular initiative aimed at the improvement of the rights of immigrants in Switzerland, the FCLIS became one of the central forces of the movement. It succeeded in encouraging 'a large process of mobilisation within the migrants' (D'Amato, 1997, p. 145) which was characterised as a real 'coming out' of immigrants in the sense of 'a radical turn of the political perception of foreigners as not only economic-functional, but also cultural and social' (Cattacin, 1996, p. 72). The aims of the initiative were simple: that immigration control should continue, but the foreigners once admitted to Switzerland should quickly get the same rights as the Swiss (excepted the political rights). That meant the right of free movement, immediate family reunification and the same social and civil rights as Swiss had (Mitenand, 1981). The government agreed that the initiative made some legitimate demands, but criticised the abolishment of the status of the seasonal workers (*Saisonniers*) and the right for immediate family reunification, as exorbitant. It recommended rejection of the initiative and presented as an alternative its own project for a reform of the Foreigners' Law, which was discussed in Parliament. This project tried also to improve the legal status of foreigners, but in a less ambitious way than the Mitenand initiative.

The two projects were submitted to a popular vote: in April 1981, the Mitenand initiative was rejected by a very large majority of the voters (84 per cent) and by all the cantons. This outcome strengthened the position of right-wing parties in the political struggle over the new Foreigners' Law that was still discussed in Parliament. A compromise in Parliament was reached in favour of more restrictive views, but the National Action nevertheless launched a successful referendum. In June 1982 the new project was rejected in a popular vote, this time however by a narrow majority of 50.4 per cent. The failure was also due to the hostility of the left, which judged the project too restrictive.

This clear defeat led the FCLIS to change its strategy: from then on it addressed its claims to the local – the cantonal and the municipal – level. In Zurich, political rights increasingly became the central focus of its struggle. At the beginning of the 1970s, however, another domain had already become the field of conflict between the authorities of Zurich and the FCLIS: schools. Two reasons explain this development: on the one hand a generation change of the organisation's leadership led to a strategy more oriented to the migrants' life in Switzerland. On the other hand, more and more children of Italian migrants entered the education system. In 1973 the FCLIS published a booklet *Gli Emigrati e la Scuola*, which tried to encourage immigrants to send their children to Swiss schools and not to Italian ones (FCLIS, 1973). In order to help the migrants to cope with the Swiss system and in order to represent also their interest to Swiss authorities, many *Colonie* set up parent committees (*comitati di genitori*). As in other countries, education became therefore one of the most important issues which brought the migrants in a close negotiation process with the authorities of the country of settlement (see Layton-Henry, 1990, pp. 100-2).

The most important issues became the rights to set up courses for migrant children in Italian language, the organisation of courses after the regular school to help them make their homework (*dopo scuola*) and the treatment of migrant pupils with learning difficulties by the Swiss education authorities. This third issue was the most controversial: the cantonal education system was at this time not adapted to linguistic and cultural differences and, therefore, many Italian children who had problems in following the classes in German were sent to special classes for pupils with learning difficulties (*Sonderklassen*). Italian parents regarded this treatment – which relied on linguistically-biased intelligence tests (Schuh, 1977) – as discriminatory, but they did not have the means to challenge the decisions. In 1973 the CLI therefore founded the Centre for School Information (Centro Informazioni Scholastichi delle Colonie Libere Italiane). Directed by a psychologist and in the beginning only financed by the CLI itself, this institution became the focus of the struggle against the discrimination of Italian children in the education system of the Canton of Zurich, and increasingly also of other cantons.

The Centre tried to resist the assignments of Italian children to *Sonderklassen* primarily by making appeals on the ground of counter-expertise and by launching petitions. However, these activities, coming from a migrant institution which was perceived to be leftist, were considered to be an affront by the relevant authorities during the 1970s. Nevertheless, already in 1976, the claims of the Centre became included in the recommendations of the Federal Conference of the Cantonal Directors of Education (Eidgenössische Konferenz der Erziehungsdirektoren, EDK) through the bilateral treaties between Italy and Switzerland. Furthermore, the support of the Italian Consulate, which was for a long time the most important financial source of the Centre, as well as the increasing consciousness of the authorities that the institution did a very valuable work, considerably increased the official recognition of the Centre during the 1980s. In 1988 the city contributed to its funding for the first time. It is now definitely considered to be a pioneer in the education of migrant children.

One can therefore observe an increasing adaptation of the institutions to the problems of migrants in education. In 1984, for example, the first consultative commission for foreigners regarding education questions was set up. But by contrast, the accreditation of new rights failed several times. During the mobilisation for the Mitenand initiative, the FCLIS, together with the Spanish organisation Asociaciòn de Trabajadores Emigrantes Españoles, had organised a petition for local and cantonal voting rights in fifteen cantons. The petition, however, got nowhere. At the end of the 1980s the CLI participated in a new campaign for local voting rights at the cantonal level. A petition with 5,400 signatures of foreigners collected in Zurich was handed to the authorities in February 1989. This campaign also took place in other municipalities of the Canton, but none of them received a positive answer (Marquis and Grossi, 1990, pp. 24-5). However, the claims of the petition were taken over by a popular initiative on the cantonal level, supported by representatives from labour unions, left-wing parties, the churches and migrant organisations. The initiative aimed to introduce local voting rights for foreigners who had a permanent residence permit for at least five years.[9] The vote took place in September 1993: 75 per cent rejected the initiative. In several other Swiss cantons similar initiatives also received negative answers by strong majorities in the same period (Cueni and Fleury, 1994, pp. 15-17).

Since then, the CLI has contributed to a number of initiatives in which different migrant associations, but also Swiss organisations, participate. One can find its members in two groups: on the one hand, in the group Political Rights for Migrants (Politische Rechte für Migrant(-innen)) which announced a week before the municipal elections of March 1998 that it would once again try to struggle for the issue of political rights. During the election campaign the principal aim of the group was to support Swiss candidates with a migrant background, but it has since then launched a new petition for the right to vote on the local level. On the other hand, there are members of the CLI in the SP-Migration, a number of persons who during the discussion around the *Leitbild* have decided to form a group within the Social Democratic Party in order to defend the interests of migrants. They have made the question of naturalisation their leading topic. Finally, the CLI has also participated in the debate on the *Leitbild* (see above): its two most important claims are the *ius soli* for foreigners born in Switzerland and the right to vote in local affairs after 10 years of residence (CLIZ, 1998).

Conclusion

If we return to our initial question of whether the peculiarities of Zurich's political opportunity structure had a positive impact on the inclusion of migrants, we have to answer clearly: no. Our study of the municipality's immigrant policy and of the Italians' struggle for political rights shows that the failure of attempts for more inclusive policies can neither be imputed to a lack of mobilisation of the migrants nor to the unwillingness or resistance of local policy-makers. It has to be explained principally by the opposition of important parts of the population who can articulate their hostility towards migrants through the instruments of direct democracy. The opportunity structure of a political system that guarantees greater participation opportunities to citizens than the institutions of purely representative regimes, was not the ground of an inclusive dynamic towards migrants, but of a restrictive one. An interesting parallel can be drawn to the granting of voting rights for women in Switzerland: in this case too, the instruments of direct democracy can be considered responsible that women acquired the right to vote only late, in 1971 (Linder, 1999, p. 62).

The reasons for this phenomenon are of course the contradictory grounds of liberal democracy itself. As we mentioned in the introduction, modern democratic regimes are built on the *democratic* principle, the right to participate in political decisions, and the *liberal* principle, the guarantee of human rights. The actual balance between the two is the result of the political history of a nation-state: in Switzerland, the democratic element is clearly stronger than the constitutional one (Häfelin and Haller, 1984, pp. 43-4). In other words, in Switzerland, decisions on the inclusion of migrants – at least in the domain of political rights – can be considered as a zero-sum game. As Linder (1999, pp. 60-2) argues in the case of voting rights for women, in a political regime of the representative type there are inherent incentives for the political elite to promote voting rights for denizens because parties can reasonably expect that the new citizens will vote for the political organisations which defended their interests. Furthermore, parties can present the issue in their programmes together with other aims, which attract the votes of people not necessarily in favour of voting rights for a new group. In a direct democracy, on the contrary, 'package deals' are not possible because important issues are voted upon separately. The decision on political rights for new members becomes therefore a zero-sum game, that is a loss of privilege without compensation for the ones who are already citizens.

However, the argument that granting political rights to immigrants is a zero-sum game must be questioned on the ground that a society which excludes some of its members from participation will be confronted with serious problems, such as political segregation and social unrest, and that therefore inclusion of all members profits all citizens of a society. Obviously this view is not shared by a majority of the population of Zurich. Our findings correspond therefore to a certain extent to Patrick Ireland's conclusion on the mobilisation of migrants in Switzerland in general: according to him, 'Swiss political institutions, (...) have channelled away the immigrants' protest potential, fragmenting their political energies and neutralising their threatening aspects' (1994, p. 270). However, if there is no doubt that the political systems' opportunity structure *blocked* the claims of migrants so far, we cannot find evidence that it *channelled* the struggle of Italian migrants *away*. On the contrary, our study shows that for more than thirty years now Italian associations have kept the issue of political rights on the agenda. Explaining the form of their mobilisation by Switzerland's opportunity structure seems therefore not appropriate: the migrants' struggle for political rights seems much more to be based on the universalistic commitment that all members of a society should have the right of participation. Or as the representatives of the Colonia Libera of Zurich formulated it: 'We want to participate in the social-political life because we are citizens of this city' (CLIZ, 1998).

Notes

1   The popular initiative permits the launching of a political idea in the form of a project for a constitutional article, which is then submitted to the Swiss people. In order to succeed, a popular initiative must gather the signatures of at least 100,000 voters in a period of 18 months. It is then followed by a popular vote (*Volksabstimmung*); on the level of the city 4,000 signatures are necessary to launch an initiative.
2   The referendum permits each law adopted in Parliament to be submitted to a popular vote, if 50,000 signatures are collected in the three months following its adoption; on the city level, 4,000 signatures must be collected during the twenty days following a decision of the city's executive.
3   The units of the Swiss Federal State are the 23 cantons.
4   However, because of the country's federal political culture the economically less important City of Bern became the political capital.

5   We will speak in this text in general of 'migrants' or 'immigrants'; however, if we are
    using statistical data, we will always speak of 'foreigners'.
6   According to the census 1.5 per cent of Zurich's Swiss population was Jewish.
7   The years spent in Switzerland between the 10th and 20th birthdays count double.
8   Municipality here refers to the City of Zurich and not the other 260 municipalities in
    the whole Canton.
9   Because most of the foreigners living in Switzerland obtain a permanent residence
    permit only after 5 years of residence, this means that they had to wait at least 10 years
    to get local voting rights.

References

Ah, M. von and Dobler, C. (1998), 'Befragung von Ausländerorganisationen', in Leitbild,
    Integrationsleitbild Zürich, Band II, Beilagen, Ethnologisches Seminar der Universität
    Zürich, Zürich, pp. 217-45.
Arend, M. (1991), 'Housing Segregation in Switzerland', in E.D. Huttman (ed.), *Urban
    Housing Segregation of Minorities in Western Europe and the United States*, Duke
    University Press, Durham and London, pp. 155-67.
Bartal, et al. (1998), 'Stadtstrukturen', in Leitbild, *Integrationsleitbild Zürich*, Band II,
    Beilagen, Ethnologisches Seminar der Universität Zürich, Zürich, pp. 29-175.
BFA (1998), *Die Ausländer in der Schweiz: Bestandsergebnisse Dezember 1998*, Bundesamt
    für Ausländerfragen, Bern.
BFS (1997), *Statistisches Jahrbuch der Schweiz 1998*, Verlag Neue Zürcher Zeitung,
    Bundesamt für Statistik, Zürich.
Bokovska, N. (1999), 'Feindbild Jugo', *Tages-Anzeiger Magazin*, no. 19, pp. 22-9.
Bolzmann, C., Fibbi, R. and Garcia, C. (1987), 'La Deuxième Génération des Immigrés
    en Suisse: Catégorie ou Acteur Social?', *Revue Européenne des Migrations Inter-
    nationales*, vol. 3, pp. 55-72.
Bresadola, G. (1974), 'Le Colonie Libere', *Il Ponte*, vol. 20, pp. 1490-9.
Cattacin, S. (1996), '"Il federalismo integrativo": Qualche Considerazione sulle Modalità
    di Integrazione degli Immigrati in Svizzera', in V.C. Lusso et al., *I Come Identità,
    Integrazione, Interculturalità*, FCLIS, Zurich/Messina, pp. 67-82.
Centlivres, P. (ed.) (1990), *Devenir Suisse*, Georg Editeur, Genève.
CLIZ (1998), *Oggetto: Leitbild zur Integrationspolitik der Stadt Zürich*, Colonia Libera
    Italiana di Zurigo, Zürich.
Cueni, A. and Fleury, St. (1994), *Stimmberechtigte Ausländer: Die Erfahrungen der
    Kantone Neuenburg und Jura*, Nationale Schweizerische UNESCO-Kommission, Bern.
D'Amato, G. (1997), 'Gelebte Nation und Einwanderung: Zur Transnationalisierung von
    Nationalstaaten durch Immigrationspolitik am Beispiel der Schweiz', in H. Kleger
    (ed.), *Transnationale Staatsbürgerschaft*, Campus, Frankfurt am Main, pp. 132-59.
De Marchi, B. (1972), *Gli Immigrati Italiani in Svizzera e il Ruolo delle Colonie Libere*,
    Tesi di Laurea, Università di Bologna, Bologna.
EKA (1998), *Die Einbürgerung der Ausländer in der Schweiz*, Eidgenössische Ausländer-
    kommission, Schönbühl.
FCLIS (1973), *Gli Emigrati e la Scuola*, Federazione delle C.L.I. in Svizzera, Zurigo.

Freeman, G. (1995a), 'Modes of Immigration Politics in Liberal Democratic States', *International Migration Review*, vol. 29, pp. 881-902.

Freeman, G. (1995b), 'Rejoinder', *International Migration Review*, vol. 29, pp. 909-13.

Grossi, G. (1985), 'Brevi Cenni Storici sulle Colonie Libere Italiane', *'Passaporti, prego!'*: *Ricordi e Testimonianze di Emigrati Italiani*, FCLIS, Zurigo.

Guiraudon, V. (1998), 'Citizenship Rights for Non-Citizens: France, Germany and the Netherlands', in C. Joppke (ed.), *Challenge to the Nation-State: Immigration in Western Europe and the United States*, Oxford University Press, Oxford, pp. 272-318.

Häfelin, U. and Haller, W. (1984), *Schweizerisches Bundesstaatsrecht*, Schulthess Polygraphischer Verlag, Zürich.

Hagmann, R. (1995), *Aspekte der Jugendarbeit*, Verein Zürcher Jugendfoyers, Zürich.

Hartmann, H. and Horvath, F. (1995), *Zivilgesellschaft von Rechts: Die (Unheimliche) Erfolgsstory der Zürcher SVP*, Realotopia Verlagsgenossenschaft, Zürich.

Haug, W. (1980), *'... und es kamen Menschen': Ausländerpolitik und Fremdarbeit in der Schweiz 1914 bis 1980*, Z-Verlag, Basel.

Haug, W. (1995), *La Suisse: Terre d'Immigration, Société Multiculturelle*, Bundesamt für Statistik, Bern.

Hitz, H., Schmid, Chr. and Wolff, R. (1995), 'Boom, Konflikt und Krise: Zürichs Entwicklung zur Weltmetropole', in H. Hitz et al. (eds), *Capitales Fatales: Urbanisierung und Politik in den Finanzmetropolen Frankfurt und Zürich*, Rotpunkt Verlag, Zürich, pp. 208-82.

Holliefield, J. (1992), *Immigrants, Markets and States: The Political Economy of Postwar Europe*, Harvard University Press, Cambridge MA.

Ireland, P. (1994), *The Policy Challenge of Ethnic Diversity: Immigration Politics in France and Switzerland*, Harvard University Press, Cambridge MA.

Koordinationsstelle (1997), *Ausländerinnen und Ausländer in Zürich*, Städtische Koordinationsstelle für Ausländerfragen, Zürich.

Layton-Henry, Z. (1990), 'Immigrant Associations', in Z. Layton-Henry (ed.), *The Political Rights of Migrant Workers in Western Europe*, SAGE, London, pp. 94-112.

Leca, J. (1996), 'La Démocratie à l'Épreuve des Pluralismes', *Revue Française de Science Politique*, vol. 46, pp. 225-79.

Leitbild (1998a), *Leitbild zur Integrationspolitik der Stadt Zürich: Ziele und Massnahmen zur Integration der Ausländischen Wohnbevölkerung*, Entwurf zur Vernehmlassung, Zürich.

Leitbild (1998b), *Integrationsleitbild Zürich*, Band II, Beilagen, Ethnologisches Seminar der Universität Zürich, Zürich.

Leuenberger, G. (1984), *Der Antifaschismus in der Italienischen Emigration in der Schweiz 1943-1945: Die Entstehung und die Gründung der Federazione delle Colonie Libere Italiane in Svizzera*, Lizentiatsarbeit Universität Zürich, Zürich.

Linder, W. (1999), *Schweizerische Demokratie: Institutionen, Prozesse, Perspektiven*, Verlag Paul Haupt, Bern.

Looser, H. (1986), 'Zwischen "Tschinggenhass" und Rebellion: Der Italienerkrawall von 1896', in *Lücken im Panorama: Einblicke in den Nachlass Zürichs*, Geschichtsladen Zürich, Zürich, pp. 85-107.

Mahnig, H. (1998), 'Between Economic Demands and Popular Xenophobia: The Swiss System of Immigration Regulation', in A. Böcker et al. (eds), *Regulation of Migration: International Experiences*, Het Spinhuis, Amsterdam, pp. 174-90.

Marquis, J.-F. and Grossi, G. (1990), *Einwanderer: Minderheit ohne Politische Rechte?*, Schweizerischer Gewerkschaftsbund, Bern.

Meyrat-Schlee, E. and Gafner, A. (1998), *Soziale Entmischung in der Stadt Zürich*, Fachstelle für Stadtentwicklung, Zürich.

Mitenand (1981), *Weissbuch: Die Ausländer in der Schweiz*, Arbeitsgemeinschaft 'Mitenand', Zürich.

Morach, M. (1979), *Pietro Bianchi: Maurer und Organisiert*, Limmat Verlag Genossenschaft, Zürich.

Mostert, F. (1999), *Netwerken van Immigrantenorganisaties als Sociaal Kapitaal: Een Netwerkanalyse van Migrantenorganisaties in Zurich*, Universiteit van Amsterdam, Amsterdam.

MPMC (1997), *Multicultural Policies and Modes of Citizenship in European Cities (MPMC)*, http://www.unesco.org/most/p97.htm.

Neidhart, L. (1998), 'Nebeneinander von Kirchturm- und Weltpolitik: Die Rolle des Parlaments in der Stadt Zürich', *Neue Zürcher Zeitung*, April 24, 1998, p. 31.

NZZ (1996), *Neue Zürcher Zeitung*, July 13-14, 1996.

Ochsner, P. (1998), 'Ökonomische Integration der Ausländischen Wohnbevölkerung', in Leitbild, *Integrationsleitbild Zürich*, Band II, Beilagen, Ethnologisches Seminar der Universität Zürich, Zürich, pp. 272-326.

Penninx, R. (1998), 'European Cities and their Citizens: Problem, Challenge, Opportunity?', Introductory lecture for the Conference Ethnic Minorities and Local Government, Municipality of Amsterdam, Amsterdam.

Rath, J. (1988), 'La Participation des Immigrés aux Élections Locales aux Pays-Bas', *Revue Européenne des Migrations Internationales*, vol. 4, pp. 23-35.

Schlaepfer, R. (1969), *Die Ausländerfrage in der Schweiz vor dem Ersten Weltkrieg*, Juris-Verlag, Zürich.

Schmidt, M.G. (1982), 'Does Corporatism Matter?: Economic Crisis, Politics and Rates of Unemployment in Capitalist Democracies in the 1970s', in G. Lehmbruch and P. Schmitter (eds), *Patterns of Corporatist Policy-making*, SAGE, London, pp. 231-56.

Schuh, S. (1977), '"Was ist Aufgabe der Polizei?": Intelligenztests und Ausländerkinder in der Schweiz', *Tages-Anzeiger Magazin*, September 24, 1977.

Schulsynode (1983), *Ausländerkinder in Unseren Schulen*, Berichte zur Synodaltagung vom 10. November 1982 in der Kantonsschule Freudenberg, Schulsynode des Kantons Zürich, Zürich.

Statistisches Amt (1996), 'Die Ausländische Wohnbevölkerung in der Stadt Zürich 1970 bis 1995', *Zürcher Statistische Nachrichten*, no. 7, Statistisches Amt der Stadt Zürich, Zürich.

Statistisches Amt (1997), *Statistisches Jahrbuch der Stadt Zürich 1997*, Statistisches Amt der Stadt Zürich, Zürich.

Truniger, M. (1995), 'Interkulturelle Pädagogik in der Lehrerbildung: Entwicklungen im Kanton Zürich', in E. Poglia et al. (eds), *Interkulturelle Bildung in der Schweiz*, Peter Lang Verlag, Bern, pp. 223-7.

Vuilleumier, M. (1992), *Flüchtlinge und Immigranten in der Schweiz: Ein Historischer Überblick*, Pro Helvetia, Zürich.

Wittwer, P. (1996), 'Muslime in Zürich: Unruhe um Ruhestätte', *IRAS-Panorama*, no. 1, July, pp. 7-8.

12 Afterword: Citizenship and its Modes

JOHN CROWLEY

Is it possible to develop a concept of 'local citizenship' that is *coherent, usable,* and *useful*? The condition of coherence is that local citizenship should be identifiably a species of the genus *civitas* – one that includes other manifestations that differ from it in scale (e.g. national citizenship) or in structure (e.g. social citizenship), but have nonetheless a genuine family resemblance. For such a concept to be usable, it must be possible, on the basis of it, to develop empirical research protocols capable of ascertaining whether it is actually extant in any particular habitat. And finally, the exercise might as well be useful, in the sense of telling us something about complex societies that we might miss if the concept of local citizenship were not deployed.

That a coherent and usable concept of local citizenship would be useful if available can reasonably be assumed. There are two major strands in traditional theories of citizenship. The first is centrally concerned with the idea of a *political community*. It asks how we can make conceptual and institutional sense of the democratic principle that the subjects of law should also be, jointly and severally, its authors. Its polar figure is Jean-Jacques Rousseau, who, while deeply divisive, is as important for the liberals who reject him as for the radical democrats who embrace him. The second strand is centrally concerned with the idea of an *integrated society*. It asks how we can make conceptual and institutional sense of the idea that membership of society means the same thing for large numbers of otherwise unrelated people who occupy very different positions in it, command unequal resources, and have often sharply divergent views of what is going on. Durkheim is its often-unacknowledged ancestor, but T. H. Marshall may be conveniently taken as a fairly consensual father figure. These strands of theory differ in many ways, but they share an important feature. They locate citizenship at the level of social entities that are, at least empirically, large-scale and, more importantly, conceptually homogeneous.

With respect to contemporary European societies, this feature looks like a defect. Rousseau could, for his purposes, make a sharp distinction

247

between law and administration, and relate the former unequivocally to a unique, concrete political process. *Pace* Jürgen Habermas, the distinction seems grossly implausible in a world of statutory instruments, ministerial instructions, quasi-autonomous administrative agencies, and semi-secret corporatist accommodation, where the political meaning of 'law' can be highly elusive. Furthermore, a political community's self-government – in the sense of its exclusive right to give itself laws – is not synonymous with its effective control of its own destiny. What it might mean for the citizen to be a 'lawmaker' thus becomes unclear. Furthermore, partly but not solely because of the blurring of law, the levels of political authority in contemporary states are increasingly diverse – both above and below the traditional state – and their hierarchy is less clearly defined. Each level necessarily raises questions of citizenship that do not fit together in a neat pattern. Finally, perfect symmetry between lawmakers and subjects of law is illusory. It is of particular significance for the issues raised in this volume that legal rules defining membership of the political community – which are unavoidable in principle, but are in practice needlessly restrictive in many European countries – interact with migration to produce inequalities of status that a pure theory of citizenship has difficulty accounting for.

A more sociological approach avoids some of these difficulties because it does not postulate a single nexus of law that uniquely defines citizenship. To that extent, it seems promising to tie together the two strands of traditional thinking and to take as units of analysis *societies organised as political communities*. However the Marshallian paradigm of citizenship, even as adapted by later writers, leaves us lumbered with an implicit presumption of homogeneity. Citizenship, says Marshall,

> is a status bestowed on those who are full members of a community. All who possess the status are equal with respect to the rights and duties with which the status is endowed (1950, p. 18).

The core of his analysis is the extension of full membership, or citizenship, to an ever-wider group of people and its enrichment by attachment to it of an expanding bundle of rights and duties. There is thus a structural presumption that full membership is uniform and homogeneous, however diverse may be forms of exclusion. It may be that this analysis is empirically correct in the sense that modern societies do tend towards uniformity of membership. But it would be deeply unsatisfactory to build it into the very concept of citizenship. A differentiated concept would thus be useful in making it possible to take account of a greater degree of heterogeneity than the Marshallian framework allows for.

Granting the exercise to be useful, it is therefore worth considering whether the idea of *local* citizenship – as an issue for any differentiated perspective on citizenship – can be made coherent. Using as a working definition of citizenship 'the form of membership peculiar to *societies* organised as *political communities*', this implies assessing the *idea* of a 'local society' and of a 'local political community' – leaving aside for the moment the question of their empirical existence. Prima facie, the idea makes a lot of sense. Once we view it in differentiated terms, citizenship combines, in complex ways, a set of legal statuses and relationships, including rights; a set of institutions and practices; and a set of ideas that give meaning to all of this. Because of this complex structure, there is nothing absurd in the idea that citizenship might differ from time to time and from place to place. It may evolve, as in Marshall's analysis of Britain. It may also be expressed differently at different institutional levels, for instance in the context of European integration. It is possible in principle, therefore, that at a local level, for example at the level of the city or city neighbourhood, a specific form of membership may be identifiable that can be called 'citizenship' without doing violence to the concept.

There are, furthermore, empirical reasons to make such an assumption. One aspect of citizenship is the relationship between a political authority with territorial or functional jurisdiction and the group of people subject to it. Some such authorities are specifically local in both senses of the word: they are defined territorially, and they are of comparatively small scale within a larger territorial system. Indeed, there is a tendency in countries such as the UK and France, which are perceived to be over-centralised, for the importance of local jurisdiction to increase in response to concerns about both administrative efficiency and democratic accountability. The relevance of the local idea is also apparent if we consider patterns of mobilisation, which are a constitutive dimension of citizenship as defined here. Their very existence expresses the dual relationship between the people subject to political authority (or a sub-group of them) and between such people collectively and the institutions that embody authority. Furthermore, to the extent that mobilisation involves challenges to existing arrangements or proposals for new arrangements, it is necessarily framed in a political language (in the broadest sense, including not just verbal deliberation but also a whole range of modes of communication of which violence is equally part) that reflects the prevailing meaning of citizenship – or, more likely, the set of possible meanings within which a particular political community argues about citizenship. Now, by its very nature, mobilisation has a geography. This may be tightly defined – when it is framed by a territorial issue, or involves specific uses of physical space, such as demonstrations, occupations, etc. Or geography may be of minor significance in understanding a process of mobilisation, when it merely brings together some of the people who happen to occupy a particular territory. From either perspective, however, local territories that are endowed with structures of political authority, and within which specific issues and mobilisations emerge, may be thought of, prima facie, as possible spaces of citizenship.

These points are sketchy, and each of them would require both conceptual expansion and empirical substantiation. They do however suffice to show that to talk of 'local citizenship' is not simply to make a sloppy category mistake. On the contrary, the need for critical appraisal of our habitual, and sometimes taken-for-granted, 'scaling' of democracy emerges from the very conceptual structure of citizenship. In addition, formulating citizenship in terms of the articulation between society and political community points us towards the kinds of empirical work that might make the concept usable. In particular, this formulation shows the fruitfulness of a focus on contestation, on the mobilisation of claims about political exclusion – interpreted here as the denial of full membership – not as the only mode of citizenship, or even necessarily the most important, but simply as a crucial indicator of tensions of scope and scale within formally democratic systems. The contributions to this volume, which focus on the nexus of multiculturalism and citizenship at the city level – on the position of ethnic and cultural minorities within societies organised as political communities of which they are at best ambiguously members – are exemplary in this respect.

To refer to such 'tensions' serves to remind us that the scale and scope of democracy are normative issues of considerable contemporary significance. Indeed, it is fair to say that interest in local spaces of citizenship, even in its most ethnographic forms, is invariably – not least in this volume - normatively charged. In the background of most recent social-science literature on citizenship lurks the 'crisis of the nation-state', serving as both a diagnosis and a prescription. Simplifying for my purposes here, the supposed crisis is the inability of actual states to guarantee the citizenship they claim to embody. One set of arguments, not directly relevant to the issues raised in this volume, is that globalisation is depriving the state of so much of its capacity for action that legal sovereignty has ceased to constitute self-government. The second, often related, set of arguments

– for which 'multiculturalism' is a convenient generic label – stresses the absence, or the purely rhetorical nature, of the convergence between the ethnic and civic dimensions of nationhood that the nation-state model postulates and on the basis of which it defines legitimacy (Crowley, 2000). The normative critique, correlatively, is that this inability is not simply an accidental or transitory defect of currently existing nation-states but a necessary feature of the nation-state model itself, which, as a consequence, is conceptually irrelevant. Furthermore, the tension between the ethnic and civic dimensions of nationhood gives rise to real and damaging processes of exclusion, of which the difficulties experienced by most European countries in responding to the presence of substantial immigrant communities in ways compatible with basic liberal democratic principles is exemplary. Subscription to such arguments leads logically to a normative defence of non-national forms of citizenship – what we might call generically 'post-nationalism'. The 'local' is one of these forms (alongside the European and the cosmopolitan), and is perhaps peculiarly significant because its smaller scale and very concrete issues make it easier for people to identify with it. Such arguments are offered, in particular, in defence of the view that resident foreigners should be granted local, but not national, voting rights. A number of countries have granted such rights to foreigners generally, and the principle has been enshrined in European law – for citizens of the European Union only, on the basis of reciprocity – since the Treaty of Maastricht.

As far as possible within the limits of the present brief discussion, we may be satisfied that there are no insuperable obstacles to the development of a concept of 'local citizenship' that might be coherent, usable, and useful – and perhaps, indeed, of considerable conceptual importance. We also have at least a sketch of what that concept might look like once we take seriously the idea of citizenship as membership of a society organised as a political community. Nothing in the concept, however, presupposes that local citizenship actually exists. We need therefore to consider empirically, in the light of the findings presented in this volume, how politics is actually structured at the local level.

In any system as complex as a contemporary European state, there will be different levels of political authority and administrative competence, issues that are inherently territorial because they involve among other things contested appropriations of physical space, forms of mobilisation that depend on pre-existing structures within civil society, types of identification defined mainly or partly in terms of pride of place. If we take seriously the concept sketched in previous paragraphs, our working hypothesis must therefore be that citizenship will manifest itself in a distinctively local key or mode to the extent that these four dimensions tend to overlap. Conversely, the mere fact of localisation, of being *somewhere*, cannot be considered decisive. Mobilisation directed at the holders of political authority and framed in terms of legitimacy is, prima facie, an expression of citizenship. This does not mean, however, that citizen mobilisation about local issues directed at local authorities is necessarily an expression of *local* citizenship. That will depend on how closed the local political system is and how distinctive is its repertoire of political language. Local manifestations of citizenship are thus questions of degree, and crucially of scale. The very existence of a territorially circumscribed focus of administrative authority, especially if it is at least partly accountable to some elected body, will tend to stimulate a specific mode of citizen activity. However, depending on the kinds of issues, the forms of mobilisation and the types of identification involved, points other than official territorial subdivisions may be more relevant, or the 'local' itself may prove illusory. It is possible, in particular, that what *takes place* at the local level can be adequately understood only at the national level.

In fact, this theoretical possibility does seem to be substantiated empirically. A range of evidence, including the research reported on in this volume, clearly indicates the importance of local political activity and its particular significance for groups whose membership of the society and the political community is institutionally incomplete or normatively contested. Thus, many things that ethnic political activists care about – certain aspects of education, access to facilities for religious and cultural activities, relations with law-enforcement agencies, housing issues – are, in practice, most effectively addressed at municipal or neighbourhood level. Furthermore, exclusion itself creates political resources that can be mobilised, often as explicit or implicit threats, in certain local contexts. Nonetheless, despite the internal connection – illustrated in this volume – between local modes of citizenship and the politics of multiculturalism, it would be premature to conclude that properly local citizenship is thereby shown to exist (and even more premature to consider that local citizenship is thereby proved to be the answer to the problems raised by multiculturalism). There is, of course, no strictly uniform political space corresponding to the legal limits of the state. However it is misleading to view the local as simply the opposite of the national. A more adequate interpretation is rather that *multiple* dynamics of territorialisation or localisation are at work without converging on *any* uniform space. Because representative and administrative structures, substantive issues, forms of mobilisation, and identities relate to different sub-divisions and bring into play different dynamics, there is no uniform, homogeneous level or scale that is truly 'the local'.

Undoubtedly, mobilisation around some territorially inscribed issue – housing regeneration, say – will generally be local in at least three senses: it involves people that can be attached to a fairly small-scale social space, it is expressed by forms of action (demonstrations, petitions, squatting, etc.) that occupy an identifiable and limited space, and it is addressed at institutions and policy processes that are reasonably 'close'. Furthermore, there is often a fair degree of overlap between these three forms of 'locality'. There are, however, two reasons to be wary of talking here of specifically local citizenship. First, such overlap is an empirical fact rather than a necessary feature of any particular political configuration. It is sometimes more effective to mobilise for local purposes at national level because doing so facilitates the forging of coalitions and enhances media impact. Conversely, of course, issues for which the state is solely responsible – the legal status of aliens, say – may, for tactical reasons, be the objects of local mobilisations. And, finally, transnational mobilisation does occur, although it remains unusual. The local is part of a repertoire of political activity that is never strictly determined by the nature of the actors or of the issues involved. An important implication is that there are no strong reasons to believe that local citizenship stands in a specifically coherent relation to multicultural concerns. Empirical analysis shows the inadequacy of policies premised on the claim that multiculturalism is about 'community' issues that are best solved locally of the basis of specific forms of political participation. Such policies tend to be undermined or overtaken by mainstream participation, and have often been abandoned or downgraded in countries such as the UK, the Netherlands and Sweden where – in different ways – they had in the 1970s and 1980s been at the heart of official multiculturalism (Crowley, 2001). This is hardly surprising: multiculturalism is essentially a critique of the nation-state, and many of the issues it raises – involving the symbols and institutions of nationhood – can, by their very nature, only be addressed at the level of the state. There are many good reasons for the multicultural agenda to be strongly expressed at municipal level, but all of them depend on detailed empirical considerations of political sociology rather than any necessary conceptual connection.

The second reason to be wary of exaggerated claims for local citizenship is that the observable 'leakage' of local political systems has a conceptual and not simply an empirical basis. Mobilisation of the kind referred to in the previous paragraph cannot be adequately characterised solely in terms of the interests and material resources of the actors involved. Comparatively weak actors – such as those who speak for ethnic or cultural minorities, but most actors, after all, are comparatively weak – are always necessarily engaged in a process of justification that calls upon the discursive resources of a shared political language. To say that it is shared is not to say that it is uniformly subscribed to – multiculturalism is, among other things, a critique of the hegemony of the liberal language of political justification. What make it shared, and therefore generally although not uniformly available, are the institutions and practices in which it is embedded. Citizenship, in other words, once understood as membership of a society organised as a political community, is intimately entwined with participation in what is generally called, following the work of Jürgen Habermas, a 'public sphere'. The existence of local citizenship in a strict sense is therefore equivalent to that of a local public sphere, implying among other things a locally shared language of political justification.

While nothing in the idea of a public sphere implies that it should necessarily be located at the level of the state – still less of any particular state – it is an empirically observable and historically intelligible fact that the language of political justification in Western Europe is predominantly state-centred. It is, therefore, no surprise that politics should be set within different scales depending on whether one focuses on discourse, interests, resources, or activities, and that, as a consequence, the 'local' should prove ultimately almost impossible to pin down. What remains to be seen is how strong this argument is. Is the fragmentation or diversification of political language a conceptual possibility that might, indeed, be expressed by empirically observable dynamics, such as those diagnosed under the rubric 'crisis of the nation-state'? Or is there, on the contrary, something conceptually incoherent in the idea of an autonomous local language of political justification?

My suggestion is that such an idea is, indeed, conceptually incoherent. In order to sketch the reasons for this answer, it is necessary to consider the idea of a public sphere in a more sociological way. Its essential normative feature is that it is structured by a language of political justification based on impartial argument. What sociological features might guarantee the emergence and stability of such a structure? The first is what Habermas (1992) puts at the centre of his analysis: the fact that the public sphere relates politics to law. Lawmaking involves defining general rules for persons and circumstances unknown, or at least imperfectly known. Impartiality is thus a natural, internal feature of discussion about rules, not a separate, independently grounded constraint on it. This is plausible enough, and indeed it is not too difficult to find supporting evidence. The shift from bargaining (about resource sharing) to deliberation (about rule drafting) is characteristic of the way in which local claims become nationalised. In practical local politics, the typically observable claim is that the council should provide resource X for group Y: the planning and use of physical infrastructure, such as housing and leisure facilities, offer numerous examples. Such infrastructure obviously occupies specific spaces, and issues of access, quality, etc., are themselves highly localised. It may, however, be more politically effective to mobilise at a higher level, and one would expect in that case to encounter the claim that the *state* should provide (or order the council to provide) resource X for group Y (or for some broader coalition group Ψ). Examples can of course be found, but they are not typical, and tend to be transitory and unstable. Forms of mobilisation that succeed in federating a durable coalition usually have a rather different character, expressing more abstract, more generalizable – in a word, more political – concerns. Typically, the revised claim is that law A should be passed in order to guarantee equitable access to resource X (or some broader class X of resources) for all groups (including, of course, Y). In other words, claims that are legislative in the generic sense that they are about the *rules* of politics are political in a way that typically does not make sense 'locally' because the local is by definition not so much a space as a sub-space. It is of its nature to be embedded in a larger-scale entity.

What is important sociologically is that the politicisation of claims, and the corresponding shift from bargaining to deliberation, depends on the dynamics of mobilisation rather than on the good intentions of the actors involved. Otherwise, the idea of a public sphere would be purely wishful thinking. Whether the dynamics of mobilisation suffice to impose deliberation on actors who do not have an interest in generalising and politicising their claims is, however, doubtful. The process sketched with reference to the nationalisation of local claims depends crucially on the comparative weakness of the initial mobilisation and the structural necessity to change scale, because of the lack of legislative capacity at the local level. Pure bargaining may be a perfectly stable format for other kinds of claims. Habermas himself would of course argue that the dynamics of *argument* – even within a bargaining format – force the participants towards deliberation. But this is inadequate, since it leaves willingness to participate in good-faith argument ungrounded within the dynamics of mobilisation.

The problem for a sociological analysis of the public sphere is therefore to specify the structural conditions that make participation in deliberation a rational political strategy even for actors who are unreasonable in the

Rawlsian sense that they are not motivated by a desire for just co-operation. Such conditions cannot, of course, provide guarantees, or even impose enforceable constraints on political participation. Arguably, indeed, democracy *depends on* the absence of guarantees or constraints of this kind. The conditions are simply those that make it more probable that membership of a society organised as a political community should take the form of participation based on public-spiritedness – in other words what one would usually call, for normative purposes, *citizenship*.

The sociology of political participation, of which work inspired by the theories of Pierre Bourdieu is exemplary, is generally regarded as – and to a real extent is self-consciously constituted as – a critique of and alternative to the 'idealism' of Habermas and other proponents of *Öffentlichkeit*. What Bourdieu calls the 'political field' (*champ politique*) coincides empirically with the 'public sphere': it is characterised by the expression of interests, the mobilisation of resources and the articulation of justificatory language (Bourdieu, 2000). It is, in the sense in which I have been using the phrase, the forum in which membership of a society organised as political community is constituted; in other words, the forum of citizenship. In Bourdieu's interpretation, however, the political field is also the point where political domination converges, in mutually reinforcing ways, with economic and symbolic domination to arrange and justify unequal participation. It is the place, in other words, where domination dresses up as citizenship. As people confronted with cross-dressing tend to, Bourdieu views this with a mixture of technical admiration and moral revulsion.

At first sight, no two things could be more different than a public sphere and a political field. Without being able to go into much detail here, I wish to suggest that they are in fact, *pace* both Bourdieu and Habermas, mutually reinforcing. What prevents citizenship being simply a sham in the political field is the competitive pressure to which those who attempt to monopolise it – the 'political class' – are subjected. And what prevents *Öffentlichkeit* being merely wishful thinking in the public sphere is *precisely the same competitive pressure*. What develops, in other words, is an uneasy balance between the tendency of public-spiritedness to emerge from cynical politics and the tendency of even the most idealistic politics to close in on itself. This balance, like citizenship itself, is a question of empirical degree: there are no knockdown arguments, sociological or quasi-transcendental. Effectively, a public sphere is an open political field: one from which nothing – no person, no issue, no mode of discourse – is excluded *a priori* and in which practical limits to inclusion can be overcome if people care about them enough. Meaningful citizenship is the correlate of such openness.

While the general theoretical implications of this hypothesis cannot be explored here, it has direct and important consequences for the notion of local citizenship. I have suggested that the latter depends on the existence of a local public sphere in which the language of political justification is not entirely reducible to a usable higher-level resource. It now appears that such a local public sphere would necessarily be related to a local political field. This relation does not threaten the theoretical coherence of the idea of local citizenship: everything said earlier remains valid. But empirical evidence that local politics might constitute a local political field is woefully lacking. Political career structures, modes of political organisation, relations between politics and the media, all these features continue to shape a predominantly national and state-centred political field. The 'local field' is one of its modes of expression, not an autonomous alternative to it. (The same is true, for much the same reasons, of politics at the European level.) Nor is there any strong evidence that multicultural issues offer an exception to this pattern. The European research reported on here hardly contradicts Kymlicka's claim, made in a North American context, that

most polyethnic demands are evidence that members of minority groups want to participate within the mainstream of society (1995, p. 177).

And for political purposes, the mainstream is the national and state-centred field sketched earlier. The 'local' offers a mode of citizenship that is valuable, perhaps deserves enhancement, and possibly has a specific affinity with the interests of certain groups within contemporary European societies. But, conversely, *confinement* to the local arena, to the extent it exists, is the expression not of citizenship but precisely of exclusion from it.

References

Bourdieu, P. (2000), *Propos sur le Champ Politique*, Presses Universitaires de Lyon, Lyon.

Crowley, J. (2000), 'France: The Archetype of a Nation-state', in L. Haagendoorn, G. Csepeli, H. Dekker and R. Farnen (eds), *European Nations and Nationalism: Theoretical and Historical Perspectives*, Ashgate, Aldershot, pp. 67-106.

Crowley, J. (2001), 'The Political Participation of Ethnic Minorities', *International Political Science Review*, vol. 22, pp. 99-121.

Habermas, J. (1992), *Faktizität und Geltung: Beiträge zur Diskurstheorie des Rechts und des Demokratischen Rechtstaats*, Suhrkamp Verlag, Frankfurt.

Kymlicka, W. (1995), *Multicultural Citizenship: A Liberal Theory of Minority Rights*, Oxford University Press, Oxford.

Marshall, T.H. (1950), 'Citizenship and Social Class', reprinted in T.H. Marshall and T. Bottomore, (1992), *Citizenship and Social Class*, Pluto, London, pp. 3-51.